THE PLEASURE
OF READING

THE PLEASURE OF READING

Edited by Antonia Fraser

B L O O M S B U R Y

NEW YORK · LONDON · OXFORD · NEW DELHI · SYDNEY

Bloomsbury USA
An imprint of Bloomsbury Publishing Plc

1385 Broadway	50 Bedford Square
New York	London
NY 10018	WC1B 3DP
USA	UK

www.bloomsbury.com

BLOOMSBURY and the Diana logo are trademarks of Bloomsbury Publishing Plc

First published in Great Britain 1992 in commemoration of
the bicentenary of WHSmith
This paperback edition published in Great Britain 2015
First U.S. edition published 2015

Editorial © Antonia Fraser Victoria Gray, 2015
Introduction © Antonia Fraser, 2015
Text © 1992 and 2015 by Individual Authors

ISBN: TPB: 978-1-63286-228-0
ePub: 978-1-63286-229-7

Library of Congress Cataloging-in-Publication Data has been applied for.

2 4 6 8 10 9 7 5 3 1

Typeset by Newgen Works (P) Ltd., Chennai, India
Printed and bound in the U.S.A. by Thomson-Shore Inc., Dexter, Michigan

To find out more about our authors and books visit www.bloomsbury.com. Here you
will find extracts, author interviews, details of forthcoming events, and the option to sign up
for our newsletters.

Bloomsbury books may be purchased for business or promotional use. For information on
bulk purchases please contact Macmillan Corporate and Premium Sales Department at
specialmarkets@macmillan.com.

This new edition is dedicated to the memory of
Simon Gray and Harold Pinter

Contents

Preface

by Victoria Gray

In the summer of 2009, the year after my husband Simon died, I found myself in a small bookshop in upstate New York. The young man at the checkout asked me if I'd like to give someone a book. They had a local scheme collecting books for single mothers. There were three titles to choose from. I gave a copy of *Great Expectations* to a single mother I never met living in a trailer park in rural New York State. I hope it did something for her; I know it cheered me up.

Back in the UK I became convinced that there would be a way of doing something like this through the internet. I tested the idea on more experienced acquaintances, and wrote to a bookseller suggesting that the moment when the world is worried about the future of the book was the perfect time to celebrate giving a book. All reactions were positive.

Give a Book (UK registered charity no. 1149664) went live in May 2011. Our firm belief is that to give a book, to pass on a good read, is a transaction of worth – not something thrown away, but a gift that is thought about and passed on out of generosity and respect. Our initial aim was to offer books where they would be of particular value in such places as Maggie's Centres, Age UK and First Story – for escape, companionship, imagination and challenge. We were adamant that we would not get involved with primary schools or prisons – they were too huge for us and there were plenty of long-standing organisations who knew what they were doing.

Three years later, our largest projects are in prisons and primary schools. We almost always go in with the long-established organisations who indeed know what they are doing – we have been privileged to learn from such places as The Reading Agency, National Literacy Trust, Beanstalk and Booktrust. Give a Book is very much needs-led and project-based. We go wherever the gift of a book will make a difference.

There is more information about our projects and partners on the website www.giveabook.org.uk. We go on donating books for book groups in Maggie's Centres and Age UK. But the groups that Give a Book connects to mainly come from language-deprived worlds. Our work ranges from setting up Magic Breakfast Book Clubs for primary school children who come to school hungry in all sorts of ways, to helping make a library at a mother and baby refuge and supporting Prison Reading Groups. We also give mini-dictionaries to prisoners who complete the Six Book (Adult Literacy) Challenge and supply book bags for children visiting on prison family days.

The people who support us take having and giving books for granted, as second nature. It is the sea we swim in. This is also why we have our Book of the Month slot on the website where new guests tell us about the book that they particularly like to share. Every reader has one – or more than one – as you can see in this wonderful collection. There are people just around the corner who are nothing like as lucky, for whom such 'pleasurable addiction' is behind a closed door. Giving a book to a person who really needs one helps open that door – introducing them, in short, to the pleasure of reading.

Give a Book is delighted that Bloomsbury have decided to republish and refresh this excellent and timely volume, at the suggestion of Antonia Fraser, its original editor. And of course we are immeasurably grateful to all the contributors who have so generously shared their work.

Victoria Gray
London, 9 December 2014

Introduction

by Antonia Fraser

'WELL, what books has anyone brought?' Thus my father, at the beginning of the Second World War, on a journey to the Isle of Wight for an Officers' Training Course; intending to break the ice in the most conventional manner possible. There was complete silence. Finally one of his companions said in a voice of complete amazement: 'Books? But we'll find a book when we get there, won't we . . .?' This story has always seemed to me to sum up the deep division that exists in the human race, regardless of any other more obvious distinction, between those for whom books are an obsession, and those who are prepared, good-humouredly enough, to tolerate their existence.

Belonging to the former category, I too have always been fascinated by other people's reading. I am that irritating person who reads your book over your shoulder in the train or tube; somehow, you feel, purloining its secret. I have to admit that for a while I was baffled by Kindles (although very happy with one myself, as an essential weapon of travel). Then one day, swimming frustratedly in a hotel pool surrounded by Kindle-readers, I decided to move with the times. I rose up out of the water like an inquisitive mermaid and questioned each reader in turn. All answered politely and nearly all answered: 'John Grisham.' (I began to think it was some kind of code.)

What *do* other people read? In profiles of public figures I always home in on their reading matter – if any – and make judgements accordingly. But of course the reading of other writers is the most fascinating of all; a truth is here revealed, as when looking at the houses in which famous architects actually live.

In this way, I came to suggest a collection of pieces by writers about their own reading for WHSmith, who wanted an appropriate volume to celebrate its bicentenary in 1992. This new version is being published twenty-three years later, with equal appropriateness, in aid of the charity Give a Book. Its detailed aims are related by Victoria Gray in her Preface: but its motto could be summed up by the title of this book: the pleasure of reading.

Originally it was decided to invite well-known writers (using the English language) of all ages and from back-grounds as diverse as possible. Very few refused – and generally for the good writerly reason of needing to get on with their own work. The brief was simple. Writers were asked to describe their early reading, what did (or did not) influence them, and what they enjoy reading today. They were also asked 'if possible' for a list of their ten favourite books. Some did not find this possible – there were groans of 'I hate lists' – but however odious to compile, other people's lists do make intriguing reading. Who could resist learning that J. G. Ballard rated the Los

Angeles *Yellow Pages* among his favourite reading, or that for Paul Sayer it was the *Timeform Black Book No 19, 26 February 1978/9*?

For this new version, five additional writers were invited, born in the 1970s and 80s, and respectively a novelist, a travel writer, a biographer, a poet and a playwright: Kamila Shamsie, Rory Stewart, Katie Waldegrave, Emily Berry and Tom Wells. Fittingly, Tom Wells, the youngest contributor, calls attention to the phenomenon of the J. K. Rowling books. 'Everything is different when you're in love. And I absolutely loved *Harry Potter*.' That was something I encountered for myself when I watched my granddaughter Atalanta reading the first book of the series at breakfast. Her eyes were glued to the precious page held in front of her nose: in order not to stop reading for a moment she attempted to spread marmalade on toast with her other hand without looking (with disastrous results).

So here are forty-three writers whose dates of birth range over seventy-six years. The countries in which they were brought up include Canada and China, Ireland and India, New Zealand and Nigeria, Syria and Southern Rhodesia (now Zimbabwe), even Germany during the 1930s – followed by a flight from Hitler for Judith Kerr, for whom Dr Dolittle's pushmi-pullyu still remains its German version of a *Stossmichziehdich*. In Kamila Shamsie's childhood memory for example, the Neverland of J. M. Barrie was 'just off the coast of Karachi . . . So although Peter might fly into rooms in London he ended up just off the coast on which I lived; a comforting thought.'

Backgrounds are as varied as Stephen Spender's 'family of journalists: I was brought up among people who read

and wrote much' to Roger McGough's Irish Catholic
working-class world and his father's 'working man's
fear' of entering a library. Sometimes reading emerges as
prophetic of a future career – Philip Ziegler, biographer of
Lord Mountbatten, read Macaulay and Hume, and loved
Lord David Cecil's life of Lord Melbourne – and sometimes wildly at variance – Dr Robert Burchfield, the
distinguished lexicographer, coming from 'a working-class
environment in New Zealand without books'.

Yet for all these differences, certain common themes do
emerge: and strongest of these is of reading as a childhood
or youthful passion, amounting to an addiction. Melvyn
Bragg actually uses the word: alone in his parents' 'overdressed' front parlour, with its 'shapely womanly paraffin
lamp', he found in books first a refuge, then an addiction.
Jane Gardam was promised 'a porter' (contrary to expect-
ation it turned out to be a book – a Beatrix Potter) and
after that there was no stopping her. Here is John Fowles:
'it was impossible to think of life without reading' or
Emma Tennant, in a remote Victorian Gothic 'monstrosity'
of a castle in Scotland: 'I read up and down house.' Brian
Moore: 'at a very early age I became an avid reader'. For Sue
Townsend 'reading became a secret obsession'.

A. S. Byatt boldly describes herself as 'greatly blessed by
very bad asthma' which meant that she spent most of her
childhood in bed reading. Katie Waldegrave writes of 'a
wicker basket (still beside her bed) full of children's books . . .
it is the first possesion I would rescue in a fire.' Emily Berry's
conclusion was specially evocative: 'I suppose for me, the
"pleasure of reading" is in feeling safe . . . when you read
something that speaks to you, it's a reminder that everything,

even and especially the hardest things, has a precedent. So you're not alone, not "lost in a forest" after all.' While it is Rory Stewart who points to the awesome power of the reader: 'Once you have taken possession of a book, you can inspect a writer's mind, in all its shades and dimensions. You can establish a relationship, which would be intolerable to a living individual: you can wake the writer at three in the morning, switch her off in mid-sentence, insist she continues for six hours unbroken, skip, go back, repeat the same paragraph again and again, impertinently second-guessing her vocabulary and metaphors, scrutinising her structure and tricks.'

Carol Ann Duffy, finding escape through reading in a 'virtually bookless house', was, however, among the many contributors whose prolonged immersion was somehow felt to be unhealthy or even subversive. 'Get your head out of that book!' was a command frequently issued – without being obeyed. Prohibition led Jeanette Winterson to the memorable discovery that seventy-seven paperback books is the maximum number you can hide under an average single-bed mattress without the level rising dangerously.

Of course there are interesting exceptions to prove this rule. Tom Stoppard declared himself as 'quite shifty' on the subject of other people's precocious early reading since he did not share it, Michael Foot was 'a late developer' and Alan Hollinghurst sitting surrounded by books in his father's library preferred 'the abstraction of music'. Patrick Leigh Fermor, however, stood for the great majority, when he described how learning to read at the age of six turned him from 'an unlettered brute into a book-ridden lunatic'.

An addict myself, who learnt to read extremely early (taught by my mother who had time to spare since I was her first child), I certainly shared this preoccupation. There is a letter from Evelyn Waugh to Lady Diana Cooper describing a visit to my parents, then Frank and Elizabeth Pakenham, in September 1932, when I would have been a few weeks old. 'So I saw F. Pakenham's baby and gave it a book, but it can't read yet.' My first reaction when it was pointed out to me in 2014, by Robert Gottlieb, was not amusement but indignation: I learnt pretty soon, I wanted to cry! I also had the advantage – as it seemed then – of reading extremely fast, so much so, that my mother and I have speculated whether she did not by mistake teach me speed-reading. At any rate my speedy reading used to earn me a useful income, trapping the grown-ups to unwise bets on the subject of my prowess. The grown-up would select the book (to avoid cheating) and I then retired to whizz through it. There followed a searing examination of the contents. For some reason grown-ups tended to choose the lesser-known works of Sir Walter Scott; in this way I acquired good cash profits from *Kenilworth*, *Peveril of the Peak* and *The Talisman* – as well as a grateful love of Scott himself. Alas, speedy reading, so useful in youth for passing examinations, is a double-edged weapon in an age of security: I used to have to travel on holiday with luggage that aroused instant suspicion at airports: 'Are you suggesting these are all *books*?' – hence the aforesaid convenience of Kindle.

The second theme which emerged from this collection is an encouraging one to those parents who fear that their children read nothing but 'rubbish'. It seems that what children read is less important than the fact that they do the reading in the first place. The stirring of the imagination is the important thing. Doris Lessing learnt to read off a cigarette packet at the age of seven and Simon Gray from comic-strip cartoons in wartime Canada where he was an evacuee. Enid Blyton was forbidden by Hermione Lee's 'high-brow middle-class' parents: and also, incidentally, by my own. (I passed on the ban to my own children, only to find – naturally – a wardrobe bulging with the forbidden volumes, imported from a friend with a more tolerant mother.) Yet the frequent mentions of Enid Blyton in this volume give another side to the picture. For Ronald Harwood, as a child in Cape Town, too young to see her deficiencies, her work represented the 'magic world' of England.

Similarly, the popularity of the *Just William* books is a marked feature of these contributions: in the original list of most-often mentioned books, *Just William* ranks fourth, just after *Treasure Island*, with only *Alice's Adventures in Wonderland, Jane Eyre* and *Winnie-the-Pooh* ahead. Evidently devouring what are now perceived as less good books does not preclude devouring good books too: as Sally Beauman, an avid reader, put it: 'I loved them all.' Jan Morris was probably right in suggesting that most of what we read is thrown into 'a mental waste-paper basket', leaving stored on 'some indestructible disk of the sensibility only the works destined permanently to influence us'.

A third theme also relates to the question of the imagination. There seems to be a kind of creative fear which children – those who grow up to be writers, at least – actually enjoy feeling. J. G. Ballard was among many who loved *Treasure Island*, finding it 'frightening but in an exhilarating and positive way', just as John Mortimer, reading it under the bedclothes with a torch, felt 'reassuringly afraid'.

John Mortimer also pointed out that Dickens is our greatest novelist, not only for his mastery of comedy but also because of the way 'he alarms his readers'.

Creative fear can be experienced from sources which are at first sight surprising. Margaret Atwood referred to Beatrix Potter's 'Dark Period (the ones with knives, cannibalistic foxes and stolen babies in them)'. Ruth Rendell remembered an Andrew Lang *Fairy Book* with a shudder: 'The picture I can still see in my mind's eye,' she wrote, 'is of a dancing gesticulating *thing* with a human face and cat's ears, its body furred like a bear.' She knew exactly where the picture was, knew that she must avoid it, and yet 'so perverse are human beings, however youthful and omniscient' that she was also terribly tempted to peep 'and catch a tiny fearful glimpse'. One of my own favourite books was *The Enchanted Castle* by E. Nesbit. On the one hand, the terror of the moment when the Uglie-Wuglies (created as an 'audience' for the children's play out of overcoats, gloves and walking-sticks) come to life and start to clap their gloved 'hands' with a horrid muffled sound, still haunts me sufficiently to make me give racks of old coats hanging in back corridors a wide berth. On the other hand, it was probably creatively buried in my mystery-writer's unconscious.

The appearance of books, as opposed to their contents, turned out to be very important to contributors. The first book Edna O'Brien ever treasured was made of cloth 'reminding me in some way of the cloth of the scapulars we wore inside our vests and which contained a relic of the saints'. In her Irish childhood, she continued to love 'the feel and smell of them, ravelled old books, growing musty, in a trunk but full of secrets'. John Carey loved the red and gold look of a *Chums* annual, inherited from previous generations of his family. Germaine Greer spiritedly denounced *The Water-Babies* (another of my own favourite books – oh, Ellie's white bedroom! – but one which arouses very mixed reactions here). However she did at least commend the red morocco feel of the edition she read. One cannot help wondering if this visual and tactile advantage is something which books might still retain for young children over videos, iPads and, of course, television.

Reading aloud gets a good press here. Some contributors of course, like Buchi Emecheta, brought up in Nigeria, come from cultures where stories were naturally read and told. Rana Kabbani, with one grandmother who could read and one who could not, described the 'harem world' of her youth in Damascus, where women were constantly telling stories. Then there were British parents who believed in reading aloud as a matter of principle (like my own mother, who by skipping a great deal of description in *The Last Days of Pompeii* gave me the erroneous impression that Lord Lytton was an action-packed author to be compared only to Baroness Orczy). Of such parents, Candia McWilliam wrote: 'My first reading was of course not *mine*', as she painted a picture of her father chain-smoking Senior Service as he read, so taken up with the wickedness of Samuel Whiskers that he might burn his fingers or her nightdress.

One of the unexpected delights of editing this collection was being reminded of forgotten favourites – Harrison Ainsworth's historical epics for example (hated by some but adored by me – *Old St Paul's*! Oh Amabel – betrayed by her seducer!), or Geoffrey Williams and Ronald Searle's Molesworth in *Down with skool!* who, as Wendy Cope recalled to me, defined poets as 'weedy people [who] say la and fie and swoon when they see a bunch of daffodils'; Timberlake Wertenbaker reading *The Three Musketeers* 'twenty or thirty times', a subject on which I too could once have passed an examination.

The other gratification came from completely the opposite direction: finding windows opened onto a very different view from the academic world of my childhood when my father was a don at Oxford. Gita Mehta in India *heard* about the pleasures of reading, even before she could read herself, from booksellers working from carpets spread out by the roadside, or jumping on the steps of moving trains in their enthusiasm: '*Anna Karenina*, sahib, *Madame Bovary*. Hot books only this very minute arrived. Believe it or not, sahib. Tomorrow no copies remaining!' (In a continent where illiteracy was so widespread, the ability to read was greeted with 'awe'.) Readers will undoubtedly share both experiences: the shock of recognition and the shock of the new.

Lastly, I am indeed grateful to Bloomsbury for making it possible for this book to live again, in order to benefit such an excellent cause as Give a Book. As for the contributors, both old and new, I thank them for enabling us to peer into the various magic worlds of the past which made them what they are – writers.

Antonia Fraser
London, 8 January 2015

Stephen Spender

I COME from a family of journalists – my father and two uncles were all on newspapers – and my mother wrote verse. My great-grandfather, Sir Hermann Weber, was a famous Victorian physician who had left the Rhineland, where he was born, and come to England because (so my grandmother told me) it was the country of Shakespeare.

Thus I was brought up among people who read and wrote much, though only my mother (who died when I was eleven) tried to write poetry. My journalist father and uncles revered poetry but distrusted the imagination. However, my uncle Alfred – J. A. Spender – the best-known of them, as editor of the famous *Westminster Gazette* – published Georgian poets such as Walter de la Mare and Rupert Brooke in the weekly supplement to that newspaper. He regarded poets with sympathy, as though they were sufferers from some mildly debilitating illness which prevented them from ever earning a decent living.

Uncle Alfred discouraged me from being serious about writing poetry, saying that he himself could easily have chosen to write what he called 'word patterns', but found himself under the obligation to 'sing for his supper'. Supper, that is, being obtained by writing newspaper articles, and not by writing slim poems bound in slim volumes. What my uncle really meant was, I think, that unless someone is a great poet or at least living in a period when writing poetry is a major enterprise, it may prove a sadly self-deluding occupation, giving that dim figure the 'minor poet' a false sense of his superiority over mere journalists who write to earn a decent living. There is some truth in this. However, my mother thought that to be a poet was the highest of callings, an almost sacred vocation.

During the First World War we lived in a house on the cliff's edge at Sheringham where I made friends of caterpillars and knew the names of butterflies and wild flowers. I wanted to become a naturalist with a long white beard, like Charles Darwin. But zeppelins dropped some bombs near Sheringham and when the family was evacuated to a farm on Lake Derwent Water near Penrith in the Lake District, nature became for me Wordsworth, whose poems our parents, seated in deckchairs on the lawn below the open windows of our – the children's – bedroom at Skelgill Farm, took turns in reading out loud to one another. Wordsworth was only the murmur of their voices, which for me, not hearing the words, merged into the lapping of the waves of Lake Derwent Water and the waiting silence of the mountains. From then on poetry had this mysterious fascination for me. At my prep school when I was given textbooks on composition I turned compulsively to the examples chosen from poems:

> *The Ettrick Shepherd was my guide.*
> 'Extempore Effusion upon the Death of
> James Hogg', William Wordsworth

For some reason this line was chosen to illustrate some point, and it has haunted me ever since. When we were children, our father read aloud to us, usually after supper. What he read mostly was Dickens, Robert Louis Stevenson (*Kidnapped*) and Tennyson (*Morte d'Arthur*). My grandmother would read Walter Scott and fall asleep in the middle of some long description of a rugged moor or heath. (I have never been able to read Scott since. Perhaps I should have one more go before I die.) There were, before this, children's stories: Hans Andersen, *Grimm's Fairy Tales*, George MacDonald. Of these, I liked most Hans Andersen's ballet-like stories of fairy creatures in snowy landscapes. There was also the creepily well-illustrated *Struwwelpeter*, a book written by Heinrich Hoffmann, a German physician who wished to edify children with stories of how they will get their fingers cut off if they bite their nails or their home burned down if they light matches.

This was still the time when some Victorian boys' books were considered improving literature for the young. The most maudlin of these was surely Dean Farrar's sado-masochistic novel *Eric, or Little by Little*, in which the author traces the decline of Eric, an angelic-looking

small boy who goes to the bad at his public school, band-
ing together with bullies in 'crusting' (throwing crusts
at) Mr Rose, the schoolmaster who has been so kind to
him. He ends up as boy on a ship where the captain flogs
him with a rope's end, after which he dies, repentant and
speaking, or having spoken over him, a poem. This, at all
events, is how I remember *Eric, or Little by Little*, which
made a great impression on me. *Tom Brown's Schooldays*
by Thomas Hughes was supposedly less sadistic (indeed
The Oxford Companion to English Literature tells us that
Hughes meant to condemn bullying), but what got
across to me when I read it was scenes of older boys
'roasting' younger ones over fires, and so on. When a few
years ago *Tom Brown's Schooldays* was serialized on TV,
it was received with protests of outrage by many view-
ers. Children's stories are crammed with coded messages
from authors 'sublimating' their desires to molest children, though the authors themselves may not be aware
of this. And a list of the books that someone most loved
when he or she was a child might be as revealing of his
or her psychology as a Rorschach test. The fact that I
preferred Ballantyne's *The Coral Island* to the military
tales of G. A. Henty, though I never quite sank to the
depths of Barrie's *Peter Pan,* is a sure sign that in later life
I would prove to be a Cissy.

Shakespeare? The fact is that Shakespeare does not reveal
in his plays a sublime ego, like Milton's or Wordsworth's,
but a world. For this reason children encounter his plays as
they do something 'given', like the landscape or a fun-fair.
At the age of nine, when I was at the preparatory school

of Gresham's School, Holt, I seem to have had some diminutive non-speaking role in a school performance of *A Midsummer Night's Dream* in which Puck was played by a boy who later became a famous actor – Sebastian Shaw. What I remember was simply a world – Shakespeare's Athens, the Duke, Titania, Oberon – but most of all the two girls (played, of course, by boys), Hermia and Helena, squalling at one another.

As an adolescent I read novels voraciously: Dickens, Thackeray, Charles Reade, Thomas Hardy – but not, I am afraid, George Eliot. Then later I became rebellious and read Shaw (whom my father strongly disapproved of) and Samuel Butler's *The Way of All Flesh*. Butler's novel is an outstanding example of novels which express what one might term 'the politics of adolescence'. For my generation these were books which expressed one's fantasies about sexual freedom, one's rebelliousness against institutionalized religion, one's anarchist yearnings. A later generation had much spicier stuff. On the day in which the Penguin paperback edition of Lawrence's *Lady Chatterley's Lover* was released for publication, my son, then a schoolboy at Westminster, was commissioned by the other boys in his dormitory to buy for them six copies of *Lady Chatterley* and two pounds of toffee.

From the time when we were in the Lake District I was, as I suppose I still am, a sucker for romantic poetry. Romantic poetry treats poetry as a kind of absolute – an experience beyond all other experiences, which are valuable only as gateways leading to the supreme experience which is the poetry.

Romanticism also leads to the exaltation of the poet: for the poet experiences his life supremely at the moments when it becomes his poetry. The romantic does not, as does the classicist, regard himself as a craftsman standing outside the artefacts which he makes, which are his poems. The romantic *is* the poetry, the artefact, the record of a particular moment in the biography of the poet when the lived experience is transformed into the poetry, which replaces it.

When I was an undergraduate at Oxford I read voraciously Shakespeare's tragedies; also Webster and Tourneur. I then discovered modernism: above all James Joyce's *Ulysses.* It is difficult to remember what I got out of Joyce except a kind of intoxicated excitement. I certainly thought of *Ulysses* as an exercise in free association. 'Inspired' by it, I wrote a great deal of whatever-nonsense-came-into-my-head in the hope that it would result in work of genius like *Ulysses.* The fact that *Ulysses* was banned made it seem a great deal more readable than it may seem today to a younger generation, now that, at certain universities, it is compulsory reading. Bracketed with *Ulysses* as modern was T. S. Eliot's *The Waste Land.*

At Oxford I also read novels by D. H. Lawrence. Lawrence is one of those writers who either excite you enormously or leave you cold. I happen to be, on the whole, rather bored by descriptive writing. But with Lawrence, I can read his descriptions of the countryside near Nottingham in *The White Peacock,* or near Volterra in *Etruscan Places,* or of Mexico, and (there is no other way of expressing this) feel simply more alive. He is a master of selective precise observation within a wider luminosity, like one of the great impressionists – Monet – or perhaps like Cézanne. There is a comparable excitement in some pages of Ruskin, and of Carlyle.

In old age I go back to masterpieces. Recently I reread Tolstoy's *War and Peace,* Boswell's *Life of Johnson,* and Pascal. I find myself very interested in the history of the third and fourth centuries AD, and in the books of Peter Brown; his *Life of St Augustine,* and the more recent book, *The Body and Society,* about the contrasting attitudes of Christians and pagans to the body. I read the Greek dramatists in various translations, and Catullus, in Latin, with the help of cribs. After the 'greats', I have come to think of Catullus as my ideal poet, of uninhibited energy, driving forward-moving rhythm and straightforwardness.

I read a lot of books by my friends (they seem to write a lot, and several are very good writers) and a good deal of my time is taken up with reading critical essays and reviews in various publications. These contain some of the best and also some of the worst writing of our time. Like many of my friends, I am a Proust addict. The reason for this is, I think, that there are at least twenty characters in his great novel whom one knows – but never quite well enough, and whom one never tires of going back to. Even Tolstoy's characters seem to come forward to meet you, very conscious of the impression they are making on one another and on the reader. Proust's characters seem to escape down alleyways, and the reader follows them, never knowing what he will find them up to in some corner, at the bottom of some staircase, meeting a social equal or unequal, or indulging some hitherto unrealized propensity.

My favourite books

In making a list of my favourite books, I leave out the Bible and Shakespeare, which can be taken for granted. Here are some others:

The Prelude, William Wordsworth; *Poems* and *Letters,* John Keats; *Bleak House,* Charles Dickens; *Daniel Deronda,* George Eliot; *Huckleberry Finn,* Mark Twain; *The Christmas Garland,* Max Beerbohm; Poems by Ben Jonson, George Herbert, Alfred Lord Tennyson, Robert Browning, T. S. Eliot, Cavafy, W. H. Auden, Seamus Heaney etc, etc; *Between the Acts,* Virginia Woolf; *Women in Love,* D. H. Lawrence; *A Single Man,* Christopher Isherwood; *Chatterton,* Peter Ackroyd.

Michael Foot

SINCE my own father was the greatest reader who ever read – the case for the few rival claimants to the title may be considered later – and since in the houses where I was born and reared books were properly honoured, seductively displayed and piled high to the heavens, any suggestion that my taste for reading could be traced to some other source may seem an affectation. But it was so: what he gave me, and what he still gives, was an elixir of his own concoction which could guarantee a touch of instant relief but also an assured and lasting rejuvenation of the spirits. I will try to unravel these secrets later.

I was a late developer; maybe I stubbornly thought that there might be other interests allowed to compete. But any deficiency in this respect was more than made good by my beloved sister, Sally, just one year older than myself, who was already captivated by my father's imaginative excursions and volunteered to take me along too. She was my white witch, mischievously good, and she would always find room for me on her broomstick.

She had already started, in her early teens, as all children should, with the great novelists, while I was still stuck with the *Magnet*, the *Gem* and the *Popular*, and the elaboration of such schoolboy themes in Talbot Baines Reed's *The Cock-House at Fellsgarth*. Was this an early sign of a confirmed preference for the world around me? What puritan instinct held me back from Sally's next expedition to the realms of gold?

Even at Oxford, as I can now recall with amazement and shame, I had not learnt the lesson. Politics and economics and philosophy, to be studied together according to the innovation of the time, should have provided the ideal instruction and incitement. Just a few real writers were starting to intrude. Bertrand Russell would teach all these mighty subjects at the same time and much else besides. Indeed, he could parade for young people the whole armoury required for the translation of the good old liberal cause into democratic socialist triumph, for the conquest of happiness. He had the further virtue of writing the only book on philosophy I could comprehend. But the link between the way he wrote and what he wrote was not then so startlingly apparent as it should have been. *The Conquest of Happiness* was indeed the title of one of his very best books on morals and political conduct, and when I went to an Oxford meeting and saw the author himself, beaming with happiness and presenting his case on every subject with the same combined simplicity and wit, I became a convert on the spot. Moreover, Bertrand Russell offered an independent, original criticism of the great intellectual creed of Marxism which, not merely in

Oxford debating societies, but across the Western world, seemed to be sweeping all before it.

For the rest, the best book I read at Oxford – the one that sticks out in my mind and still retains its place on my shelf – was *The Early History of Charles James Fox* by G. O. Trevelyan and the accompanying volume on the later Fox by J. L. Hammond. These two offered political history as it should be written, confounding the Namierite school which was so fashionably enforced at that period. The old Whig interpretation of history had passion and wit and thorough grounding in the revolutionary traditions of the nation. The new Tory interpretation looked like some kind of parody of what was happening before our eyes in the age of Baldwin or Chamberlain. But real reading – I still hardly knew what it was. And, sin against the holy ghost, I actually sold some of the books I had acquired. Thereafter, I never ceased to curse my folly. Somewhere or other in the second-hand shops may still be found the first edition of J. M. Keynes's *Treatise on Money*, volumes which I thought I had inwardly digested and which at least spared me ever afterwards from succumbing to the kind of excuses for mass misery and unemployment suggested by the economist Hayek, which were already prevalent at the time.

Soon after that Oxford *auto-da-fé*, I found myself in Paris with my brother John, celebrating my twenty-first birthday and preparing for an adventurous journey across Europe towards what was then Palestine. But it was the book I shared with him which I remembered much more even than the glories or the temptations of Paris. We were reading H. G. Wells's *Tono-Bungay*, and soon after we had discovered its original delights, we rationed ourselves to about thirty pages a session, so that the ecstasy should not pass too soon. It is still, I believe, the very best of all Wells's novels, although there is no lack of competition. On my way home from that expedition, I made an unspoken resolve to explore the whole world of H. G. Wells. I was beginning to learn.

Was it Wells who introduced me to Arnold Bennett or the other way round? As a book-lover, Bennett would beat the lot – with the exception of my father. My guess is that Bennett did more than any other English writer in this century to teach people how to read, how to find time for reading, and how to set about building the personal library essential for the purpose.

He did so particularly in two little manuals of no more than a few thousand words, each published round about the year 1908, one called *How to Live on Twenty-Four Hours a Day*, and the other, *Literary Taste: how to form it*. The first, which became much the more famous – it went through six editions before 1913 – was not solely directed towards the art of book-reading. It set out to prove to the common man, on the best, commonsensical grounds, how much of his twenty-four hours a day he was wasting, and how, by taking thought, he could add intellectual cubits to his stature – change his whole life, indeed. Only in the last chapter but one did he reach the real subject of 'serious reading'. I do think that little book, literally, changed my life.

Four gods just at that time had been starting to take possession of my Valhalla, and I worshipped them daily by turns – H. G. Wells, Bertrand Russell, Bernard Shaw and Arnold Bennett. (Rebecca West, I discovered many years later, had called these four her literary uncles, or maybe she had Galsworthy instead of Bennett.) Bennett did not offer quite the same political inspiration as the others, although he was not deficient in that quality either. But his practical advice could be applied at once, and his way of reading could be applied to the others. I soon captured for reading the Arnold Bennett hours – on the bus, on the way home, every available period previously and recklessly squandered: *real* reading, reading for relaxation, reading in utter absorption, as if one were playing chess or watching Plymouth Argyle or falling in love or suchlike comparable pursuits.

But turn now from his *Twenty-Four Hours,* which might be regarded as no more than a brilliant mental trick, to his *Literary Taste,* which deserves an even louder and more lasting acclaim. He sets out in language no less plain, in sentences which follow hard and sharp and incontestable one upon another, how to come to love what you read. 'The aim of literary study is not to amuse the hours of leisure . . . It is not to affect one hour, but twenty-four hours. It is to change utterly one's relation with the world.' Then: 'Do not worry about literature in the abstract, about theories as to literature. Get at it. Get hold of literature in the concrete as a dog gets hold of a bone.' He introduces you to one man and writer, writer and man, Charles Lamb: 'He is a great writer, wide in his appeal, of a highly sympathetic temperament; and his finest achievements are simple and very short.'

Who could resist such an enchanting invitation? Charles Lamb's reputation is not quite what it was when Arnold Bennett wrote those words. But no one who makes the Lamb–Bennett entry into the limitless adventure of literature is ever likely to feel that their first steps have been misguided.

I reread both these little classics the other day, and happily recall my first reading of them – in the early 1930s – just after Bennett's own death, just after I had left the suffocating study of economics and philosophy at Oxford, and was turning to more joyous topics such as socialism, sex and the other truly liberating themes hinted at in the choice of authors listed above.

I recalled vividly considerable chunks of the momentous advice Bennett had offered. But there too, to my astonishment, was another name which later became to me more treasured than any other: William Hazlitt. I had thought it was my own father who, a few years later, had taught me to read him, and the first Hazlitt books I ever read certainly came from his library. But his advice must have mingled with Arnold Bennett's. For here too are a few sentences which could surely incite any receptive mind to read Hazlitt. 'If you chance,' he writes in *Literary Taste,* 'to read Hazlitt on *Chaucer* and *Spenser,* you will probably put your hat on instantly and go out and buy these authors; *such is his communicating fire.*' And then again, a few pages later: 'Read William Hazlitt's essay *On Poetry in General* . . . He has put the truth about poetry in a way as interesting, clear and reassuring as anyone is ever likely to put it. I do not expect, however, that you will instantly gather the full message . . . After a week's interval read the essay again.'

Good advice, for sure; *that*'s the way to read things worth reading. And then again I noticed a reference, this time in his *How to Live on Twenty-Four Hours*, which is much less a book about specific books. There too he returns to Hazlitt, prizes him almost above anyone else: 'If poetry is what is called "a sealed book" to you, begin by reading Hazlitt's famous essay on the nature of *Poetry in General*. It is the best thing of its kind in English, and no-one who has read it can possibly be under the misapprehension that poetry is a medieval torture, or a mad elephant, or a gun that will go off by itself and kill at forty paces.' At which point, I should make it clear that one of the main purposes of the two books together is to make you read *poetry*; literature in general but poetry in particular. Read it all, again and again, as he prescribed, and like the greatest poems it will offer fresh discoveries at each reading.

But these are just glimpses. Neither William Hazlitt nor Arnold Bennett were poets, but each believed that poetry was the highest form of artistic expression and each had an overpowering passion to share his own discovery with others. Of course, Arnold Bennett could never be seen as a critic of the Hazlitt quality: what he did share with him was the *gusto*, the zest for books, the eagerness to share his excitement with all he could persuade to listen. His power of literary persuasion was very strong indeed. And one further essential part of the recommendation was that his readers should *buy a library*, and he showed in *Literary Taste* how it could be done, intelligently and cheaply.

Which brings me back to my father, and the way books should be read, and the way new authors should be honoured, and the way everything about them should be disinterred, and how preferably they should be assembled on shelves inviting the reader to return to the old favourites as whim or accident might prompt him. He combined the Hazlitt method and the Bennett method and what seemed to be an extra dimension of his own. Once upon a time, in his impecunious youth, my father, as he walked to work, would read a Shakespeare play or a book of *Paradise Lost* every week. Still, at the age of fourteen, he started to build a library: the Penny Poets and some pamphlets of Edmund Burke set him on his way. Thereafter, he reared seven children, pursued a full political life but made sure that time would always be available, whatever the pressures, whatever the cost, to enable all his chosen authors to have a fair chance to put their case, and by that he usually meant everything they have to say and everything said about them. They would become in turn his inseparable, living companions. He had, as Montaigne put it, 'a singular curiosity to know the soul and natural judgements of my authors'. He came to Montaigne only comparatively late in life, but they were fellow-spirits or fellow-souls on the first acquaintance. Each knew how books should be treated.

My favourite books

So my list of necessary books starts with Montaigne, happily included in the one-volume translation by Colin Frame.

Every follower of Montaigne has acclaimed the new translation, and Montaigne would have done the same, since he read the soul of many of *his* authors in translation.

Two who acknowledged their debt to Montaigne in the next period – leaving aside his pupil Shakespeare, for no good reason – were Jonathan Swift and Alexander Pope.

A hundred years later Hazlitt and Byron, argumentative rivals in some other fields, united in their homage to Montaigne. Hazlitt's *Essays* may best be seen as a giant autobiography, like Montaigne's, and Byron was making up for lost time on his way to Greece in the end, reading an essay by Montaigne or a poem by Swift every day. Byron and Swift, of course, were both bookworms from infancy to the day of their deaths.

Who can conceivably be mentioned in the same breath as these? But there are some: the socialist writers who saw that this delight must be decently shared, like all the other good things of this earth. Some of their sacred names have already been cited: Bertrand Russell, H. G. Wells, Bernard Shaw, Arnold Bennett. But another must be immediately added to the list, as all these would concur: Robert Blatchford, editor of the *Clarion*, showed more working-class readers the way to read than anyone else. So his *My Favourite Books*, often to be found in the second-hand shops, should be in every library, alongside Montaigne. He was, naturally, a devoted follower of Montaigne too.

Patrick Leigh Fermor

Left on the Locker

'"TWANG!" A clothyard-shaft struck the banqueting-board and stood quivering. A message was twisted round it, and, starting up, the Sheriff and the barons looked at each other aghast . . .' (It would be an insult to the reader to name the legendary tales this exclamation comes from, and most of the books mentioned later need no author's name. With less familiar books, especially foreign ones, I hope that the absent names, when they are unknown, will prove that exciting treasure-hunt and stimulus to curiosity which always lead us on to literary exploration and further delights.)

Pretending to read, I was really reciting by heart – I had followed the words often enough, after badgering people to go through that particular page aloud; for, though I was six, reading was still beyond me. I was ashamed that others could manage at four, the whole thing was a sham, I was unmasked when told to turn over and sighs of pity and boredom went up. It wasn't the first time.

Books, on one's own, still meant pictures. It had been all right earlier on. *Jemima Puddleduck* could do without the text, so could the contemptible *Chicks' Own* and *Little Folks* and the sophisticated 'Bruin Boys', and my hero *Little Black Sambo* too. (I gazed for hours at Henry Ford's illustrations in the *Coloured Fairy Books*; those wide-eyed kings' daughters, ice-maidens and water-sprites were exactly the sort of girls, later on, that I would pine for and pursue.) Luckily, there was a lot of maternal reading aloud: all Kipling's books for children, *Treasure Island*, *Black Beauty*, *The Heroes*, *Alice*, *Wet Magic*, *Three Men in a Boat*, *The Midnight Folk*, *The Forest Lovers*, Somerville and Ross, Surtees, scenes from Shakespeare and *Oliver Twist*. (Dulac and Rackham illustrations moved on to Phiz, Cruikshank, Tenniel and du Maurier and then, downhill, to Sheppard and Hugh Thompson.)

The miracle of literacy happened at last, it turned an unlettered brute into a book-ridden lunatic. Till it was light enough to read, furious dawn-watches ushered in days flat on hearth-rugs or grass, in ricks or up trees, which ended in stifling torchlit hours under bedclothes. Book-ownership was the next step. To assuage a mania for Scott, I was given four Collins pocket Waverley novels every birthday and Christmas and my father sent sumptuous works about animals or botany from India, wrapped in palm-leaves and sewn with a thousand stitches by Thacker and Spink in Calcutta or Simla. When the Scott craze died, I tried Thackeray, loved *Vanity Fair* but failed with all the rest. Dickens became a lasting passion and there was no looking back with *Pride and Prejudice* and *Wuthering Heights*. Moments of illumination followed fast: falling scales and initiations – epiphanies unloosing journeys of discovery that rushed away and branched and meandered all through the years between six and eighteen.

Untimely ripped from school at sixteen-and-a-half and sent to an Army crammer in London, I read more in the next two years than ever before or after: but, instead of Sandhurst, I suddenly longed for Constantinople, caught a boat to Holland and set off.

My literary state of play on departure is best approached through contemporary poetry. I knew nothing about Pound or Eliot, and of Yeats only 'Innisfree', one sonnet and 'Down by the Salley Gardens' – which, anyway, belonged to singing – and nothing at all about younger poets now venerable. My favourites were Sacheverell, Edith and Osbert Sitwell and in prose, Norman Douglas, Aldous Huxley and Evelyn Waugh. I judged earlier poets now by whether I knew anything they had written by heart that I could recite as I slogged along the roads of Swabia and Bavaria. At home and at school there had been much learning by rote, both compulsory and by choice. The young learn as quick as mynahs, at an age, luckily, when everything sticks: and the list starts with two or three Shakespeare sonnets, a few speeches and choruses from *Henry V*, some Marlowe ('Ah, Faustus . . .'), Milton (*Lycidas*), and Spenser's *Prothalamion* ('Sweet Thames! runne softly . . .'). Then came stretches of Tennyson, Browning and Coleridge, bits of Shelley's 'West Wind', most of Keats's odes (no Byron; Keats was still the yardstick): and fragments of Gray and Pope. Some of Scott's verse survived, with Rossetti as a medieval aftermath, though fading fast. Several border ballads were next, then 'The Burial of Sir John Moore at Corunna', patches of 'The Scholar Gypsy' and *Hound of Heaven*: 'Cynara': *The Dead at Clonmacnois* from the Irish, a lot of Kipling, *Hassan*'s serenade of Yasmin: plenty from *A Shropshire Lad*; and (part of a recent metaphysical addiction) passages of Donne, Ralegh, Wyatt and Marvell, Carroll and Lear abounded, but, for some reason, not Chesterton or Belloc. *Horatius* and most of *The Battle of Lake Regillus* were the longer pieces: *Granchester*; and, more or less in sequence, *The Rubaiyat of Omar Khayyam*. I loved French, but the entries are soon over: one poem of de Banville (*'Nous n'irons plus au bois'*), two of Baudelaire, a bit of Verlaine (*'Les sanglots longs des violons'*), Ronsard's original of the famous Yeats sonnet, and another by du Bellay (*'Heureux qui comme Ulysse . . .'* etc), and finally, Villon, starting with the *Ballads of the Dead Ladies and of the Hanged Men*; a recent and all-absorbing mania.

Moving back and changing step, tracts of Virgil, hammered into my head by countless impositions at school, now boomed out over the snow, a few odes of Horace and some Catullus, including a bit of the *Attis*, six lines of Petronius and Hadrian's five lines to his soul. Next, two Latin hymns, remnants of a spasmodic religious mania, and some recently learnt verses from the Archpoet and the *Carmina Burana*. I ended with snatches from Homer, two or three epitaphs of Simonides and two four-line moon-poems of Sappho.

Roughly speaking, the date of this giveaway rag-bag is the winter of 1933, when I was just short of nineteen. The general intake is approached through verse because the inevitably larger prose corollary, by a shadowy logic, automatically suggests itself.

Now, with an unknown language and shifting scenery, something quite different was on the way. The language assault was through village talk and Schlegel and Tieck's *Hamlet, Prinz von Dänemark*; Austrian inns, Vienna, and a *Schloss* or two in Slovakia; German poets were turning into something more than names. It was a season of inklings; I was put on the track of Hölderlin, Rilke, Stefan George and Morgenstern; and by the time I got to Transylvania that summer, I could arduously and very slowly hack my way through *Tod in Venedig*. (I never got much further.) They were haymaking in Hungary, the dactylic canter of Magyar was mettlesome and stirring, yet little remained; but Romanian, a Latin tongue with some of the vowels Slavonically fogged, seemed much easier and enough of it stuck to help with the poems of Eminescu and Goga later on. Across the Danube that autumn a Bulgarian smattering and a grapple with Cyrillic came and went with the speed of measles: and over the next border, the agglutinative harshness of the Turks, laced with genteel diaereses, sounded like drinking out of a foeman's skull with a little finger raised.

Suddenly it was winter again. Constantinople was already astern, snowflakes were falling fast, and I was landing in Mount Athos, impelled there by the books of Robert

Byron. (I had met him, before setting out, in a nearly pitch-dark Soho nightclub where everyone was clouded by strong drink.) I knew by instinct that Greece was going to mean much in the coming years; but, in Cretan caves during the war it was *David Copperfield* – read and reread and falling to bits – which kept us going. The other resources – literature without letters – were complex Cretan mountain songs and their spontaneous fifteen-syllable rhyming couplets to the notes of the three-stringed rebeck. Sometimes, for strange smoky hours, as we lay round on brushwood under the stalactites, while our old shepherd hosts intoned a few miles of the marvellous *Erotokritos* myth. It is longer than Homer's *Odyssey* and, like iron age Dorians reciting Homer before the alphabet, they could neither read nor write. But there was never a falter.

These two years of wandering ended with a backward loop to Romania. I settled there for a long time in a rambling country house where the dales of Moldavia sloped away to Bessarabia and the Ukraine. As in the Russia of Tolstoy and in pre-war Poland, some Romanian families, often to their regret, spoke French more readily than their own language and so it was here.

An octagonal library held the whole of French literature; encyclopaedias and histories beckoned in vistas; and, during two winters with snow to the windowsills and miraculously cut off except for horses and sleighs, I tried to advance deeper into this transplanted French world than earlier steps had allowed. It was a dominating and – or so I felt – somehow a debarbarizing passion.

Books were a paperchase. *Le Grand Meaulnes*, left invitingly open, led to haunting new regions where *Le Potomac* and *Le Bal du Comte d'Orgel* were landmarks, until, totally at random, I would find myself up to the neck in *Le Lutrin, Mademoiselle de Maupin, Bajazet* or *Illusions Perdues* – or, indeed, in *Arsène Lupin*; or Giono or Panait Istrati: Charles d'Orléans, Hérédia, Mallarmé, Verhaeren, Apollinaire and Patrice de la Tour du Pin followed, and many others, and thanks to the fluke of my whereabouts, Russian literature first impinged in French translations. Matila Ghyka, the author of *Le Nombre d'Or*, often came to stay, bringing the latest issues of *transition, Minotaure* and *Verve*; also fascinating gossip about Valéry, Léon-Paul Fargue, Paul Morand, Saint-Exupéry, Eugène Jolas and his other friends in Paris: he pointed the way to *Là-Bas, Axel, Les Diaboliques* and *Sylvie* and let the names of Corbière and Laforgue hang in the air. *L'Aiglon* was read aloud and *Les Fourberies de Scapin*; and now and then, to change from *analogies* and *bouts rimés* after dinner, somebody would take down the literary parodies of Reboux and Muller; the glow of shaded petroleum lamps lit the faces of the readers and the listeners. The four chief English-language milestones of that time were D. H. Lawrence, Virginia Woolf (*Orlando*), Hemingway and Joyce. *Paludes* and *Les Caves du Vatican* were the break-in to Gide: very excitingly, many people in Romania seemed to have been friends of Proust. Once I had begun, allegiance was immediate and for good.

This house, then, resembled a chaotic and abounding waterfall. I was there when war broke out in September 1939, so there was plenty to think about, at the Guards'

Depot two months later over the buttonsticks and the Brasso. (When I went back to Moldavia recently, the house had completely vanished. Some industrial buildings, already abandoned, had taken its place, and the trees had been cut down long ago.)

'The eleventh edition of the *Encyclopaedia Britannica*, Fowler, Brewer, Liddell and Scott, Dr Smith, Harrap, Larousse, Lempriere, Duden, the whole DNB, *Hobson-Jobson*, a battery of atlases, concordances, dictionaries, Loeb classics, Pléiade editions, Oxford Companions, Cambridge Histories, anthologies, and books on birds, beasts, plants and stars – ' I was looking through a list made years ago, when planning a house on a remote headland of the Morea: 'If you are settling in the wilds, ten reference shelves are the minimum.'

All right for a house, perhaps, but not for a desert island. Not under the present rules. Curiosity is half the pleasure of reading, so what's to be done? As I brood, my lids began to sink . . . and my faculties lose hold . . . If it were Prospero's island, a wave of the wand could float an illicit and watertight trunk ashore, enough to fill ten sand-proof shelves in the hut . . . but if that's the way things are, Danaë might emerge, holding Perseus . . . I shake myself. There will be no trunk, no Danaë, no Perseus, no Miranda, no Calypso, no Man Friday even, and no puff of smoke on the horizon.

We are allowed Shakespeare and the Bible as well as the choice ten books; but how many actual *volumes*? I plan to start with Auden's five-volume, brilliantly chosen

Poets of the English Language: it runs from Langland to Yeats. No Eliot, of course, and, indeed, no Auden: but Maurice Baring used to savage a dozen books to glue in reams of extra pages, and I shall do the same . . . In goes *The Decline and Fall of the Roman Empire*, all seven volumes, with Bury's notes, followed by Evelyn Waugh's *Decline and Fall*. (But what about *Vile Bodies, Black Mischief, Scoop*, and *Put Out More Flags*? I've got to have them. Perhaps they could be microfilmed or stitched together. If this won't do, it will have to be the first on the list and the same applies to *Antic Hay, Crome Yellow* and *Those Barren Leaves*). *Old Calabria* goes in without a shadow of doubt; it's a particular style and cast of mind here that one can't do without, so Cyril Connolly follows. Next comes the Temple Classics Dante, with its crib, *Kim*, read about every two years; the habit is too old to break. The *Odyssey*, certainly (glued to the *Iliad*?). No good without a parallel text, alas, so I'll get them stapled to Robert Fitzgerald's translations, or Richard Lattimore's. *Ulysses* comes next, and lastly *À la recherche du temps perdu*. When I finish the last page, I can start all over again.

Later

I stack them on the locker.

As it turns out, the crew are lenient about the definition of 'book', and indulgent about staples and glue, but they are inflexible about number: 'There are eleven here, I'm afraid, sir.' At this moment the siren goes and a voice shouts: 'Island in sight!' All eyes turn to the porthole and with a conjuror's speed a slim volume flies into my bush shirt pocket: *The Unquiet Grave* is safe! And all goes well at the recount. The books are tidily arranged in the portman-teau, zipped up, padlocked and carried on deck.

A desperate moment! What about Saki, *Bleak House*, Walpole's letters, Burckhardt, Sheridan, Horace, *Nightmare Abbey*, Raby's *Christian and Secular Latin*? I'll never learn about *Hisperica Famina* now (for a second I think I catch the faraway, accusing, millionfold moo of the unread; then it faded . . .); Gerard Manley Hopkins, Browning, Pius II's *Memoirs*, *War and Peace*, Plutarch, la Rochefoucauld, *Les Fleurs du Mal*, Chaucer, Donne and Montaigne – there they lie higgledy-piggledy on the bunk. ('Five minutes now'; I stroke *The Wings of the Dove* for the last time.) They remind me of Saint Augustine's lifelong sins on the eve of his conversion: they plucked at his garments and twittered: 'What! Are you leaving us now? All your old friends? And forever?' ('Stand by'). *Tristram Shandy? Mr Sponge's Sporting Tour? Huckleberry Finn?* Boswell? *Torrents of Spring? Phineas Redux? Far from the Madding Crowd?* ('Steady there') Lorca? *Uncle Fred in the Springtime? Urn Burial? Tintin* . . .?

'We'll have to look sharp, sir. They are putting the boat down now. O, thank you, sir!' (I shan't need it) 'and the best of good luck to you sir.'

Doris Lessing

Because I left school when I was fourteen, a drop-out before the word was minted, I educated myself through reading. An autodidact. An ugly blocky little word for a free-ranging unhedged condition. The advantages and otherwise can be (over) simplified like this . . . If you have taught yourself through books then every one has been chosen by you, as part of a personal Odyssey, has been absorbed and becomes part of your substance. But later you keep unearthing areas of ignorance, and have to spend time catching up on information every schoolchild has. Perhaps, these days, I should say: every schoolchild ought to have. What dulls my regret is that I would not have chosen rightly at eighteen, for I would certainly have been channelled into literature and history. But anyone can discover literature and history for themselves: all you need is a library ticket and some advice. I most sorrow-fully and passionately regret not knowing mathematics and languages. Maths is essential for understanding all the starry and turbulent research that goes on, overturning all our ideas about ourselves: not having maths is like being half-blind, half-deaf. And languages are what we need for this world that gets smaller every minute. And, no, it is not easy to learn languages after you are young.

I began reading at seven, off a cigarette packet, and almost at once progressed to the books in my parents' bookcase, which would be found in any middle-class household then, and, for that matter, the yeasty section of the working class who saw books as a key to a better life. Sets of Dickens, Walter Scott, Stevenson, Rudyard Kipling. Some Hardy and Meredith. The Brontës. George Eliot – English classics but, interestingly, none from the eighteenth century. There were anthologies of poetry, a collection of Impressionist pictures, many books of memoirs and histories of the First World War. I read, or tried, most of these before I was ten or so. The books I responded to then are not those I would choose as best now. You have to read a book at the right time for you, and I am sure this cannot be insisted on too often, for it is the key to the enjoyment of literature. I read children's books, some unknown to today's children. The Americans: L. M. Montgomery's *Anne of Green Gables* books, Susan Coolidge's *What Katy Did* series, the *Girl of the Limberlost* by Gene Stratton Porter and its sequels. Louisa Alcott. Hawthorne. Henty. The English classics were Lewis Carroll, who I like better now than I did then, and Milne's *Winnie-the-Pooh*, which I adored then, but feel uneasy about now. The hero is a stupid greedy little bear, and the clever animals are ridiculous: good old England, I sometimes think, at it again. But there was Kenneth Grahame's *The Wind in the Willows*, and a wonderful children's newspaper, and a magazine called *The Merry-Go-Round* that printed Walter de la Mare, Eleanor Farjeon, Lawrence Binyon, and other fine writers. Walter de la Mare's *The Three Royal Monkeys* entranced me then, and still kept some of its magic about it when I recently reread it.

I was lucky that my parents read to my brother and me. I believe nothing has the impact of stories read or told. I remember the atmosphere of those evenings, and all the stories, some of them long-running domestic epics made up by my mother, about the adventures of mice, or our cats and dogs, or the little monkeys that lived around us in the bush and sometimes leaped about in the rafters under the thatch, or the interaction between our domestic animals and the wild ones all around us. For that was before the wild animals were driven out. Recently I was describing my childhood to a young black man and he asked: 'Did you live in a safari park?' At school a couple of the girls told stories after lights out, lurid and wildly funny tales. Parents who read to their children or who make up stories are giving them the finest gift in the world. Do we too often forget that tale-telling is thousands of years old, whereas we have been reading for a trifling number of centuries?

I believe that children are very bright when young and become more stupid as the hormones boil and bubble. I read more difficult books when I was eight, nine, ten, eleven, than I did until I was sixteen, when it occurred to me (probably because of the eruption into my bloodstream of some chemical or other) that I had been in a doze and a daze for years, reading the same things over and over. I have taken tiny children, of three, four, five, to films like *2001*, *Star Wars*, *Close Encounters of the Third Kind*, and I have watched a four-year-old boy listen to an Ivy Compton Burnett dramatized on radio for an hour-and-a-half, not moving a muscle. By the time they are eleven or so they can only understand *Neighbours*.

At sixteen, with my mind exploding, I thought, there is that world of books out there, and I began on the trajectories of discovery that will end when I die. What did I begin with? As it happened, H. G. Wells and *The Shape of Things to Come*, but it could have been any serious book lying around. Wells and Shaw – what excitements, what ferments, what delicious iconoclastic reversals of everything currently being taught and thought around me . . . this was in old Southern Rhodesia, now Zimbabwe, and it could hardly be described as an intellectually stimulating place. Mostly, I was on my own, though I kept coming on people in this or that farmhouse in the bush with rooms full of books, many of them awkwardly-cornered eccentrics who would never slot into England. I used to track down books mentioned in other books – a novel, history, memoirs.

Then I heard of the Everyman Library and sent to London for parcels of books that took weeks to arrive. I'll never forget the intoxication when I opened the parcels. Some of them I was too young for, they bored me: Ruskin, Carlyle, Hazlitt, Dr Johnson. But I discovered the then modern English writers, my contemporaries, if my elders; Virginia Woolf, D. H. Lawrence, Aldous Huxley, Lytton Strachey.

The classic Russians, Tolstoy, Dostoyevsky, Chekhov, Lermontov, Turgenev. The modern Russian novel *And Quiet Flows the Don* by Mikhail Sholokhov, which introduced me to the Russian Revolution for the second time: the first was in a comic strip of Pip, Squeak and Wilfski (I think) full of stage bolsheviks with bombs, modelled on Trotsky. This surely shows that early conditioning does not necessarily go deep? Soon I discovered Thoreau and Whitman, Proust and Thomas Mann, Balzac and Conrad. The modern Americans, Dreiser, Henry Miller, Steinbeck, Faulkner. And then, at last, to the eighteenth century for Fielding's *Tom Jones* and Richardson's *Clarissa* and Sterne's *Tristram Shandy* and Defoe's *Moll Flanders*. Stendhal – *To the Happy Few* and *La Vie de Henri Brulard*.

The delicious excitement of it all . . . the discoveries . . . the surprises . . . I was intoxicated a good part of the time. I make this point because it is possible, not to say usual, for young people to 'study' literature, and never be told that the point of literature is pleasure, and not the dreary analysis that can be of interest only to academics who, some think, have captured literature. It seems there was a point in this country when it was debated whether to make literature a university subject. Some said no – too frivolous. Others said, with Jane Austen, that through novels you may learn about human behaviour. These won. This has led to the university departments, literary prizes, and literary festivals and conferences on structuralism and post-structuralism. 'Every stick has two ends': on the one hand, literature is a serious matter, but on the other, some academics think literature is their property. The results can be seen in the attitude of some young people to books. Asked what they read, if they read at all, their replies are often variations on: 'No I don't read, because I didn't study literature at university,' or: 'We had to do *Macbeth* at school and that put me off for good.' This is enough to have any writer weeping and moaning and tearing her or his hair. Literature is for everybody. It does not need professors and teachers. Yet there are teachers who inspire generations of children to read. If you meet an adult who does read, very often they say: 'There was this wonderful teacher who . . .' I meet them as I travel around. For instance there was this Australian, a young woman who said she was working-class, had been brought up in a house without books, but had had a marvellous teacher. She now taught children brought up in homes without books, disadvantaged and, until she worked with them, half-illiterate. They read Shakespeare and classics and Patrick White and Henry Handel Richardson and wrote stories and plays.

The libraries are treasure-houses of stories, poems, essays, from every country in the world and from all times, and literature shades off into history and magic and mystery and religion, into sociology and anthropology – into nearly every subject you can think of, and it is there for everyone. There for the trouble of finding someone who loves books ready to make suggestions. A public library is the most democratic thing in the world. What can be found there has undone dictators and tyrants: demagogues can persecute writers and tell them what to write as much as they like, but they cannot vanish what has been written in the past, though they try often enough. In my paranoid

moments I wonder if the neglect, amounting to persecu-
tion, of libraries in this country now is because people who
have access to good libraries, to history, ideas, information,
cannot be told what to think. People who love literature
have at least a part of their minds immune from indoctri-
nation. If you read, you can learn to think for yourself.

When I say literature shades off into history and so
on, this means looking at novels from the point of view
of the information in them which we tend rather to
take for granted. One may judge novels and short stories on their excellence and otherwise, but one may also
learn about the societies they describe. How do we know
about pre-revolutionary Russia? From the writers of that
time. Tolstoy's *Anna Karenina* describes social conditions,
attitudes to women, no longer existing in the West – but
women like her are persecuted now in many parts of
the world. How do we know about the various stages
of the United States? From the writers. If you are studying the social conditions in the English countryside in
the nineteenth century, what better than Hardy's novels?
Greece . . . Rome . . . Medieval Europe? Nor do they
have to be 'great' writers. I have known more than one
child faced with history examinations who has taken adult
advice to read popular historical novels set in the period.
Authors of historical romances usually take trouble to get
facts and details right. To take an analogy from music: one
may enjoy everything from Beethoven and Berlioz to the
Beatles and the blues. Some young people are put off reading the best because they aren't ready for it. Not everyone
has had the luck to be brought up on a solitary farm in

the bush without television, with a crackling radio fit only for a strained listening to the BBC News – but a bookcase full of classics. What is wrong with reading Shakespeare as a comic book, and then going on to reading, or seeing, Shakespeare? There is a short step from Mills and Boon to *Jane Eyre*, if it is one that takes you from one country to another. Perhaps students should be told that an effort is always required, when you start to read a serious author, to overcome mental laziness and reluctance, because you are about to enter the mind of someone who thinks differently from yourself. And that is the whole point and the only point: the literary treasure-house has many mansions.

I see that I have written from the point of view of encouraging children, young people, and this is because I do feel pain, because of what they are cut off from, deprived of – and refuse because no one has encouraged them. Particularly now, with at least one generation of badly taught youngsters becoming adults, they could be persuaded that deficiencies may be made up in libraries – with the proper advice.

What do I read now? What I always have read, for I reread continually. Luckily I read fast. I don't know how I would manage otherwise. I try to keep up with what is being written, but it is not possible, there is so much good writing coming out in so many countries. Also, like all writers, I get sent books from publishers, sometimes nine or ten a week, because they hope for 'quotes' that will help to sell the books. I try to read enough of each at least to get a taste, but it is an unfair business, for if you are absorbed in your own work, or tired, then the book may strike you less attractively. Besides, if you were to 'puff' even one book a week, what would your recommendations be worth? I read a lot of the books that give information. For instance, James Gleick's *Chaos*, about how, independently, in separate countries and universities, physicists overturned current ideas of physics. Barbara Tuchman's books. *New World, New Mind* by Robert Ornstein and Paul R. Ehrlich. *Sufi Thought and Action*, pieces collected by Idries Shah – for this way of looking at the world seems to me by far the most rewarding of any I have met in my life. Then, history. Nirad Chaudhuri, *The Autobiography of an Unknown Indian*. Michael Holroyd's biographies of Lytton Strachey and Bernard Shaw. I have been rereading the essays of Loren Eisley, the American anthropologist. Chekhov's *The Island* – about the prisoners on Sakhalin. Neil Sheehan's *The Bright Shining Lie*. Jean Cocteau's *Opium* . . . where does one stop? How about Schama's *Citizens,* and his *An Embarrassment of Riches* – both overturn set ideas, 'received opinion'.

My favourite books

My favourite ten books. I'll make a list provided it is understood I could as easily choose another, then another, then . . . *The Overcoat*, by Gogol. It is short, compressing into itself a picture of the life of the civil servants of St Petersburg, all the heartbreak and grim humour of poverty. And it not possible to say whether it should be on a shelf with 'realism' or the one marked 'fantasy', and this I like, because I increasingly think these divisions are arbitrary. It is a miracle of a novel. *Fathers and Sons*, by Turgenev, with characters that foreshadow some who have come into their full development only now. A prophetic book that helps us to understand our times, like Dostoyevsky's *The Devils*, about violence and perversity for fun, for pleasure, and out of a need for ever stronger sensations. *The Red and the Black*, by Stendhal. My favourite writer, I think, when I haven't decided on Joseph Conrad. Homer's *Iliad*. *To the Lighthouse*, by Virginia Woolf. Another miracle of poetic compression. *Tom Jones*, by Henry Fielding. This country becomes every day more like the eighteenth century, full of thieves and adventurers, rogues and a robust and unhypocritical savagery, side by side with people lecturing others on morality. *Huckleberry Finn*, by Mark Twain. *Remembrance of Things Past*, by Marcel Proust. *The Fortunes of Richard Mahoney* by Henry Handel Richardson, the Australian woman writer, for some reason ignored. A great writer by any standards. We all know that writers go in and out of fashion like hem lengths and ostrich feathers, but surely this little bit of literary whimsicality has gone on too long.

Brian Moore

SOME people seem to have total recall of their early reading. I do not. But I vividly remember something about one of the first stories I ever read. I was in primary school and, having mastered the alphabet, was being taught to read aloud. I do not remember the name of the story and have forgotten its resolution. I remember that it was a 'giantkiller' story in which a boy wore a belt engraved with the legend 'Seven Have I Killed With One Blow'. As I read on I found that his boast was a form of deception, for he had killed seven flies, not men, with this momentous blow.

I was excited by this tale and, for the first time, I wanted to read other stories. The alphabet, which I had mastered without knowing why I should, had opened up a world more intriguing and mysterious than the world I knew. Written words could deceive. Through them, people could be made to believe untruths. And of course, although I did not know it, I had been introduced to hyperbole. Or was it irony?

And so, at a very early age I became an avid reader. Our house was filled with books, but when I think back to those days of my first reading I remember only long-ago boys' papers like the *Gem* and the *Magnet* and a serial called *The Wolf of Kabul*. I think my first and most important introduction to great writing was at the age of eleven when I read, in school, Shakespeare's *Macbeth*, *Julius Caesar* and *The Merchant of Venice*, set plays for school examinations. Being introduced to these great thunderstorms of language, to characters as vivid and strange as Lady Macbeth, Shylock and Mark Antony, and being forced to memorize and recite aloud the set speeches led me to a belief I have held ever since. The pleasure of reading exceeds the pleasure of watching even the greatest performance.

But while I bless my teachers, priests at a blinkered Irish Catholic boarding school who made me learn those lines by heart, I know now that they could also be wreckers of the true and the good. Not only did they never mention any author or book which was not on the school curriculum, but they seemed to have no feeling for the works they taught. I remember our English master droning these lines from 'The Lake Isle of Innisfree': 'Nine bean-rows will I have there, a hive for the honey-bee/And live alone in the bee-loud glade.' 'That is onomatopoeia, boys. You can hear the sound of the buzzing bees.' I did, and for years associated Yeats's poetry with the memory of falling asleep.

In fact modern poetry might have passed me by in my early years had I not, at the age of sixteen, discovered *The Faber Book of Modern Verse* edited by Michael Roberts,

which became for me as for many of my generation our
introduction to Eliot, Auden, MacNeice, Wallace Stevens,
Hart Crane and others. Reading *The Waste Land* made me
realize that the books in my father's house and the books
I was being given in school lacked the excitement of the
new.

And then, on one never-to-be-forgotten Sunday afternoon, while I watched my sisters play tennis in the back
garden of my uncle's house in Belfast, an older cousin
surreptitiously passed me a book which he had just smug-
gled in from Paris, opening it at a page which, he said,
was 'a hot bit'. I read the passage he showed me, erotically
excited at first but, gradually, reading on with an interest
which had nothing to do with the book's sexual content.
It was a novel unlike any I had ever read before and, aston-
ishingly, it dealt with Ireland, its religion, and its people. I
borrowed it from my cousin and never returned it. It is the
one and only book I ever stole and is still in my possession,
the two-volume Odyssey Press edition of *Ulysses.*

And then, at the age of eighteen, never having been
out of Ireland, I lay one day on the top of Cave Hill, the
mountain which overlooks my native city. I was reading
The Sun Also Rises, lost in Hemingway's perfect evocation
of a Spanish bullfight fiesta and the Left Bank café life of
expatriates in the 1920s. I read about a man called Jake
Barnes and his doomed sterile love affair with a beautiful
woman called Brett Ashley. I realized that Jake Barnes, like
Stephen Dedalus, was a writer of sorts and that both were
half in love with lands which were not their own. Looking

back now I think that reading these two books formed my desire to leave Ireland and become a writer. Which I did.

My favourite books

A Personal Anthology, Jorge Louis Borges; *Ulysses,* James Joyce; *Anna Karenina,* Leo Tolstoy; *At Swim-Two-Birds,* Flann O'Brien; *Madame Bovary,* Gustave Flaubert; *The Heart of the Matter,* Graham Greene; *Mémoires d'Outre-Tombe,* Chateaubriand; *Collected Poems,* T. S. Eliot; *A Handful of Dust,* Evelyn Waugh; *The Sun Also Rises,* Ernest Hemingway.

Robert Burchfield

Yes, she thought, laying down her brush in extreme fatigue, I have had my vision.

To the Lighthouse, Virginia Woolf

In a well-ordered life a catalogue of the books that have given one special pleasure should fall neatly into periods – pre-school books, those read at primary school, at secondary school, at university, and in later life – and into genres. It might start with nursery rhymes and Beatrix Potter, continue with *The Wind in the Willows* and Kipling's *Puck of Pook's Hill,* and move on to *Ivanhoe* by Walter Scott and *Pride and Prejudice.* Theoretically no university should admit a student to a course in English language and literature who does not possess a prior working knowledge of numerous classics like *Peter Pan, Robinson Crusoe,* and *Jane Eyre.*

If you happened to be born in a working-class environment in a small city in New Zealand in 1923, as I was, such an ideal plan was out of the question. Life was full of all sorts of pleasures, but there were no books in the house, and for me reading was strictly and narrowly directed towards passing examinations. Mastering the elements of geometry and chemistry was as important as reading and understanding Tennyson's 'The Charge of the Light Brigade' or Coleridge's 'The Rime of the Ancient Mariner'. The only book that I can recall my father pressing me to read, apart from the Bible, was a socialist tract called *The Struggle for Existence* by Walter Thomas Mills. He possessed (and I have inherited) a copy of the eighth edition, 1904. It was all about inequality and iniquity: it had sectional headings like 'Inherited Mastery and Servitude' and 'The Collective Struggle'. I was unimpressed by it then as now. At the beginning of 1940 I moved away from my provincial town to the examination-ridden book-filled world of the university in Wellington.

I was in my second year at university when the war swept me into the army in 1941. What reading I did then was of two kinds. By day it was army-issue manuals about surveying and some elementary principles of trigonometry. These were necessary because I found myself in a Survey Troop. My companions and I trudged the neighbouring hills with theodolite and plane table and brought back data for the draughtsmen to turn into Ordnance Survey maps. By night it was Balzac, Flaubert, Victor Hugo, and the major English writers of the eighteenth century, so that I could finish my degree. New Zealand BA degrees at that time were three-year affairs and I was 'majoring' (though we didn't use that word) in French and English. It all worked out and I completed my BA while in uniform.

In June 1944 a troopship took my unit and some 1,200 other New Zealanders to Egypt, and then to the front line, which at that time was near the principality of San Marino. It was in March 1945, when I was billeted with the other members of a Survey Troop of the Royal New Zealand Artillery in the grounds of a villa just outside Forli (near Faenza), that I became dimly aware of a fork in the road ahead. When the war was over I would need to make a direct choice between a career in English literature and one in English language, if, indeed, I was free to return to university at all.

A chance suggestion drew my attention to the need. A friend from another unit, hearing that I was a graduate with an interest in philology, thought that I should read a recently published book, *The Loom of Language* (1943) by Frederick Bodmer and Lancelot Hogben. He gave me the address of a London bookseller (John Bumpus), and I wrote off for the book. It reached me in Forli and two months later, when the war ended, I read it in my tent in a field on the outskirts of Trieste. At the time, and in the circumstances of war, it seemed to me that this remarkable book was some kind of omen for the days ahead.

When I was eleven, I was awarded a 'First Class Prize' for languages and mathematics at my local school in New Zealand. The prize was the poetical works of John Milton, with an introduction by Henry Newbolt. That book more than any other had taken me into the realm of higher literature. From then on, and particularly at university, my literary deities were increasingly those of the seventeenth century – the later works of Shakespeare, the *Songs and*

Sonnets of John Donne, Sir Thomas Browne's *Hydriotaphia*, and so on. Their world brought me ceaseless pleasure from a resonant unending fountain:

> *The Barge she sat in, like a burnisht Throne,*
> *Burnt on the water: the Poope was beaten Gold,*
> *Purple the Sailes . . .*
> Antony and Cleopatra, 2, ii, 191–3

The dramatic opening lines of Donne's poems – 'Busie old foole, unruly Sunne' ('The Sunne Rising'), 'Blasted with sighs, and surrounded with teares' ('Twicknam Garden') – and his extraordinary metaphysical conceits (as in 'The Flea') buried themselves in my brain. And so did the richly fashioned haunting language of Browne:

> *What Song the Syrens sang, or what name Achilles assumed when he hid himself among women, though puzzling Questions, are not beyond all conjecture.*
> Hydriotaphia, chapter 5, Sir Thomas Browne

A Rhodes Scholarship took me to Oxford in 1949, and the 'problem' that I had become dimly aware of in Forli four years earlier came to the surface in a dramatic way. A choice of syllabus had to be made. I opted for a severely philological course. Close textual knowledge of Old and Middle English works and their language would be required. Arrestingly difficult Old Norse texts formed part of the syllabus, including some of the most opaque poetry ever written, that of the scaldic poets. These ancient Scandinavian poets had imposed on themselves a disciplined code of versifying, characterized by alliteration, rhyme, and the use of *kenningar* (e.g. *the dragon's bed* = gold, because Fáfnir, a dragon, dwelt on his goldhoard).

I knuckled down to it all, only half realizing that the die was cast. *Beowulf, The Battle of Maldon, Hrafnkelssaga*, and the domestic wisdom of the Old Norse poem *Hávamál*, all wove their spell on me, as did the works of Chaucer, Langland, the *Gawain* poet, and many others. My wartime knowledge of Italian made it possible for me to read some Boccaccio, Dante, and Petrarch. It became the most natural thing in the world to wrestle with the text of medieval English works and their analogues, and to come to grips with the great handbooks of historical phonology and grammar. I had moved unreturnably away from my seventeenth-century gods, and had acquired a yearning to worship new gods in the field of medieval philology.

Where was I to break into the web of scholarship? Which Old Norse saga needed re-editing? What medieval concepts required further consideration? I made an improbable choice of text and had the extraordinary luck to be placed at the feet of J. R. R. Tolkien, who became my supervisor. I decided to transfer all my scholarly attention and affection to a forbiddingly long late-twelfth-century set of versified homilies written in or near Lincoln by an Augustinian canon called Orm or Ormin. The *Ormulum,* as the author himself called it, was written semi-phonetically in that all consonants were doubled after short vowels:

Icc hafe wennd inn till ennglissh/Goddspelless hallʒhe lare.
Affterr þatt little witt tatt me/Min drihhtin hafeþþ lenedd.

('I have turned the Gospel's holy lore into English, in accordance with the small understanding that my Lord has entrusted me with.')

I haunted the Bodleian Library, where the only manuscript of the poem, Junius 1, is deposited, and had almost completed a new edition when, in 1957, I had to put it aside 'for the duration' while I prepared *A Supplement to the OED.*

It soon became clear to me that the pursuit of lexicography precluded the reading of books simply for pleasure. I continued to read monographs on medieval themes and dutifully kept up with the learned journals and the new editions of Old and Middle English texts that were being published in ever-increasing numbers. But the task before me in preparing *A Supplement to the OED* was very formidable. Lurking in everything I read were words or meanings relevant to the dictionary. Any reading that I did became strictly practical. It was rewarding if it produced unregistered words and meanings. It had to be diverse – issues of *Black World* and *Village Voice* vied with *Encounter* and *The Times* as productive sources. For nearly thirty years – between 1957 when I embarked on the *Supplement* and 1986 when the fourth and final volume was published – apart from books and articles about medieval literature, I was virtually unable to read anything at all for its own sake rather than for the lexical material that it might contain.

After the completion of the *Supplement* I was free to give my attention to the language of the 1980s. For the new version of Fowler's *Modern English Usage* that I am preparing it was essential to build up a wide-ranging database of current English usage. I embarked on an ambitious programme of extracting a large corpus of suitable material from the novels of writers like Iris Murdoch, Anita Brookner, and Julian Barnes, American writers like E. L. Doctorow, Tom Wolfe, and John Updike, Australian writers like Peter Carey and Thomas Keneally, and so on, as well as all the journals and newspapers which I subscribe to and read as a matter of course. The pleasure of reading has remained an indirect one. A book is of primary interest to me in so far as it yields a rewarding amount of evidence about modern English usage. For example, apart from my admiration for Iris Murdoch as a writer, I have been struck by her addiction to what is called the comma splice, that is the loose linking of sentences by commas instead of by a strict regimen of semi-colons and full stops. And it is interesting to observe how fastidious Anita Brookner is in matters of English usage – how incomparably traditional and safe – compared with the scant respect for tradition shown by relaxed journals like *The Face*.

Given reasonable luck, the new version of *Modern English Usage* should be ready in 1994. It is giving me immense pleasure to be forced to find out what my views are on pressing matters of English usage: *comprise* distinguished from *compose* and from *include*; *compare to* or *compare with*; the relationship of *may* and *might*; methods of word-formation at the present time; rhetorical terms like *anacoluthon* and *aposiopesis*; prosodic terms like *acatalectic* and *anacrusis*; transferred epithets; double possessives; and all those other matters that I encountered and half-mastered more than half a century ago in the grammatical textbook that we happened to use at my secondary school, a book called *A Practical Course in Secondary English* by George Ogilvie and E. A. Albert, published in 1913 by Harrap. This unforgiving textbook was an essential prop and stay to many people in pre-Saussurean days. I realize now that it gave me real enjoyment at the time. Or am I deluding myself, and it is really the whole amount of linguistic experience that I have undergone since then that is giving me pleasure as I proceed with my restructuring of H. W. Fowler's famous book?

What is the further outlook? The passing of time could provide no greater gift than the chance to reread in a leisurely way, and without lexical or grammatical imperatives, the various works mentioned in this essay (except for my father's favourite tract) and the two volumes that begin:

'Whether I shall turn out to be the hero of my own life, or whether that station will be held by anybody else, these pages must show.'

David Copperfield, Charles Dickens

and

Let us go then, you and I,
When the evening is spread out against the sky

Like a patient etherised upon a table . . .
                    'The Love Song of J. Alfred Prufrock',
                        Collected Poems 1909–35, T. S. Eliot

and many another work.

My favourite books

Beowulf (eighth century); *Ormulum* (late twelfth century);
Geoffrey Chaucer, *Canterbury Tales* (fourteenth century);
The *Collected Works* of Shakespeare (sixteenth–seventeenth
centuries); The Bible (Authorized Version, 1611); The
Songs and Sonnets of John Donne (*ante* 1631); Charles
Dickens, *David Copperfield* (1849–50); Virginia Woolf, *To the
Lighthouse* (1927); The *Collected Poems* of T. S. Eliot (1936);
Iris Murdoch, *The Message to the Planet* (1989).

Judith Kerr

I FIRST learned to read in German, which is easy because spelling is phonetic. I don't remember being taught. I do remember sitting on one of Berlin's yellow trams with my mother and pointing to shop signs, posters, anything with letters on it, and endlessly asking: 'What does that say?' She always told me, and one day something must have clicked and I found I could read.

Like any German family, we had *Struwwelpeter*, whose horror-comic qualities did not bother me at all because I knew none of it was real. The thing I remember about it most clearly is my disappointment at being told that what I had hopefully identified as an aeroplane in one of the pictures was only someone's hat blowing off. This may have been due to my ignorance of what aeroplanes looked like. They were rare in those days and I couldn't have seen many. Or it may really have been as badly drawn as I remember it. In any case, it was a terrible let-down and I've always tried, now that I do illustrations myself, to make them as clear as I can.

Far more interesting than *Struwwelpeter* was a Victorian picture book which had once belonged to my mother. It contained among a medley of stories, rhymes and riddles a brisk half-page dealing with the transmigration of souls. There was an illustration to show how it worked. The souls, which were vaguely fluffy, ascended a staircase after they had died. At this point they were pale blue. On a sort of landing at the top they began to turn purple, and by the time they came down another flight of stairs on the opposite side of the page to be reborn, they were a very pretty pink.

I remember thinking this recycling process both credible and sensible and am ashamed to say that it is still the first picture I see in my mind when hearing anything about the rights and wrongs of abortion. If only one could be sure of those stairs and that landing it would be easier to make up one's mind.

There must have been a dearth of good German children's books because, apart from Grimm's fairy tales (which, like *Struwwelpeter*, I found totally unfrightening), nearly all the 'real' books I liked were translations. Andersen, of course, and the varicoloured books of fairy tales translated from the English. And *Dr Dolittle*. (Did he really have a pushmi-pullyu? To me it was always a *Stossmichziehdich*.) Then Kipling's *Just So Stories* which my mother read to me after an operation for appendicitis and which made me laugh so much that I had to plead with her to stop because it was so painful. Sadly, I tried many years later to read them to my own daughter but found that neither of us could any longer enjoy them.

I loved *Tom Sawyer* – I can still recite the opening lines in German – and *Huckleberry Finn*. Also *Oliver Twist* and the first part of *David Copperfield*, though these were probably abridged versions. And finally Jack London's *Call of the Wild*.

I had again been seriously ill. As was not unusual in those days before antibiotics, I had had a high fever for several weeks, but it had at last come down and an older child who came to visit me lent me this book. By the time I had read the first few chapters I was so excited by the half-wild dog Buck's race-memories of life among the wolves that my temperature shot up again and my mother took the book away, to be finished when I had reached a more stable condition. I thought it the most thrilling thing I had ever read and am glad that when my daughter read it at school she liked it too.

I did not know then that all these books had been written in English. The only English book I recognized was *Alice's Adventures in Wonderland*, which a benighted 'Miss' who came to our house once a week forced me to read in the original in order to learn the language. Needless to say, after having to have all the puns laboriously explained to me, I loathed it, and swore that English was one language I would avoid at all costs.

The only books which frightened me were by Johanna Spyri. Not *Heidi*, but two or three minor ones in which children were apt to die of nothing in particular with alarming frequency. Sometimes they coughed a bit first, but mostly it just seemed to happen. The children were all very good – clearly a dangerous condition – and as was

usual then, there was always a paragaph or two explaining
that God had taken them.

I found all this very unsettling. I had been brought up
as an agnostic and God was more mysterious to me than
to most. While I was sure in the daytime that no one who
really knew me would be mad enough to take me for
my goodness, alone in bed at night I thought, suppose
God made a mistake? Suppose He got it wrong and took
me anyway? It was a terrifying possibility and I remember lying awake long after my brother had gone to sleep,
listening to my heart and wondering whether I would still
be alive in the morning.

Johanna Spyri was one of the three authors I read who
actually wrote in German. The other two were Erich
Kästner (whom I liked at the time but now find embarrassing) and a lady called Else Ury.

Else Ury must have been a bestseller. She wrote unde-
manding but inventive stories, and all of us at my primary
school devoured them, borrowed them from each other,
discussed them and acted out the more dramatic episodes
in the playground. There must have been a dozen of them,
all dealing with one *Nesthäkchen*, an affectionate term for
the baby of the family. Nesthäkchen was the daughter of a
doctor, and what was unusual about these quite thin books
was that they covered her existence from pre-school to
grandmother – though I do remember that the last one
entitled *Nesthäkchen with White Hair* was a bit short on
incident.

When Else Ury had finished with Nesthäkchen, she
embarked on another series called *The Professor's Twins*,

presumably to extend her readership, since Nesthäkchen was read only by girls. However, the twins had barely made it to secondary school in 1933 when Hitler came to power and my family fled to Switzerland, leaving him to confiscate all our possessions including, I suppose, my books by Else Ury. In any case, I had probably grown out of them by then.

However, months later in a Zürich bookshop I became very excited at seeing a new book by my favourite authoress. My parents must have thought that it would be a bit of home, for they bought it for me even though by then they could ill afford it.

I was interested to see that she had abandoned her usual middle-class academic setting for one of working-class hardship. The heroine was the daughter of an unemployed artisan and she and her family had a tough time until one day a new factory opened in the district, the father got a job there, they had money again and everything was fine. The heroine, of course, was involved in some way which I have now forgotten at every stage of the action. On the last page she went out into the street with the other locals to cheer the man who had brought all this about. And for a moment, while Adolf Hitler's eyes looked deep into hers, she knew that only happiness lay ahead.

As I said, I'd really grown out of Else Ury by then. But it was a bit of a blow.

At the end of 1933, when I was ten, we left our village near Zürich for Paris. My brother and I learned to speak French in French schools, but I remember reading almost no French fiction. We were assured that *Les Petites Filles modèles* and *Les Malheurs de Sophie* were French children's favourite reading, but if this was indeed so, we thought, they must be a very funny lot. Probably they, like us, had little time to read because the school day was so long. At my elementary school one of the teachers used extracts from Daudet's *Lettres de mon moulin* for our dictations and though I enjoyed his use of the French language (which I loved once I understood it) I never found the content very exciting.

We still spoke German at home and in the holidays borrowed books from a little German library in the middle of the red-light district at the Place Pigalle. It must have been there that I discovered Sherlock Holmes. I read everything and some of Conan Doyle's other novels as well. Later my son devoured them at the same age. It seemed odd then that when I first met that sinister band it was not speckled but *'getüpfelt'*.

When I was twelve, my parents ran out of money. They decided to try to move us to England and while they battled for a foothold from icy digs in Golders Green, my brother and I were sent to stay with our grandparents in the South of France. It was a bad time. I hated being away from my parents and wondered if we'd ever be together again. So when it was suggested that I should improve my English in case I had to live in London, I was keen to do it. It seemed somehow that if I was prepared for this new life, it was more likely to come about. I tried to forget the horrors of *Alice in Wonderland* and allowed my grandmother to introduce me to the English library in Nice, where an entire corner was devoted to the works of Angela Brazil.

At first I was stumped by her vocabulary. 'Ripping' was defined in my Anglo-German dictionary as a form of tearing and 'topping' didn't appear at all. However, I gradually got the hang of it and managed to stagger through four or five different volumes, even with some enjoyment. I haven't tried to read Angela Brazil since, but she must have had something. She certainly helped my English, even though, when I did get to London a few months later, my vocabulary was received with some surprise.

And from then on I became English and read all the books everyone else reads in the language in which they were written. I read avidly, indiscriminately, out of love for an author, out of boredom or to stave off depression. I still do. I can't say that in all that welter of reading I have been influenced by any particular author. Except, perhaps, for one.

Whenever I hear of *Tintin* or *Little Black Sambo* or even *Oliver Twist* being banned from library shelves; when I read articles insisting that children's books should be about tower blocks or one-parent families or fathers doing the chores; whenever children's authors are enjoined to follow whatever the trend of the moment may be, I remember Else Ury. I wonder what became of her.

Postscript After writing this I thought I would find out. I wish I hadn't. I did not want this article to end on a note of horror, but it is what happened.

Else Ury was Jewish. I don't know why she praised Hitler in that last story, but it did not help her. Soon after it appeared, she was forbidden to write any more books. Not just to publish but to *write* them. After that nothing is known of her except that she disappeared in 1943. It is assumed that she died in a concentration camp.

John Mortimer

Each year the shops are flooded with tons of children's books, all bright, amusing, alluring and attractively illustrated. When opened, their sparsely covered pages tell of mischievous little aeroplanes, playful dragons or mildly pixilated bright red tractors. They are all, or almost all, unnecessary. Childhood, thank goodness, isn't long enough to cope with them. If no more children's books were to be produced for the next twenty years, if the ingenious inventors of wilful little fire engines or anthropomorphic hedgehogs were to give their imaginations a rest, if the charming illustrators could lay aside their brushes, would it be any great loss? Children, for heaven's sake, have got quite enough to read already in the short timespan between putting down *Winnie-the-Pooh* and picking up *Jane Eyre*, or sliding from Mary Norton's *The Borrowers Afloat* by way of James Bond and Biggles into Dickens's *Bleak House*.

If we no longer treat children as second-class citizens we still patronize them. We, of course, like to read 'good books' but, provided it's glossily packaged and prettily

illustrated, children, we assume, will put up with any sort of
rubbish. So a completely artificial distinction has grown up
between 'good books' and 'children's books'. The truth of
the matter is that good children's books are as good at any
age. *Alice's Adventures in Wonderland, Treasure Island*, Conan
Doyle's *The Hound of the Baskervilles*, John Buchan's *The
Thirty-Nine Steps*, Wodehouse's *Good Morning, Jeeves* and
Wells's *The War of the Worlds* are as satisfactory to old age
pensioners as they are to ten-year-olds. The same cannot
be said of *Ted the Naughty Little Tractor*.

I can remember not being able to read, and gazing, in
considerable frustration, at a book with pictures of scenes
from history. Everyone seemed to be dying; Harold had
an arrow stuck in his eye, General Gordon was about to
be speared by angry Arabs in Khartoum and a pale, one-
armed Nelson was bleeding to death in the arms of Captain
Hardy on the poop deck. When the words gradually made
sense I had graduated to *Struwwelpeter*, where boys who
sucked their thumbs had them cut off by a 'great big scissor man'. I also have a vivid memory of a story about a
boy who is put off the allegedly cruel sport of fishing by
a bizarre kitchen accident in which he gets a meat hook
stuck in his mouth. It is, I think, part of the power of
books that they inspire fear, particularly in those not used
to them: as witness the panic caused to certain Muslims
by *The Satanic Verses* or the trepidation with which self-
appointed censors face much of literature. In time the fear
gives way to a kind of pleasurable unease, which accounts
for the enduring popularity of stories of crime, mystery
and suspense. Dickens is our greatest novelist not only

because he was a master of comedy, but also because of the ruthless way in which he alarms his readers.

So far as I remember, the *Pooh* stage passed quickly. I was sent away, as was the practice in middle-class families in the 1930s, to a boarding prep school. It was thought that I needed company, but at school I endured a loneliness which made my life as an only child in what was then the remote countryside seem overcrowded. Books were not a luxury, but a necessity. I desperately needed to inhabit another world, far away from the icy dormitories, the bleak changing rooms that smelt of dirty gym shoes, and the numbing boredom of organized games. I wanted a brighter, more adventurous, funnier and more elegant world; above all I wanted a world in which I could be the hero, something I was certainly never going to achieve on the soggy north Oxford playing fields.

I suppose all parents introduce children to the books they loved, and my father, in a South African childhood, had read Rider Haggard and adventures among the Zu-Vendi people with Umslopogaas, who wielded the great axe Inkosi-kaas, and Alan Quatermain. He also knew many of the *Sherlock Holmes* stories by heart and told them to me as we went on long country walks. On the whole I preferred the London pea-soupers, cloak for so many mysterious crimes, the hansom cabs which brought clients in distress to the Baker Street rooms, to the witches and bloody battles on the veldt.

I took over and added to my father's favourites. I had all the *William* books by Richmal Crompton, their covers picturing the hero with his cap and tie askew and his socks like concertinas around his ankles. But I didn't really want to read about schoolboys, I had quite enough of them in real life, and I certainly didn't want to think of myself as a schoolboy. I much preferred to become the sage of Baker Street, wearing a dressing gown, playing the violin and shooting the pips out of playing cards stuck up above the mantelpiece. A few years later, when I had become more sophisticated than during my prep-school years, I liked to think of myself as Noel Coward, still in a dressing gown but smoking cigarettes from a long holder instead of a meerschaum pipe. One of Sherlock Holmes's great attractions, for me, was that I was quite sure that he never took any part in organized games. Bulldog Drummond, on the other hand, the somewhat butch hero of the Sapper books I read voraciously, had no doubt played rugby football for England, which character defect was only just offset, in my childhood eyes, by the fact that he wore impeccable light grey suits and lived in Half Moon Street, Mayfair. Bulldog Drummond was never an intellectual giant; if he saw an animal run against a wire fence and die immediately the hearty detective was slow to realize he was probably facing a high charge of electricity. On the whole I preferred to identify with Sapper's cosmopolitan villain, the dastardly Carl Peterson, who was never without his beautiful side-kick Irma.

I also read my way steadily through P. C. Wren, whose hero Beau Geste joined the French Foreign Legion, an institution which I thought must have been preferable to school. I enjoyed P. G. Wodehouse so much that I both wanted to become a valet like Jeeves and a young man about town like Bertie Wooster. I saw myself, ink-stained, lanky and with pebble glasses, sharply dressed in Prince of Wales checks, calling in to the Drones Club for a snifter to cure the hangover. I even wrote up to Gamages for a monocle, which I wore in secret, or during school holidays, and earned the derision of my mother.

While not much better dressed than William, I fancied myself as Beau Brummel, whom I had in a collection of cigarette cards called 'Great Dandies Of All Time'. I was extremely fond of *Rodney Stone* by Conan Doyle, which was full of Regency rakes and bare-knuckle prize fighters. I think it was an early interest in rakes and the Regency that led me on, when I arrived at Harrow, to Lord Byron, whose manuscripts and Turkish slippers were preserved in the library and whose illegitimate daughter was buried outside the church. I tried to sit on the tomb where he used to lie to write poetry, but found it covered with an iron grid and overlooking a somewhat depressing view of Ruislip. Perhaps for these reasons no talent for writing poetry ever rubbed off on me.

Long before that I had admired another languid dandy with a heroic secret, the Scarlet Pimpernel, who would discuss the finer points of the tying of a cravat with apparent frivolity in one chapter and turn up, disguised as an old peasant woman, rescuing aristocrats from the guillotine in the next. I was alarmed by the sound of tumbrils on the cobbled streets of Paris and the dark plottings of Citizen Chauvelin, but never by the antiseptic murders in Agatha Christie, who also figured high on my list of childhood bestsellers. What frightened me most in her books were the solutions, the eerie way in which the improbable facts were fitted into a tidy pattern in the end. 'Of course,' I remember my father turning to me and saying in an impressive whisper when I read one of her books aloud to him in his blindness, 'it must have been done with a blow pipe and a poisoned dart.' Dorothy L. Sayers seemed to me much better at scaring the wits out of you, and Lord Peter Wimsey had a reassuring resemblance to Bertie Wooster, although without the jokes.

So this was childhood reading, and of course I have no space to include all the books. They included great works like *Treasure Island*, which are unforgettable; indeed I still can't read the opening chapter about Blind Pew and the Black Spot without remembering reading it in bed by the light of a fading torch and feeling reassuringly afraid. It included rubbish like Sapper and Edgar Wallace, good melodramas like Anthony Hope's *The Prisoner of Zenda* and works of art like *David Copperfield* and *Three Men in a Boat*. I missed, fortunately, the Hobbits and the works of C. S. Lewis and I never engaged with good books like Nesbit's *The Railway Children* or Blackmore's *Lorna Doone*. By the time I got to Harrow I was ready for Evelyn Waugh, Aldous Huxley, T. S. Eliot and Auden, as well as more detective stories and the plays that I read because my ambition was, one day, to become an actor.

Most of what I read would no doubt be deeply disapproved of by child psychiatrists. A lot of it was concerned with violent crime and sudden death. My heroes might not be considered admirable by social workers; Sherlock Holmes took drugs and Bertie Wooster was apparently born without a social conscience. I read to be entertained and to find laughter. I read to escape from boredom. I read, in part at least, to be scared. All the books I read may not have been great literature, but they were an important part of the world of fiction which I now inhabit. And they led to the time when I read almost all of the books which have stayed in my mind for ever. This I did in my early teens, when I had time on my hands and everyone else was out playing football.

My favourite books

I think it's impossible to name just ten favourite books, and I assume the Bible and Shakespeare are already there. All I can do is make a list from the many books that are important to me: *Bleak House* and *Great Expectations*, Dickens; *The Last Chronicle of Barset*, Trollope; *Resurrection*, Tolstoy; *Selected Letters*, Byron; *Plays*, Chekhov; *Decline and Fall*, Evelyn Waugh; *The Portrait of a Lady*, Henry James; *The Jeeves Omnibus*, P. G. Wodehouse; *The Complete Sherlock Holmes Stories*, Conan Doyle.

John Fowles

M Y first instinct, when I read the letter asking me to contribute to this collection, was to say no. It isn't that books haven't been important in my life, both a delight and fodder (one lives to eat and eats to live) and things that I have never been able to do without, however much I may pretend I can. Indeed they have been so important, almost like love and nature, that saying what they truly mean defeats both summary and analysis. In any case, pretending I don't need them is nonsense. The cinema and television have proved it only too well by being, in general, so stereotyped and inferior – often just plain bad. The spectacle of how many of the young today seem dazzled and dazed by the vulgarity and cheaper tricks of those media is sad and sobering. The poor things (who do not even realize their own poverty) seem increasingly drugged, as Chinese peasants once by opium, by the 'visual' arts and their now very marked predominance over all others.

A teaching friend recently reported that her girls complained they could not 'see' the examination texts they were studying. This now very prevalent form of blindness, directly caused by the terrible and crippling atrophy of the imaginative faculty (being unable to slip down the magical passage from the little signals we call words into far richer worlds than any film or TV 'version' will ever be able to present), is surely – for all its lack of obvious cruelty and barbaric violence – one of the saddest tragedies of this already tragedy-filled century.

Our educational systems further confuse things by failing to teach the young to distinguish between the very different experiences of reading fiction and non-fiction. Their aims are diametrically opposed in many ways: learning to dream awake, against learning to absorb hard facts; almost, to be subjective, to learn to feel, to be oneself – or to be objective, become what society expects. I am a novelist, and it is that first 'skill' (or capability) that mainly interests me.

Talking about reading is like talking about flight in a world rapidly becoming flightless; like raving about music to the deaf, or about painting to the colour-blind. Nothing short of some major ecological disaster can now lead the vast majority of mankind back to the huge pleasures and consolations of reading. The power to set the mind dreaming in the entrancing orchard of its own self-created feelings and images is already menaced. I heard only the other day of how, in the United States, it is more than just theoretically possible to put the human species on the brink of a cybernetic world, where anyone (suitably 'wired in' to its powers of recreating and simulating real vision and feeling) will be potentially able to suppose himself or herself anywhere and in any circumstances. Sledding through the Arctic wastes, lounging beside a pool in the Alhambra, scoring a goal in the World Cup, being a prima ballerina on stage, slashing low over landscapes like a fighter pilot (much of the initial technology involved in creating these new cybernetic worlds apparently derives from that last); and – surely Mrs Whitehouse's ultimate nightmare – having sex how and with whom one wants. Regarded more seriously, that last 'possibility' is the one I find most chilling: humanity reduced to a mere sensation machine, endlessly apiarized, locked in little cells and stuffed with the wretched sugar of every selfish and foolish desire. It is the apotheosis of masturbation; all human love dies.

Proponents of this future 'paradise' may argue that this is only what fictional books have always done through the clumsy medium of print – taken readers 'out of themselves' and transported them to other places and events, personalities and psychologies. It is certainly what a great deal of the cheaper writing of our own age, and of some past ones, has tried to do; but it can't be defended unless the making of money totally supersedes all other motives. This new tool-world – for that is all it is – may command money, but never art. It is no coincidence that America appears the country most advanced in these potentially lucrative new techniques.

The pass was perhaps sold with the very first written or spoken text, and quite certainly with the invention of the cinema. It was at that latter time that the average man and woman turned their backs on the once formidable power to imagine in their own minds, and elected instead to depend on these still comparatively primitive means of having one's imagining done for one. The extent and size of what they have so tamely given up – in an era where humanity has supposedly become more and more jealous of its political rights and of preserving individual freedom – is as frightening as some enormous unpaid bill. Fascists and electronic engineers may rejoice; the rest of us should better weep. Alcohol and drugs can present a more exciting, or a more consoling, view of life; what they cannot offer is a greater or a wiser reality.

What influenced me when I was young, what influences me now, which are my favourite books . . . I can't really remember what affected me when I was a boy. I read almost incessantly; it was impossible to think of life without reading. I had chickenpox or scarlet fever, I forget which, at one point, and was strictly ordered not to read. I did, and duly ruined my eyesight; anything (though I've long forgotten what did the ruining) seemed preferable to the intolerable boredom of having to lie in bed without books.

I don't think the great bulk of what I read before sixteen was even remotely 'academic': I didn't much read comics, but I did get through a lot of Henty and Talbot Baines Reed, that sort of thing. My only precocity (I'm sure the world I lived in saw it as backwardness) was my strong longing, virtually lust, always for fiction: for the adventure, the insertion of the imagined to leaven the dully real. One book of this kind was vital, Richard Jefferies' *Bevis*. I must have read it once a year through all my teens. Quite simply, to the surburban child I was, it stood for paradise, all that my own world could not be. Another such 'escape' (more colourful if less intense) lay in Dumas's saga about the three musketeers. That too I must have read several times. One may smile rather ashamedly later, looking back on these fanatical 'pashes' of adolescence. I think that is a mistake. They may be below the consideration of the university departments of literature, but they mould the wax when it is at its warmest and most malleable.

In general I certainly much preferred fiction to non-fiction, the objective feeding of facts, which has long betrayed to me and in me a female alter ego. It is one (or its male counterpart) I think most novelists are best, almost necessarily, born with: that is, a strong compound familiar ghost of the opposite sex to whichever he or she outwardly belongs. Perhaps rather strangely (and, I suspect, femalely) I did not like fiction when it was *too* fantastic. I knew very little of science fiction then, but have frankly never greatly liked what I've read of it since. It somehow takes a step beyond the degree of unreality I can naturally tolerate; touches a lethal live rail, which kills all human interest.

There were, still are, two books by sisters whose early importance in my life I somehow never at the time admitted. They were *Wuthering Heights* and *Jane Eyre*. The greatness of the first I didn't really begin to grasp until I had to teach it; the second is for me like a leak in a river embankment. Always it mysteriously inundates and revivifies buried parts of one's Englishness, one's racially archetypal self. Nothing can equal the extraordinary literary and very personal vitality, the true uniqueness, of Emily Brontë, but I certainly think (I read French at university) of Charlotte's masterpiece as the most quintessentially *English* of all novels: so intensely romantic, so full both of suppressed emotion and a deep moral (*not* Christian) rectitude. There is that marvellous plot, which so subtly blends the two opposed sides of our national character: the puritanical and the poetic, the dutiful and the erotic. Somewhere between Jane and Rochester beats the mysterious deep heart of England.

My favourite books

A brief list of the novelists I have loved must suffice. Beyond the Brontë sisters and Jefferies, I must put an arm round Jane Austen, and also her contemporary Thomas Love Peacock. She has almost completely, but not quite justly, overshadowed him. I also much love Defoe, the father of the English novel; such a convincing simulator of reality, and the ancestor to whom I feel closest. From him I must leap abroad and a long way back to the greatest fiction ever written, Homer's *Odyssey*; the one book an intending writer, never mind all readers, *cannot* fail to have read. I also deeply admire the finest novel of these last hundred years, and one based on the *Odyssey*, James Joyce's *Ulysses*. Now I must move to a number of other foreign novelists . . . but this becomes impossible, as I feared.

Between ourselves, I hate lists, not so much for what they choose, but for what they leave out. I think I'd better nominate the one novel I'd pick to represent all this great fictional treasure-house of the Western world, with all its vices and its virtues, its wisdom and its wit. *Hamlet* is but a play, and this is but a tale. It was first published in 1759, written in a delicious French (many times translated), and is about a quite candidly odd young man . . . but wait a minute. What is nicer than discovering great books for oneself? Who would ever spoil that pleasure?

Jan Morris

WHEN I consider the heap of books, the *mountain* of books, that somehow or other we all programme into our experience in the course of a lifetime's reading, it seems an impossible overload of the system; but the truth is I suppose that most of it is unconsciously discarded, thrown into a mental waste-paper basket, leaving stored on some indestructible disk of the sensibility only the works destined permanently to influence us. Six such works in particular I have identified lodged there in my own inner computer – six books, from six ages of reading, recalled now with gratitude and affection as I proceed all too impetuously through my sixties.

The first book, from that misty infant's time when a decade really has no calendar meaning, is certainly *Alice's Adventures in Wonderland* by Lewis Carroll, with which I bind up, mentally at least, *Through the Looking-Glass* too. I was read no trash in my mewling age, no footling *Noddy*-type books, but was thrown in the deep end with a great classic. I was taught to regard it as a classic, too, and to realize that while it was most certainly a book to be laughed with, it was never one to be laughed at. Its nonsense was art, its characters were serious, its verses were poetry, its Tenniel illustrations could never be replaced, its humour was a universal benchmark. Getting to know it was, I was led to suppose, a *sine qua non* of a fortunate and civilized childhood – a child without *Alice* was a child deprived. I agree with this elitist theory. I have loved and honoured the book from that day to this, and for me no other work of surrealism, whether in literature, in visual art or in the theatre, can match its antic genius.

'What's that you're reading?' I can remember a teacher astutely demanding, at my very first school, as she saw my shining morning face peering through the crack in my slightly opened desktop, instead of paying attention to the blackboard. She forgave me, though, when I told her it was my grandfather's copy of *Huckleberry Finn* (which I still possess, ink-stained here and there by one generation or another). Who could not forgive a child, caught illicitly rafting upriver with Huck and Jim, instead of thinking about long division? I hear that Mark Twain is sometimes pilloried nowadays for his racial attitudes, but I read *Huckleberry Finn* as it was written, in happy innocence, and I have only to concentrate even now to feel myself back among the Mississippi tangles, to see the whites of Jim's eyes widening in the darkness, or to hear Miss Watson's voice thin and reproving from the porch. Thank God for a decent upbringing! To think I might have been reading Ransome's *Swallows and Amazons*!

Somewhere in my early youth I stumbled upon *Eothen,* by Alexander Kinglake. Nowadays everyone knows it, and many of the best travel writers acknowledge its seminal importance. Then it was largely forgotten, I think, and it was just one of the innumerable books from the house library that I read at random during the long weeks of captivity at boarding school, in between writing woeful ballads. How rich, how exotic, how carefree, how marvellously funny it seemed to me then, speaking from an almost unimaginable world of colour and adventure into the grim lonely hours after evening prep! What a friend it has been to me ever since, in editions ranging from the sumptuous coffee-table edition which Frank Brangwyn illustrated, in splashy purples and ochres, to the Oxford paperback for which, long afterwards, I was myself to provide an introduction! To mark our first ten years of life together my love gave me a first edition of *Eothen,* and of all the books in my library it remains the one I cherish most.

Sterner stuff dominated my fourth and soldierly age of reading. Finding myself with a regiment of tanks on the edge of the Sinai desert, where one would sometimes wake up in the morning to discover that a teeming company of Bedouin, with camels, dogs and black tents, had arrived during the night to camp outside the perimeter wire, I bought (from Steimatsky's in Jerusalem) an American one-volume edition of Doughty's *Arabia Deserta.* I read it there and then, at the wilderness edge, and everything about it profoundly affected me. Its contents held me in such thrall that for the next ten years the course of my life was shifted. The smell of its Random House ink (still just detectable, more than forty years on) was to become as evocative to me as any madeleine. And the stupendous style of the work was to ring so permanently through my mind that to this day I sometimes sing its opening lines aloud in the bath, to music of my own device.

The fifth age was my liberal age. I was full of saws and instances by then, of course, but in retrospect I think of it as my somewhat belated moment of literary awakening. Countless books from the period are stacked in my computer at various levels of consciousness. Turgenev, and Dickens, and Conrad, and Cheever, and Flann O'Brien, and Trollope, and a hundred other authors came to me then, and are ineradicably with me now. One great novel, though, took me so long to read, and engaged my attentions so insistently, that it impressed itself upon me more heavily than any other. I spent a whole year reading Proust's *A la recherche du temps perdu,* together with George Painter's biography of its author. My reactions varied from the ecstatic to the bored to the repelled; but at the end of it I felt I had truly been admitted into some new and translucent chamber of relativity, where the real and the sham were reconcilable, where will and destiny merged, squalor could be apotheosized into beauty, and time itself might achieve a final unity.

It took me longer still to read the dominant book of my sixth age. For half a lifetime I had resisted *Ulysses,* and had sneered at those who claimed to love it. Five or six times, starting in 1942, I had tried and failed to get through it, and I was of the opinion that most of its alleged admirers had failed to finish it too. My litmus test of literary pretension was to ask people at a bookish party what they thought of *Ulysses,* such a variety of transparent evasions did the question prompt. There is nobody, though, so zealous as a convert. In Dublin, in the year 1989, I bought a book of commentary called *The New Bloomsday Book,* by Harry Blamires; and armed with this key, spectacles on nose, I began yet again at the beginning – 'Stately, plump Buck Mulligan came from the stairhead . . .' It was a revelation. I still find parts of *Ulysses* incomprehensible and unreadable, and suspect that often Joyce was just mischievously befuddling the academics. I still disbelieve anybody who claims to have read the book with pleasure without some explanatory key, and still feel that life is too short for *Finnegans Wake.* But I bless Mr Blamires for the gift he gave me, when he opened my eyes at last to the grandeur, the complexity, the unbeatable entertainment of Bloom's day in Dublin, and programmed it for ever in my being.

And what of the seventh age, around the corner for me, looming up for us all? *Sans* eyes perhaps, *sans* teeth, but certainly not *sans* everything. In my years of mere oblivion I may not be able to store much more on the old disk. I may not even be competent to retrieve with any exactness the material stacked up there already – the titles may go, the quotations may be blurred, I may even confuse the Carpenter with the Duc de Guermantes, or send Huck Finn down the long street that is called Straight. But all those words and tales and cadences will be with me still, irrevocably a part of me, and I shall go to the grave in great company – Carroll and Twain and Kinglake to entertain me, Doughty majestically my guide, Proust and Joyce making me wonder still, as they conversationally feint and parry at the gates of paradise, whether they really have read each other's masterpieces all through.

My favourite books

There is no more fatuous exercise, in my view, than trying to name one's ten favourite books – I have a couple of hundred books, I imagine, that are all equally my favourites, some more favoured on one day, some on another. I have decided, then, simply to list ten books, out of so many, whose company I feel I would always enjoy.

I would choose for a start three of the works that have most affected me in life – Charles Doughty's *Arabia Deserta,* James Joyce's *Ulysses* (with a key to its meanings), Alexander Kinglake's *Eothen.* I would like *The Collected Jeeves,* by P. G. Wodehouse, partly just for the fun of it, partly for the literary example of its timing. From the great Russian works of fiction I think I would take, because it is as long as it is wonderful, Leo Tolstoy's *Anna Karenina* (in my copy of which, I now happen to see, at Canberra in July, 1962 I rather drunkenly scrawled the comment: 'This is the best book I have ever read'). *The Nigger of the Narcissus* seems to me the most perfect of Joseph Conrad's novels; *Kim* would have made Rudyard Kipling immortal if he had written nothing else – I was almost rash enough to say that it alone would have made the British Raj worth while; Anthony Trollope's *Barchester Towers* makes me smile with pleasure just to think of it. I have lately been bowled over by the truly sacred loveliness of the New Testament in Scots, translated by William Laughton Lorimer ('Lat the bairns come tae me, seekna tae hender them; it is een sic as them at the Kingdom o God belangs . . .'). And as a lover of my country I would not like to be without the collected poems of Dafydd ap Gwilym, together with translations of them into modern Welsh (for in the original, I am sorry to say, Dafydd's medievalism all too often defeats me).

Philip Ziegler

IN the beginning was the picture. I suppose that at some point in those unregenerate days before the Beginner Books had taught three generations of children that They Must Not Hop On Pop I must have transcribed in laborious pothooks 'The-cat-sat-on-the-mat', but if so the experience is mercifully forgotten. My earliest recollection is of books whose illustrations were sufficiently intriguing to make me spell out the exiguous text which accompanied them. There was a series which I dimly remember as being called the *Golliwog* books, featuring that now socially unacceptable but perpetually endearing anthropoid and a skeletal clothes-peg figure wearing a beret and called, I think, Peg. Was there a Meg as well? In one book in the series there were icebergs too, and polar bears. From another book comes a frieze of little black boys being chased round and round a tree by a tiger until the ravening beast churned itself into butter. Or was it marmalade? A minimum of research would establish the truth about these details, but I prefer to keep such memories impressionistic and obscure. Certainly my children never experienced them, though de Brunhoff's *Babar* books and the terrifying Long-Legged Scissor Man (from *Struwwelpeter*) successfully leapt the generation gap and survive today.

Apart from a conviction that, if no more pressing commitment arose, the proper way to spend time was with a book, I cannot pretend that these early studies affected either my prose style or my personality. Nor did the *William* books, nor, a little later, the adventures of the *Swallows and Amazons*, have much effect on me except, perhaps, to compel my reluctant admission that I lacked the boldness of the first and the resourcefulness of the second. It was the masterpieces of what, I suppose, might now be categorized as magic realism which first stirred my imagination and led me to realize that everything need not necessarily be as it seems, that the prosaic needs only to be stood upon its head to become poetic. Thackeray's *The Rose and the Ring*, E. Nesbit's *The Phoenix and the Carpet* and, most of all, the works of Lewis Carroll, opened my eyes to the latent oddity of things. Carroll in particular taught me the incredible liberties that can be taken with language without sacrificing lucidity. Without subscribing to the Humpty Dumpty doctrine that a word should mean whatever the author chooses it to mean – 'the question is, which is to be master – that's all' – I believe that rules are made to be broken and that though in *Finnegans Wake* Joyce defeats his own purpose by plunging too deep into the inspissated waters of his own unconscious, some passages of *Ulysses* are among the finest ever written in the English language.

The great wave of adventure books through which I swam between the ages of eight and fourteen gave much pleasure but left little mark. I never wanted to write like Sapper or Buchan, Rafael Sabatini or P. C. Wren. Still less did I accept or even reflect on their social and political assumptions. English schoolboys in the 1930s often indulged in a mild and unthinking anti-semitism, but this was something quite distinct from the odious thuggery of Bulldog Drummond, whose obscurantist mutterings about an international Marxist–Jewish conspiracy I either skipped or failed to notice. Nor did the subtler snobbery and prejudices of John Buchan have any noticeable effect on my social attitudes; I followed with relish the exploits of Hannay or Sandy Arbuthnot but never considered them as role models to whose thoughts, or still less deeds, I should aspire.

I can date almost to the moment the time at which I – not put away childish things, since it is only a few months since I reread Buchan's *Greenmantle* with considerable pleasure – realized that there was a world elsewhere. In February 1944, when I was fourteen, I had a bad bout of flu. I was convalescent and becoming restless but, as was the custom of the times, was condemned to another three days in bed. My housemaster, a much shrewder man than he usually allowed his pupils to perceive, looked in to my room one morning and, remarking: 'I think you might be ready for this,' tossed a copy of *Pride and Prejudice* on to my bed. Seventy-two hours later, having finished the sixth of Jane Austen's novels and realized to my outraged perplexity that there were no more to come, I got up. By the end of that year I had gulped down all the Brontë novels, much of Dickens, *Vanity Fair*, and Butler's *The Way of All Flesh*, shortly following these with George Eliot's *Middlemarch*, Galsworthy's *The Forsyte Saga* and Trollope's Barchester novels. Some time that following year I also discovered Saki; a writer who, I am still convinced, would, if he had lived, have become one of the most important novelists of the twentieth century. His masterpiece, *The Unbearable Bassington*, showed a compassion and understanding of human nature which far transcended the wit and ingenuity that are normally considered the hallmarks of his work. Since 1944 no year has gone by without my rereading at least two of Jane Austen's novels and one or more by Dickens. Inexorably over the next few years the frontiers of my reading expanded, introducing new gods to take their places in my pantheon; there have been periods when it seemed to me that no novelist could hold a candle to Dostoyevsky, others when Flaubert reigned supreme; but over the decades it is to Jane Austen and Charles Dickens that I have remained most faithful.

What Jane Austen did for fiction, Macaulay did for history. Though one ancient but inspired schoolmaster had persuaded me that it was possible for history to be taught in such a way as to amuse and excite the pupil, I must have been sixteen before it occurred to me that the same pleasure was to be derived from books. Then someone made me read Macaulay's supremely dramatic account of the Massacre at Glencoe. How closely this related to reality I did not know then and do not know now, but in its capacity to move and disturb it ranked with any of the novels I had devoured over the previous eighteen months. A few days later term ended; I raced to my father's shelves, found Macaulay's *History of England*, and had read it all within the next few days. Perverse and bigoted though I now know that it sometimes is, I still believe it to be one of the noblest flowers of historical genius to be found in the English tongue.

'Ziegler will never make a historian,' that same perceptive housemaster once all too correctly remarked. The serious reader of history, I would suppose, is one who is resolved to be informed and instructed without worrying too much about being entertained. Macaulay ended that possibility for me. Over the intervening forty-five years I have derived enormous pleasure from reading history, but always the style has been as important as the content. Grouped around Macaulay's works in my father's library were other heavily leather-bound sets of volumes. I began to explore. Prescott on the Incas and the Aztecs I relished; Kinglake on the Crimea I found rewarding but intractable; Carlyle on the French Revolution I confronted, recoiled in dismay, tried and once more emerged intoxicated but convinced that I would never broach it again except in the smallest doses. Gibbon's *Decline and Fall* was my greatest defeat. I have embarked on it at least four times, once on a long sea journey, once as a soldier marooned in North Africa on the edge of one of the largest sandpits in the world, yet even in such propitious circumstances I have abandoned the effort in despair after the first hundred or so pages. I can see all Gibbon's merits, accept his greatness, but I cannot read him.

As a biographer I should be able to identify the great works in my own field which have most inspired me, but I turned to biography only after I had failed miserably at fiction, and I view the art form through the eyes of a novelist manqué. It seems to me now that it was Lytton Strachey's *Queen Victoria* which first convinced me that the dreary three-decker hagiographies of the nineteenth century were not the only way to write of someone's life, yet I doubt if Strachey's brilliant, if perverse, study was in fact the first biography that I enjoyed, and certainly I had read precious few nineteenth-century biographies when first I encountered it. By its style and elegance no biography has given me greater delight than David Cecil's *The Young Melbourne* but the twentieth century is rich in practitioners who have combined meticulous scholarship with writing of the highest order.

Today my reading is largely circumscribed by the constraints of what I *have* to read; for reviews, in connection with the book that I am writing, or for the literary prize which I help adjudicate. I read perhaps forty new novels a year, looking forward with particular pleasure to anything by Martin Amis, Julian Barnes, William Boyd, Iris Murdoch, or further afield Bellow, Updike, Richler, Vargas Llosa, Gabriel García Márquez. This list seems dispiritingly fashionable, but on the whole it is true that the writers who best stand the test of time are those who are appreciated and applauded (if not necessarily bought extensively) by their contemporaries. I read perhaps the same number of books of biography or history, admiring particularly Holroyd, Richard Holmes, Carpenter and,

among those who write the same sort of book as I do, John
Grigg, Alistair Home, Ben Pimlott – but I could name a
dozen others without even venturing into that remarkable new school of travel writing-cum-autobiography
which includes Jonathan Raban, Colin Thubron and Paul
Theroux.

I have written only about the effect that writers have
had on my own writing or my reading – books upon
books. Has any book changed my life or notably affected
my personality? I was brought up on Bunyan's *Pilgrim's
Progress,* have reread it several times and believe it to be
one of the most moving and inspiring of human testaments. I would like to feel that it has influenced me. For
a time Forster's *Howard's End* was my bible, but I would
not dare reread it now for fear that I would find that
the philosophy had worn thin and that its potency had
departed. Dostoyevsky's *The Brothers Karamazov* I *have*
reread and will return to constantly; I know of no book
which says more about the human spirit.

My favourite books

I could not name ten favourite books, only identify ten
books which, for a variety of reasons, are of special importance to me. The books that have given me the greatest
pleasure over the longest time – both reread twenty times
or more – are Jane Austen's *Persuasion* and Stendhal's *Le
Rouge et le Noir.* The most perfectly crafted of all novels is
Gustave Flaubert's *Madame Bovary.* The two books of the

kind which I write myself and which I would most like to have written are Norman Gash's *Peel* and Duff Cooper's *Talleyrand*. The two books that moved me most and haunt me still are Hardy's *Jude the Obscure* and *Crime and Punishment* by Dostoyevsky. The richest and most delectable, for occasional sipping only, is Sir Thomas Browne's *Hydriotaphia* or *Urn Burial*. My desert island book, chosen for its length and density as well as other qualities, would be Proust's *A la recherche du temps perdu* in the original with the Scott Moncrieff/Kilmartin translation bound in on alternate pages. And finally a wild-card book, not to be categorized but irresistible, is *Tristram Shandy* by Laurence Sterne. With that travelling library I could confront eternity unafraid.

J. G. Ballard

As I grow older – I'm now in my early sixties – the books of my childhood seem more and more vivid, while most of those that I read ten or even five years ago are completely forgotten. Not only can I remember, half a century later, my first readings of *Treasure Island* and *Robinson Crusoe*, but I can sense quite clearly my feelings at the time – all the wide-eyed excitement of a seven-year-old, and that curious vulnerability, the fear that my imagination might be overwhelmed by the richness of these invented worlds. Even now, simply thinking about Long John Silver or the waves on Crusoe's island stirs me far more than reading the original text. I suspect that these childhood tales have long since left their pages and taken on a second life inside my head.

By contrast, I can scarcely recall what I read in my thirties and forties. Like many people of my age, my reading of the great works of Western literature was over by the time I was twenty. In the three or four years of my late teens I devoured an entire library of classic and modern fiction, from Cervantes to Kafka, Jane Austen to Camus, often at the rate of a novel a day. Trying to find my way through the grey light of postwar, austerity Britain, it was a relief to step into the rich and larger-spirited world of the great novelists. I'm sure that the ground-plan of my imagination was drawn long before I went up to Cambridge in 1949.

In this respect I differed completely from my children, who began to read (I suspect) only after they had left their universities. Like many parents who brought up teenagers in the 1970s, it worried me that my children were more interested in going to pop concerts than in reading *Pride and Prejudice* or *The Brothers Karamazov* – how naive I must have been. But it seemed to me then that they were missing something vital to the growth of their imaginations, that radical reordering of the world that only the great novelists can achieve.

I now see that I was completely wrong to worry, and that their sense of priorities was right – the heady, optimistic world of pop culture, which I had never experienced, was the important one for them to explore. Jane Austen and Dostoyevsky could wait until they had gained the maturity in their twenties and thirties to appreciate and understand these writers, far more meaningfully than I could have done at sixteen or seventeen.

In fact I now regret that so much of my reading took place during my late adolescence, long before I had any adult experience of the world, long before I had fallen in love, learned to understand my parents, earned my own living and had time to reflect on the world's ways. It may be that my intense adolescent reading actually handicapped me in the process of growing up – in all senses my own children and their contemporaries strike me as more mature, more reflective and more open to the possibilities of their own talents than I was at their age. I seriously wonder what Kafka and Dostoyevsky, Sartre and Camus could have meant to me. That same handicap I see borne today by those people who spend their university years reading English literature – scarcely a degree subject at all and about as rigorous a discipline as music criticism – before gaining the experience to make sense of the exquisite moral dilemmas that their tutors are so devoted to teasing out.

The early childhood reading that I remember so vividly was largely shaped by the city in which I was born and brought up. Shanghai was one of the most polyglot cities in the world, a vast metropolis governed by the British and French but otherwise an American zone of influence. I remember reading children's editions of *Alice in Wonderland*, *Robinson Crusoe* and Swift's *Gulliver's Travels* at the same time as American comics and magazines. Alice, the Red Queen and Man Friday crowded a mental landscape also occupied by Superman, Buck Rogers and Flash Gordon. My favourite American comic strip was *Terry and the Pirates*, a wonderful Oriental farrago of Chinese warlords, dragon ladies and antique pagodas that had the added excitement for me of being set in the China where I lived, an impossibly exotic realm for which I searched in vain among Shanghai's Manhattan-style department stores and nightclubs.

I can no longer remember my nursery reading, though my mother, once a schoolteacher, fortunately had taught me to read before I entered school at the age of five. There were no cheerful posters or visual aids in those days, apart from a few threatening maps, in which the world was drenched red by the British Empire. The headmaster was a ferocious English clergyman whose preferred bible was Kennedy's *Latin Primer*. From the age of six we were terrorized through two hours of Latin a day, and were only saved from his merciless regime by the Japanese attack on Pearl Harbor (though he would have been pleased to know that, sitting the School Certificate in England after the war, I and a group of boys tried to substitute a Latin oral for the French, which we all detested).

Once home from school, reading played the roles now filled by television, radio, cinema, visits to theme parks and museums (there were none in Shanghai), the local record shop and McDonald's. Left to myself for long periods, I read everything I could find – not only American comics, but *Time, Life, Saturday Evening Post* and the *New Yorker*. At the same time I read the childhood classics – *Peter Pan*, the *Pooh* books and the genuinely strange *William* series, with their Ionesco-like picture of an oddly empty middle-class England. Without being able to identify exactly what, I knew that something was missing, and in due course received a large shock when, in 1946, I discovered the invisible class who constituted three-quarters of the population but never appeared in the *Chums* and *Boys' Own Paper* annuals.

Later, when I was seven or eight, came *The Arabian Nights*, Hans Andersen and the Grimm brothers, anthologies of Victorian ghost stories and tales of terror, illustrated with threatening, Beardsley-like drawings that projected

an inner world as weird as the surrealists'. Looking back
on my childhood reading, I'm struck by how frightening most of it was, and I'm glad that my own children
were never exposed to those gruesome tales and eerie
coloured plates with their airless Pre-Raphaelite gloom,
unearthly complexions and haunted infants with almost
autistic stares. The overbearing moralistic tone was expli-
cit in Charles Kingsley's *The Water-Babies*, a masterpiece in
its bizarre way, but one of the most unpleasant works of
fiction I have ever read before or since. The same tone
could be heard through so much of children's fiction, as if
childhood itself and the child's imagination were maladies
to be repressed and punished.

The greatest exception was *Treasure Island*, frightening
but in an exhilarating and positive way – I hope that I
have been influenced by Stevenson as much as by Conrad
and Graham Greene, but I suspect that *The Water-Babies*
and all those sinister fairy tales played a far more important
part in shaping my imagination. Even at the age of ten
or eleven I recognized that something strangely morbid
hovered over their pages, and that dispersing this chilling
miasma might make more sense of the world I was living
in than Stevenson's robust yarns.

During the three years that I was interned by the
Japanese my reading followed a new set of fracture lines.
The 2,000 internees carried with them into the camp a
substantial library that circulated from cubicle to cubicle,
bunk to bunk, and was my first exposure to adult fiction –
popular American bestsellers, *Reader's Digest* condensed
books, Somerset Maugham and Sinclair Lewis, Steinbeck

and H. G. Wells. From all of them, I like to think, I learned the importance of sheer storytelling, a quality which was about to leave the serious English novel, and even now has scarcely returned.

Arriving in England in 1946, I was faced with the incomprehensible strangeness of English life, for which my childhood reading had prepared me in more ways than I realized. Fortunately, I soon discovered that the whole of late nineteenth- and twentieth-century literature lay waiting for me, a vast compendium of human case histories that stemmed from a similar source. In the next four or five years I stopped reading only to go to the cinema. The Hollywood films that kept hope alive – *Citizen Kane*, *Sunset Boulevard*, *The Big Sleep* and *White Heat* – seemed to form a continuum with the novels of Hemingway and Nathanael West, Kafka and Camus. At about the same time I found my way to psychoanalysis and surrealism, and this hot mix together fuelled the short stories that I was already writing and strongly influenced my decision to read medicine.

There were also false starts, and doubtful acquaintances. *Ulysses* overwhelmed me when I read it in the sixth form, and from then on there seemed to be no point in writing anything that didn't follow doggedly on the heels of Joyce's masterpiece. It was certainly the wrong model for me, and may have been partly responsible for my late start as a writer – I was twenty-six when my first short story was published, and thirty-three before I wrote my first novel. But bad company is always the best, and leaves a reserve of memories on which one can draw for ever.

For reasons that I have never understood, once my own professional career was under way I almost stopped reading altogether. For the next twenty years I was still digesting the extraordinary body of fiction and non-fiction that I had read at school and at Cambridge. From the 1950s and 1960s I remember *The White Goddess* by Robert Graves, Genet's *Our Lady of the Flowers,* Durrell's *Justine* and Dalí's *Secret Life*, then Heller's *Catch-22* and, above all, the novels of William Burroughs – *The Naked Lunch* restored my faith in the novel at a time, the heyday of C. P. Snow, Anthony Powell and Kingsley Amis, when it had begun to flag.

Since then I've continued on my magpie way, and in the last ten years have found that I read more and more, in particular the nineteenth- and twentieth-century classics that I speed-read in my teens. Most of them are totally different from the books I remember. I have always been a voracious reader of what I call invisible literatures – scientific journals, technical manuals, pharmaceutical company brochures, think-tank internal documents, PR company position papers – part of that universe of published material to which most literate people have scarcely any access but which provides the most potent compost for the imagination. I never read my own fiction.

In compiling my list of ten favourite books I have selected not those that I think are literature's masterpieces, but simply those that I have read most frequently in the past five years. I strongly recommend Patrick Trevor-Roper's *The World through Blunted Sight* to anyone interested in the influence of the eye's physiology on the work of poets and painters. *The Black Box* consists of cockpit voice-recorder

transcripts (not all involving fatal crashes), and is a remarkable tribute to the courage and stoicism of professional
flight crews. My copy of the Los Angeles *Yellow Pages* I
stole from the Beverly Hilton Hotel three years ago; it has
been a fund of extraordinary material, as surrealist in its
way as Dalí's autobiography.

My favourite books

The Day of the Locust, Nathanael West; *Collected Short Stories*,
Ernest Hemingway; *The Rime of the Ancient Mariner*, Samuel
Taylor Coleridge; *The Annotated Alice*, ed. Martin Gardner;
The World through Blunted Sight, Patrick Trevor-Roper;
The Naked Lunch, William Burroughs; *The Black Box*, ed.
Malcolm MacPherson; Los Angeles *Yellow Pages*; *America*,
Jean Baudrillard; *The Secret Life of Salvador Dalí*, by Dalí.

Ruth Rendell

THE picture I can still see in my mind's eye is of a dancing, gesticulating *thing* with a human face and cat's ears, its body furred like a bear. The anomaly is that at the time, when I was about seven, the last thing I wanted was ever to see the picture again. I knew quite precisely where in the Andrew Lang *Fairy Book* it came, in which quarter of the book and between which pages, and I was determined never to look at it, it frightened me too much. On the other hand, so perverse are human beings, however youthful and innocent, that I was also terribly tempted to peep at it. To flick quickly through the pages in the dangerous area and catch a tiny fearful glimpse.

Now I can't even remember which of the *Fairy Books* it was, Crimson, Blue, Yellow, Lilac. I read them all. They were the first books I read which others had not either read or recommended to me, and they left me with a permanent fondness for fairy stories and with something else, something that has been of practical use to me as well as perennial fascination. Andrew Lang began the process of teaching me how to frighten my readers.

Because I had a Scandinavian mother – I have to describe her thus as she was a half-Swede, half-Dane, with an Icelandic grandmother, born in Stockholm, brought up in Copenhagen – I was early on introduced to Hans Andersen. I never liked him. He was too much of a moralist for me. His stories mostly carried a message and a threat. Oddly enough, or perhaps not oddly at all, the one I hated most was the favourite of my mother, who had her stern Lutheran side. This was 'The Girl Who Trod on the Loaf', which is about ugsome Inger who used a loaf of bread as a stepping stone to avoid wetting her fine shoes at the ford. The result of course was that she sank down into the Bog Wife's domain, a kind of cesspit full of creepy-crawlies, and that is only the beginning of her misfortunes.

I never really wanted to read anything my parents wanted me to read. No doubt this is normal. The exception would be Beatrix Potter, but we grow out of her early and only return to our passion after twenty or thirty years. Does anyone read *The Water-Babies* today? Charles Kingsley is just as improving as Andersen but in a different way. It was social rather than moral evils he pointed out. Andersen never gave a thought to Inger's poverty and deprived childhood. The poor little chimney sweep's boys always excited my wonder and pity. I never imagined I would one day live in a house where, inside the huge chimney, you can see the footholds the boys used to go up with their brushes. The water creatures the metamorphosed Tom encountered started me on a life-long interest in natural history.

Two years after Tolkien's *The Hobbit* was published I read it for the first time. Twenty years later I read it again and experienced just the same feeling of delight and happiness and a quite breathless pleasure. That first time, when I was nine, was also the first time I remember feeling this. It is a sensation known to all lovers of fiction and comes at about page two, when you know it's not only going to be good, but immensely satisfying, enthralling, not to be put down without resentment, drawing inexorably to a conclusion of power and dramatic soundness.

While I was engrossed in *The Hobbit* I was also reading *The Complete Book of British Butterflies*, a fairly large tome by the great naturalist F. W. Frohawk — what a wonderful name that is, he sounds like a giant butterfly or moth himself. That copy I still have, can see it on the shelves from where I sit writing. I used to collect butterflies, kill them in a bottle containing ammonia on cottonwool and mount them on pins. The disapproval of a schoolfellow, whom I rather disliked but must have respected, put an end to that and I have killed hardly anything since, a few flies, a mosquito or two. Outside the pages of fiction, that is.

My father came upon me reading Thackeray's *Book of Snobs* and told me — rightly — that I should not understand it. I was only driven to it by the lack of anything else. The reader must read even if, by default, it is *The Book of Snobs* or the telephone directory. If it was the school holidays and the school library therefore closed to me, if the distance from the county library made nipping out for a book impossible, my only recourse was my parents' book-shelves. They were both teachers, both readers, but they had few books of their own. They couldn't afford to buy them. What they had were textbooks they had used as students, newish novels given as Christmas presents and two sets of the complete works of favourite authors, in my father's case Hardy, in my mother's Kipling.

I can remember one horrid wet Sunday afternoon when I struggled with *An Introduction to Palaeontology* and some-thing called *Igneous Rocks*. My father had been trained as a geologist. Rather more rewarding was Marie Stopes's *Married Love*, the only volume on the shelves to have a blank slip-on cover, so therefore marked out as of 'special interest', as dealers in porn used to put it. However, there was no porn in Stopes and very little information. It puzzled me then and puzzles me now that this book, by a mistress of circumlocution and euphemism, is supposed to be about *sex*.

Oh, the dreary evenings sitting with my father while he read Hardy aloud to me. I'm sure he read very well and with a fine rendering of Wessex speech, for he was a Devon man, but to me in my early teens there was an inexpressible tedium about those rustics under their green-wood tree. Today I find *Jude* too painful to reread and *The Return of the Native* almost suicidally grim, but there was none of that then, only stratagems milling about in my head as to how escape might be effected without hurting the feelings of a dearly loved parent.

Not that Victorian fiction was unacceptable. Far from it. A lifelong fondness for Trollope was about to begin.

Dr Thorne – a reissue of which by a pleasant irony I have just edited and introduced for Penguin Classics – I found on the shelves in the house of an aunt. I was discouraged from reading it. There were whispers about unsuitability. It seems incredible today (it was coming close to incredible *then*) that the reason for caution was that a girl in the novel has an illegitimate child and the word 'seducer' is used. But my family were like that. Without their reluctance to let me get my hands on it, I might never have opened the book. How many of us owe a lifelong devotion to an author because he or she once narrowly escaped banning? How many of us derive a permanent distrust of certain writers because a parent read aloud from them to us in our impressionable youth?

I was to get over my dislike of Hardy and have come to a reserved admiration for him. My mother's transports put me off Tennyson for good – what on earth would a Swedo-Dane see in *Maud*? – and Kipling I don't care for to this day. But the encyclopaedia called *The Wonderland of Knowledge* which my mother bought for me when I was much younger introduced me to Greek mythology, and the *Odyssey* remains a favourite book.

Another enduring favourite is *The Way of All Flesh*, the copy I still possess given me as a seventeenth birthday present by a school friend. I should like to think that I learned to avoid cant from Butler but the truth is I only learned what it is. I should like to think it taught me to eschew humbug but it only showed me how to recognize it in others. After all, at the same time as I was reading Butler I was also in love with Somerset Maugham. This was a ridiculous passion, such as a few years later the young had for pop stars. *The Painted Veil* on those profoundly influential parental bookshelves was responsible for starting this. Before I went off Maugham for good I had managed to rake up the money to buy each new book of his as it came out. This left me with a fine collection of Maugham first editions and a quasi-Maugham style, Frenchified, archaic, embarrassing, in which I wrote all my early short stories and one very bad novel. Small wonder they were rejected.

I used to boast that during those years of my late teens and early twenties I read every play ever published in English in the twentieth century. It can't have been true but I think it nearly was. Even if it is only almost so, how strange that today I would not dream of writing for the stage and resist with all my strength invitations to produce television scripts.

My favourite books

For years *The Way of All Flesh* remained my favourite book and it must certainly be included in a list of my top ten. Ford Madox Ford's *The Good Soldier* superseded it a dozen years ago and remains in prime position. I reread it every year, I love it. Its characters live in my mind's eye as if moving in some ritual dance, precise, exquisite, finely balanced. With the poor narrator I suffer afresh each time.

Jane Austen must be there and it had better be *Mansfield Park* – the fun-less one, the profoundest, the most didactic, but nevertheless the greatest. Here in fourth position, though I can't undertake to place all in strict order of preference, the *Odyssey* must come, and the edition the relatively new Robert Fitzgerald translation.

Now for *The Complete Poems of George Herbert* because he is my hero, then *Grace Abounding* because Bunyan is too. For opening my eyes to a world of wonders, and not just dreams, drugs and drawings, I shall take as my seventh favourite Alethea Hayter's *Opium and the Romantic Imagination*.

I like Proust, or I say I do and convince myself I do, but since I have only read *Remembrance of Things Past* once and don't feel like reading it again, I shall give it a miss here, remembering among my own things past what Butler has to say about humbug. But Trollope must be on the list and if it is a choice between the two masterpieces, *The Way We Live Now* and *The Last Chronicle of Barset*, the latter wins, if only because the tedious comic antics at Johnny's lodgings grate less than Sir Felix's junketings with his working-class girlfriend.

There seems no reason not to squeeze the maximum in and have a trilogy. The one that comes first to mind is Robertson Davies' *The Deptford Trilogy*, but it surfaces only to sink again. I love Henry James but I like L. P. Hartley better, he is more economical, more *readable*, less rarefied, so I will pick the three novels of his in one volume that appear under the title *Eustace and Hilda*. Number ten might be Fowler's *Modern English Usage* but Brewer's *Dictionary of Phrase and Fable* has a tiny edge on it.

Those ten will be on my desert island or my deathbed.

Edna O'Brien

M Y first sense of books is the feel and the smell of them, ravelled old books growing musty in a trunk, but full of secrets. Ours was not a literary household, there were prayer books, one cookery book (*Mrs Beeton*) and bloodstock manuals. In our village there was no public library, yet I was in love with writing before I was acquainted with it; a pre-love if you like. My mother, an artist, I do believe, in her own right, disliked books, particularly disliked fiction, believed it was redolent of sin. It was as if she herself had read Molly Bloom's soliloquy in *Ulysses* in a past life and was still reeling from the bawdiness of it.

I cannot remember the first book that I read, no matter how hard I try, but I do know that at ten or eleven I read the occasional page of *Rebecca* by Daphne du Maurier. A copy was secured in our village, no doubt by some lovelorn wife or spinster, and was loaned by the page because all were avid to read this tormenting love story and all identified with it. In my girlish dreams, star-crossed love became the pulse of life, a notion I have never quite surrendered. What a long way I had to go to find Chekhov, a fiction so imbued with truth it is to me more like a breath of nature.

The first book I ever treasured was a cloth book, a children's book perhaps, and though I have no memory of the story I do think of it as something sacred, akin to religion, the cloth of the book reminding me in some way of the cloth of the scapulars we wore inside our vests and which contained a relic of the saints. I was more addicted to words than to pictures. Words were talismanic, transfiguring, making everything clearer, and at the same time more complex. Words were the sluice gates to the mind and to the emotions. Reading for me, then as now, is not a pleasure, but something far more visceral, a brush with terror. The mythologies of my country were of invasion, battle, betrayal, barbaric events told in a supernaturally beautiful language – there were *The Red Branch Knights*, *The Laments of Corc and Nial*, *Con of the Hundred Battles*, *Mad Sweeney in the Woods*, *The Sweet Song of Diarmuid and Grainne* and *Morrigan the Goddess of War*, glorifying in the gore:

Ravens shall pick/The necks of men/Blood shall gush/ In combat wild/Skins shall be hacked/Crazed with spoils/ Men's sides pierced/In battle brave/To Erne woe/To Ulster woe.

By contrast, the language of prayer books verged on the sentimental – paeans to the mystic Christ, who was also a mortal man, a mortal man who bled on the cross for us.

Religion and literature were inextricable, so at fourteen it was something of a relief, as well as a come-down, to get to the novelettes, the gushing stories, for instance, of Miss Annie P. Smithson; tales of blighted love, elopements, embezzlements, revenge and such heady things. 'Lord Ullin's Daughter' by Thomas Campbell, 'Lucy Grey, or Solitude' by Wordsworth and Tennyson's 'The Lady of Shalott' were successive heroines with whom one identified, and of course Heathcliff and the crisp Mr Rochester were one's heroes. Peter Abelard replaced these two gents in my teens, with, as well, a morbid fascination for Dracula. It is no accident that its author, Bram Stoker, is an Irishman transmitting his countrymen's covert mania into the psyche of a Baltic count.

The greatest revelation in my reading life took place one afternoon when I was about seventeen in a chemist's shop in Dublin, where I worked, or, to be more precise, where I toiled for twelve hours a day. I received an honorarium of seven-and-six a week and, hungry for books, although not as hungry as I was for food and finery, I would devote a small portion of that grand salary to buying a second-hand book each week. At George Webb's bookstall on the quays in Dublin, I purchased for fourpence a small book called *Introducing James Joyce* by T. S. Eliot. There was a lull that afternoon in the chemist's shop and as I read the first few pages from *Portrait of the Artist,* I was myself transported to the Dedalus house, eating the Christmas dinner, seeing the brandy flame on the plum pudding, trembling at the pitch of argument about the patriot-cum-adulterer, Charles Stewart Parnell. Oh the bliss of it. It is probably true to say that for every aspiring Irish writer Joyce remains the master, Father, Son and Holy Ghost of words, although I have to say that that other great epiphanous maverick, Mr Beckett, carries his own kit of spiritual as well as literary ammunition.

I once asked Mr Beckett who his favourite author was, and rather tetchily he replied that there was no such thing. For me there is, and it is Chekhov. His stories have passed into my bloodstream, the fates of his characters as vivid to me as the happenings in my own life. I eloped from the chemist's shop and moved to a retreat in the country where I had leisure and the opportunity to read. Reading a story of Chekhov's called 'The Darling' about a woman who loved first one husband and then another and another but eventually fastened all her longings on to a little boy called Sasha, I named my son Sasha. But love of Chekhov is something more than the sentiment of a name, it is a human and aesthetic imperative. Good writing deepens or should deepen our well of humanness. Even Joyce, the cerebral William Tell, regarded it as the first prerogative of literature and it was for its human quality that he valued the story of Odysseus above any other. As an aside: he found Dante a bit boring, said that reading Dante was like looking at the sun for too long.

The great thing about reading is not just the hour by the fire or on the train, but the accumulation in the mind from moments of books, the residual thrill, the way the characters swish about in our consciousness long after we have finished the tale. Of the several moments indented in my memory I recall the jealous count in Zola's *Nana,* who, having been unfaithful all his life, suspects his wife of infidelity and stands outside a paramour's window all night, watching for one or two shadows, then tires of his vigil and falls asleep; the primordial moment when the young Marcel Proust waits for the kiss from his mother, the kiss that he will repudiate; the lethal glee when Iago plants the first seed of doubt in Othello and predicts that no drug, 'not even the drowsy syrup of the sweet mandragora', will allow him to sleep again; Becky Sharp in *Vanity Fair* protesting her innocence as her husband surprises her with Lord Steyne in a drawing room in Curzon Street; Emma Bovary's blue riding cape and the red jars in the apothecary's window, tabernacles of poison to fulfil her death wish; Anna Karenina chafing her grievances, the little red handbag on her arm, gauging the distance between the front and back wheels of the train before she jumps – drastic moments all, but literature is more eerily accurate at depicting sorrow than joy. As much as I love writing, I love writers, the demented creatures who admit us into their magic, labyrinthine worlds.

I cannot conclude without quoting from a local history card which says that Emily Brontë's death at the age of thirty was 'possibly accelerated by the failure of *Wuthering Heights* and the death of her brother Branwell' – well, as they say in Ireland, 'She's dead, but she won't lie down.'

John Carey

I WAS lucky, being born into a house with books. Not all of them were for reading. In the front room a large shiny bookcase with glass doors displayed bound sets relating to the South African war, Living Animals of the World, and other serious topics, along with the *Encyclopaedia Britannica*, in green cloth. These books were furniture. No one, so far as I know, ever ventured to disturb their austere calm. To have opened their glass prison would have been like entering a catacomb. Probably it was the same in many middle-class suburban homes of the 1930s and 40s, where there were some aspirations to culture, but not much time for it.

I have inherited that *Encyclopaedia Britannica*. It always looks a little naked on my shelves, without its glass, and it is not much good for reference, being the eleventh edition (1910–11). But it is a time-machine. Its pictures and descriptions of cities and countries show a world that two wars and modern communications have swept away. Here, preserved in photographs and tiny print, are Conrad's

Africa, and Proust's France, and the Germany of Thomas Mann's *Buddenbrooks*.

But as a child I was immune to its appeal, and would not have been allowed to touch it anyway. The real books were upstairs – perhaps a couple of hundred of them, on some old varnished shelves, in a room rather grandly called 'the study'. It also contained a big linen cupboard, in the top right-hand drawer of which, hidden under a pile of sheets, were a box of revolver bullets and a policeman's truncheon. They belonged, I suppose, to my father – the bullets left over from the First World War, in which he had fought, and the truncheon, I later surmised, from his brief period as a special constable during the General Strike. But I cannot be sure, because I never discussed these magic relics with anyone, or disclosed that I knew of their whereabouts. I would just take them out, when alone, and finger them. The truncheon was new-looking and shiny, and disappointingly free of combat-marks. But some of the bullets had been used – perhaps fired at Germans? – and the survivors rolled about and thudded importantly in their tough little cardboard box with its stoutly-stapled corners.

Their spell filled the room with past time, and so did the books. For they had been collected by my grown-up brother and sister, and seemed to me like historical documents. My favourite was a *Chums* annual from an even earlier generation – handed down, perhaps, by some vanished great-uncle. It was a huge book, in deeply embossed red and gold covers, inside which the weekly issues of *Chums* were bound together. These had no colour, just columns and columns of close-packed print, and grey-ish pictures showing schoolboys in long knickerbockers and caps with stripes going round them. What I liked were the column-fillers – jokes, fascinating facts, arresting anecdotes, each occupying its tiny paragraph. They were quite useless, but I would soak them up for hours on end, completely released from my own world, like an archaeologist at the bottom of some deep shaft.

Almost as strong a competitor for my attention was a *Hobbies Annual* from a slightly more recent era – about 1931, I think, because one of its full-page illustrations was an artist's impression of 'The Doomed R101 at its Mooring Mast'. The accompanying article described the airship, in an unforgettable phrase, as 'the crippled dirigible'. The main pleasure *Hobbies* offered, though, was not its literary style but its detailed directions about how to construct model steam yachts or electric motors or viaducts for Hornby layouts. These always carried the assurance that the neces-sary materials could be 'purchased for a few pence from any ironmongers'. I loved this phrase for the opulence it evoked. By the time I read the book the Second World War was in progress, and I knew of no likely ironmon-gers. But anyway I had no inclination to make the models. The pleasure they yielded was that of pure make-believe. I gloated over them rather, I suppose, as housewives, stinted by rationing, studied prewar cookery books.

Most of the other stuff on the shelves seemed pretty unapproachable. There was a high proportion of John Buchan and G. A. Henty, and a quick look at these put me off. More manageable was *The Boy's Book of School*

Stories, edited by the intriguingly-named Gunby Hadath. One story, which for some reason impressed me indelibly, was about an unacademic schoolboy who suffers acutely from the sarcasm of his English master. One day the boy is asked to explain the lines:

Caledonia, stern and wild,
Meet nurse for a poetic child!

He is baffled. To him the lines sound 'like a telegram from a lunatic asylum to an employment agency' (this was the story's best joke, and still seems funny to me). In despair he blurts out: 'Sir, I don't quite understand who is to meet the nurse.' The class explodes in laughter, and the master fires off some of his choicest sarcasms.

Later, in the summer holidays, the boy and his family are climbing in the Alps, and one day, high on a rock face, they come upon another climber in difficulties. It is the English master. I remember the illustration. Stuck to the rock like a starfish, in plus-fours and long socks, he is staring downwards with the whites of his eyes enlarged, to indicate fear. The boy, leaning out coolly from the rock below him, instructs him on which ledges to put his feet, to reach safety. But he is too terrified to move, so to spur him on the boy repeats the sarcasms the master had used in class. This does the trick. I suppose the story appealed to me as a triumph over the adult world – though the literary allusion also gave it a certain chic.

Contemporary writing was not represented on the shelves, so for that I had to depend on birthday and

Christmas presents, and loans from friends. My favourite modern author was Captain W. E. Johns. I must have read nearly all his *Biggles* books (though not the cissy *Worrals of the WAAF* series, of course). The *Biggles* adventures that most gripped me were the exotic ones. *Biggles in the Orient* was a marvel of deft plotting about a series of inexplicable crashes among the fighter planes operating against the Japs from a certain Burmese airfield. Inspecting the wreckage of one plane, Biggles finds a scrap of peppermint-scented silver paper. Chewing gum! All at once it dawns on him. Someone must be drugging the pilots' confectionery, so that they pass out when flying over the jungle. Sure enough, back at base, a 'moon-faced' Eurasian mess steward is found injecting the squadron's chewing gum with a hypodermic. Curtains for Moon-Face.

The scrap of pepperminty paper strikes me, even now, as a brilliant touch – like the chocolate paper William Golding's shipwrecked Pincher Martin finds in his pocket, with one agonizingly sweet crumb of chocolate still adhering to it. Perhaps Golding was a Biggles fan too.

Biggles in the South Seas enthralled me even more. I forget the plot, but in one episode Biggles's friend Ginger becomes romantically attached to a young female South Sea Islander, and they have an adventure with a giant octopus, involving a lung-searing underwater swim. The girl is clad – scantily, one gathers – in something called a *pareu*. I had no idea what this garment was, but it lingered pleasantly in my mind, eventually getting mixed up with the brief costume worn by Jean Simmons in *The Blue Lagoon*. Like many teenagers, I felt sure, as puberty approached, that my destiny was to be a poet, and Ginger's girl's *pareu* figured importantly among my early inspirations, combined with the world-weary tones of T. S. Eliot's J. Alfred Prufrock, whose 'Love Song' completely captivated me after a single reading. I wrote some wistful, elderly recollections of my youth in the South Seas, in free verse, and tapped out my poems one-fingered on my father's huge old Underwood, which lurked under a sort of tarpaulin shroud in the front room. This took a long time, as I had no way of correcting typing errors, and as soon as I made one my authorial pride obliged me to start the whole page again. At last I produced perfect copies, however, and sent them off to *The Listener* for publication. Why I chose *The Listener* escapes me, but I realize now that the then literary editor was J. R. Ackerley, later famous for his love affair with his Alsatian bitch Queenie, which he wrote up in *My Dog Tulip*. However, my tasteful blend of Biggles and T. S. Eliot must have seemed unusual, even to someone of his wide experience.

My poems were some time coming back, as I had omitted to enclose a stamped, addressed envelope. This was pointed out (in the great Ackerley's hand?) on the rejection slip, which was decorated with the BBC's crest in pastel blue. I was not as pained as I had expected. Being a rejected poet seemed somehow even finer than being published.

At school, as at home, reading was oriented towards the past – for which I am grateful. It was a boys' grammar school in south-west London, and someone had donated to the sixth-form classroom some back numbers of the

London Mercury, dating from the 1920s. They were lovely objects, printed on thick, rough-edged paper with light orange and black covers. To me, this was a modern literary periodical. Only later did I learn that it was correct to sneer at its editor, J. C. Squire, and his reactionary stance. At the time I much enjoyed the poems I found in it by Walter de la Mare, W. H. Davies, and other Georgians.

For class work we had a collection called, I think, *Shorter Narrative Poems,* which introduced me to masterpieces like Tennyson's 'The Lotos-Eaters' and Arnold's 'Sohrab and Rustum'. I had not realized till now, but the bits I liked best were nearly all about water. In 'The Lotos-Eaters' it was the waterfalls – 'like a downward smoke'; and in Chesterton's 'Lepanto' it was 'White founts falling in the Courts of the sun'; and in 'The Rime of the Ancient Mariner' and Masefield's 'Dauber' and W. W. Gibson's 'Flannan Isle', the sea. Maybe water is especially attractive to adolescents, being an alternative to the land's conventional fixed forms.

When we did Horace's *Odes* for Latin A level, it was a water-poem, *O fons Bandusiae,* that first attracted me. This caused some embarrassment when I went up to Oxford for my scholarship interview. I faced a tableful of elderly dons, one of whom asked whether I thought Horace or Virgil the greater poet. I answered, without thinking, 'Oh, Horace,' at which they all laughed, and my questioner inquired the reason for my choice. I made up some stuff about Horace's interesting use of Greek metres, which seemed to satisfy them, but actually it was because of his water. Besides, after ploughing through two books of the

Aeneid, I could not see why anyone thought Virgil a poet at all. But I felt it best not to tell them this.

My favourite books

Explaining why favourite books are favourites is always difficult, because so many private feelings are involved. It is not at all the same as choosing the 'best'. My top ten would include Lesley Blanch's *Round the World in Eighty Dishes* and L. Russell Muirhead's *Blue Guide to North-Western France*. I quite appreciate these may not be eternal monuments to the human spirit, but I have used them both so much they feel like second nature. Lesley Blanch describes various countries she has lived in and gives recipes from each. In our copy the pages on fondue and cinnamon apples (from Baalbek) are the most splashed and dog-eared. We used to take the Muirhead guide for walking holidays in Normandy, and it is interleaved with cards from little hotels we stayed in.

Also high in my favourites list would come Conan Doyle's *Collected Sherlock Holmes Short Stories,* George and Weedon Grossmith's *Diary of a Nobody,* and Stella Gibbons's *Cold Comfort Farm* – because each creates its own world, as separate as someone else's house. It is the incidentals that really count, in all three books. In the Holmes stories, for instance, the hansom cabs and the linoleum in the hallway weave the spell, rather than more sensational elements. I should certainly pick the *Collected Poems of Philip Larkin,* which are closer to me than any other poetry, and George

Orwell's *Collected Letters and Journalism,* which seem to me unmatched in English writing for intelligence and style.

As a straight novel I should choose Jane Austen's *Northanger Abbey,* because its banter and flirtation suggest the erotic charge between two young people more subtly than any other English classic, even Dickens's *Great Expectations.* There would have to be a children's book, because reading to children is so educative for the reader, so I should probably opt for Beatrix Potter's *Peter Rabbit* – not as witty as Milne's *Winnie-the-Pooh,* but children seem to understand it better, and enjoy its high style (the sparrows 'implored Peter to exert himself'). And number ten? Well, it would be a toss-up between S. J. Perelman's *The Road to Miltown,* probably the funniest book ever written (amazingly, it was never published in England), and D. H. Lawrence's *Sea and Sardinia,* which of all his books embodies most intensely the most intense personality in modern writing. So that would make ten. But luckily in real life you do not have to stop at ten.

Jane Gardam

THERE were three shelves of books in the house where I was born, on the dining-room wall between the fireplace and the wireless set. My parents moved into the house after their marriage and left it sixty-five years later when they died. During that time the books changed very little, though my father disposed of some of his physics books after Hiroshima.

My father taught mathematics and physics at Coatham School on the north-east coast for forty-seven years and the top bookshelf was filled with his textbooks. I never saw him open one of them. He taught from memory. My brother and I had our way with the top shelf. We both hated numbers and I am still afraid of measuring things. We made bridges of the books and hurled Dinky cars through them with furious sounds – sirens, firemen and imaginary blasts of smoke.

Shelf two was dominated by my father's school prizes. I can't believe that the Nelson School, Wigton was very well-endowed in 1914, for most of the boys were the sons of poor farmers of the Depression, yet the prizes are magnificent, bound in full calf, gold-tooled, with end-papers of lilac and rose marbling, bookmarks of silk, and engraved book-plates. The copperplate inscriptions are works of art in themselves. Creasy's *The Fifteen Decisive Battles of the World* (a second prize only) is the most handsome book I possess – more glorious even than the ten-volume Malone Shakespeare I found and bought for ten shillings in a backstreet in Carlisle when I was seventeen. (A curate lurking among the shelves helped me carry this home and my Aunt Mabel shut the door on him as we hadn't been introduced.) Aged eight or so I liked reading Creasy on my stomach on the dining-room floor beside the sunburst-fronted radio on which we were soon to hear Churchill's wartime speeches. The cold north-east sea-fret soaked down outside and I lay wondering what Marathon was like. Thirty years on I found myself living in the house where Creasy had written the book. His library had had its shelves ripped out by the soldiers in the Second World War and was now our breakfast room, which was a place like the cafés advertised along the motorways that serve 'breakfast all day', for we ate all our meals there except for parties, and it witnessed plenty of decisive and indecisive battles of our own. Judge Creasy's ghost sat in the window between the long white shutters, his desk looking out over the place where his Victorian tennis court had been, now called 'the hump' because it had been turned in the war into a huge air-raid shelter. I can't remember what battle it was of which Creasy said that the terrain was rather like Surrey, northward from the South Downs – little farmsteads, coppices, crops and fields. This is what he must have seen from his – now our – bedroom window which is now only a pretty view by night – a sea of lights to Epsom. Poor Judge Creasy left lovely Victorian Wimbledon to become Chief Justice of Ceylon and in three months he was dead.

The third bookshelf held my mother's books, which were nearly all holy, for she was an Anglo-Catholic and convert to the Oxford Movement. The shelf was stuffed with saints, with Keble, Pusey, Newman, Bishop Gore and Archbishop Temple, and books about sin. There were my Uncle Cyril's Winchester sermons and his mother's (a great-great-aunt Jane) edition of *The Life of St Augustine* with the pages about his wicked adolescence ripped out. There were always the hymn books my mother had brought absent-mindedly home from church and there was *The Book of Common Prayer*. This I didn't read very often, for it was a back-up book. I knew most of it by heart. Between the ages of five and eighteen I had to go to church twice each Sunday and the church was celebrated for 'the length of its solemn services'. Mother did allow herself some novels: *Jane Eyre*, Scott's *Quentin Durward*, *The Flower Patch Among the Hills* by Flora Klickmann, J. B. Priestley ('such an ugly man, but he can't help it') and Phyllis Bentley 'because she was Yorkshire'. Later, mysteriously, there was *Cold Comfort Farm* by Stella Gibbons, the first satire I ever met. I was puzzled by it at first because my mother had said that it was 'very grim'. There was another rogue in the shelf – Stephen Leacock. The same angel had slipped him in for me. There was *What Katy Did* and *Did Next,* which I adored and adore.

Of all the books I suppose *The Book of Common Prayer* has been the biggest influence. I don't think I ever once wanted to go to church as a child but on the other hand I never deeply minded going, because according to the bishops on shelf two, church was good fire-insurance, and I could gaze around at the purple camels and shocking-pink palm trees of the late Pre-Raphaelite windows and feel proud of the twelve mahogany-coloured apostles behind the high altar, painted by my Aunt Mary, and the vermilion and cobalt banners that were like an army on the march. Later on I gazed yearningly through my fingers at the older choirboys. All these years *The Book of Common Prayer* was washing over me and entangling itself in my memory for ever.

The first book I possessed arrived before all this, when I was four. My mother was going to stay for the night with a friend in York. 'Now be quiet,' she said, 'don't fuss. I'll be bringing you back a present.' The present, I was told, would be a porter.

This puzzled me. I knew porters. They were my father's enemies on our thrice-annual journeys across country to Cumberland to my grandparents' farm. 'Look alive, laddie,' my father would cry to these lugubrious men (we changed trains four times). 'By Gad, some people have easy lives. Get this lot stacked, boy – we've connections to catch. No wonder the country's finished.' But I pulled from under my pillow, the morning after my mother's late-night return, not one of my father's slaves but a small square book covered in thick shiny cellophane. Across the cover pranced an empty-headed-looking rabbit. Inside, there he was again. He and other rabbits of his acquaintance seemed to be living full and interesting lives. I can remember exactly where we sat in my bedroom, my mother and I, reading the Beatrix Potter books, how I smugly explained to her the famous word 'soporific', dazzling the world with my brilliant instant reading. All over the country hundreds of children were doing the same. A couple of times after having Beatrix Potter read to us, we were off. The few words on each page were beautifully printed and yet not in the least childish – like a missal. Those who call Beatrix Potter sickly don't know what they are talking about. They are books written by a woman who had never messed about with 'children's books'. They are full of harnessed passion, the powers of darkness, malice and terror – all the things children love – as well as the sweet comforts of ordered lives, the miraculous English landscape and the enigma of the human and animal condition. They are also very funny and this makes up for the stories being rather feeble.

The landscape of Beatrix Potter I already knew – the white farmhouses scattered on watery purple mountains, the farmyard with flowery weeds in the cobbles, sleepy beehives humming and shining puddle-ducks were at the end of the journey to Cumberland with the attendant porters. My grandparents' farm, 'Thornby End', was not very far from Beatrix Potter's 'Hill Top' at Sawrey and we spent four months of the year there – my father was expected to go back for all his long school holidays to help on the farm – and I wept in each of the five trains when it was time for us to leave for the cold north-eastern world of church and school and sea-fret and sin.

The days at Thornby End were the best in my life and about two hours long, though goodness knows what we did in them except wander about, feed the calves, gather the eggs and lie around in the hay. There was not one book on the farm except in the dining-room, on the furred green tablecloth, a family Bible with a brass clasp, and it did not attract me. One day, however, when it was raining, I decided to crawl – I must have been ten but I was very small for my age and as retarded as Peter Rabbit – along inside the court-cupboard in the dining-room, in at one door and out at the other. A court-cupboard is a piece of furniture like a long sideboard with cupboards above and below, carved in rich black oak with flowers and leaves and squirls. Ours was carved too with the date 1667 – the house had been built round it. As I proceeded along in the dark of the ground floor of the cupboard I found on a pile of rubbishy newspapers a smelly, freckly, mean little book with its cardboard covers bent back and the nastiest, smallest print I ever saw. It was called *Northanger Abbey*. 'Whatever do you want with that?' asked my grandmother. 'It's something from Crummock Bank, to do with your Aunt Jessie.' (I never discovered what this meant.) I read *Northanger Abbey* all over the farm, in the stack-yard and the Dutch barn and the bower of the red sandstone earth closet that looked down through the orchard and over the Rough Ground to the Scottish mountains. I can't pretend I doted on it – or even had much idea what it was about.

It was dry and difficult and the prickly clever people might have lived on the moon. Yet somehow I knew them.

This spring I had to write an article, for a book called *Writers' Houses*, about Hill Top, Sawrey, and saw in Beatrix Potter's sitting room a court-cupboard carved in 1667. I found in the National Trust's inventory of the house that Beatrix Potter had picked it up at a farm sale in West Cumberland – at about the time Thornby End was sold up and our cupboard disappeared. Again, it was something to do with Aunt Mabel who knew about antiques – though not as much, I'd guess, as Beatrix Potter. I felt very much as Beatrix Potter did when she saw Samuel Whiskers and his wife flitting off down Sawrey village with 'a little wheelbarrow, which looked very like mine'. But probably it's all fancy.

I should like to pretend that after my high-flown start with the Liturgy and Jane Austen, and the animal and human condition, I continued on the same plane, but I didn't. When I was ten a public library was started at home in Coatham which changed my life. I attended every day after school and often twice on Saturdays when I infuriated the librarians by bringing back the morning's book for a new one in the afternoon, which was forbidden. Who chose the books for that library? I wonder. It was said that they were bought by the yard from left-overs at sales. I never even heard of some of the children's books other children were reading at the time or the books of my mother's generation – Yonge, Molesworth, Nesbit. I read the *William* books and *Biggles*. I worshipped Biggles and would have swooned had I known that his creator,

W. E. Johns, was soon to be stationed in the RAF two miles
away – unless perhaps that had been in the war before the
one that was coming?

Biggles led me to books on flying aeroplanes and aeroplane identification and, when war was declared, to first
aid. I wallowed in wounds and soon felt that at a pinch I
could have delivered a child or done simple amputations.
I instructed my friends in the Girl Guides about tourni-
quets from illustrations of people spouting like colanders.
Of all this literature only *William* was frowned upon by
my mother, who disliked the 'bad grammar and spelling', so I read him under the sheets. Later I was smug
when I found out that Richmal Crompton had been a
classicist: beautifully constructed, unsentimental, loving,
funny stories – and still going strong. And how much
better than the milk-and-water adventures of the dreary
Ransome children of *Swallows and Amazons* in so-called
Cumberland: Cumberland without the foxy-whiskered
gentleman or smelly Mr Brock living in their dripping,
Beowulfian hovels. And where was my old grandfather
swearing behind his horses at the plough, or my Auntie
Mabel returning from an antiques jaunt to be gored by
one of her own cows? Long live *Cold Comfort Farm*. And
what names they had, those Ransome children. Titty, for
goodness sake! I knew all about that sort of thing, discussing it at length with the hired girl, Molly, as we did the
milking.

There was one splendid thing about the public library
and that was that the children's department was not separated from the rest of it and you could slide round the

end of a bookcase and in four steps be away from Arthur Ransome and *The Muddle-Headed Postman* and dismal *Worrals of the WAAF*, and be eyeball to eyeball with Thomas Hardy and Thomas Traherne (I wonder if authors were classified under Christian names?). As the years rolled on I took these across the corridor to read in the 'Reference Library', which was a quiet, nice room with a coal fire. It was wartime now and all the winter afternoons of the Christmas holidays in 1940 I sat gobbling books – all the Brontës and Dickens and a huge volume of Heath-Robinson drawings. Strangely, when the siren went, we were all tipped out on to the streets to walk home under the searchlights. I could not get the Heath-Robinson under my coat but I could pack *Villette* or *Adam Bede* into my navy-blue elasticated knickers as well as the two books we were legally allowed. I drank the books. They were tincture of rhubarb and tincture of myrrh on those bleak cold days. They were sparkling wine and *grand cru* cream soda. Soon – well, a year or so later – Hardy had emerged for me as top author. I'd never been south of York in my life and had a hazy idea of Wessex, yet like Bath in the eighteenth century with its curricles and bonnets, I somehow knew it. I've never deserted Hardy and he's never loosed hold of me.

About the same time, the first bookshop opened in the town and we were sent there from school to buy one of two possible home-readers – *Selections from the Iliad and the Odyssey* or *Selections from Don Quixote*. The shop was run by a Mr Hasty (later it became our first WHSmith), who was the slowest man I ever met. At the back of his shadowy shop he propped himself against the bookshelves and laid his arms (he was a giant) along the tops of them so that he appeared to hang immobile like a giant sloth or fruit-bat. My friend and I, each holding a two-shilling piece, were overawed by the hanging shadow and so we giggled. 'No,' he roared, 'no, I have NOT.' Moving his fingers about he detached a couple of selections from Homer and tossed them on the counter. 'I have NOT "Don QuickSOTE". I have NOT "Don QuickSOTE".' We fled, but he followed us to the step. 'DON KY-OTI,' he cried, 'Don KY-OTI.' I never read *Don Quixote* until the university (when I found it very patchy), and I still wonder why it meant so much to Mr Hasty. I'm grateful to him though, because I've loved both *Iliad* and *Odyssey* ever since.

A life without books is unthinkable to me. The three dining-room shelves were maybe an unlikely start for a love-affair for life. They were so unwanted when we cleared up my parents' house after their deaths five weeks apart that not even the church jumble sale was interested. I took nearly all of them home to live with me. God bless them – Cardinal Newman, Flora Klickmann, *Practical Physics* and *The Fifteen Decisive Battles of the World*.

My favourite books

The Book of Common Prayer; *The Tempest*, William Shakespeare; *Robinson Crusoe*, Daniel Defoe; *The Embassy Letters of Lady Mary Wortley Montagu*; *Madame Bovary*,

Gustav Flaubert; *Nicholas Nickleby*, Charles Dickens; *Tess of the D'Urbervilles*, Thomas Hardy; *The Diary of a Nobody*, George and Weedon Grossmith; *One Hundred Years of Solitude*, Gabriel García Márquez; The *Short Stories* of Raymond Carver; *Oscar and Lucinda*, Peter Carey; the thirteen-volume *Oxford English Dictionary* bought with my first royalties.

Ronald Harwood

O<small>H</small>, the excitement of the latest Famous Five adventure – with Biggles, Just William, Huckleberry Finn, Tom Sawyer and Long John Silver following close behind. I have not, except for *Treasure Island,* reread them since childhood or adolescence and I've made it a condition not to reread them now in case I am embarrassed by memory. I want to prevent the pompous adult, sensitive to what others may think, from inhibiting the impressionable child. I was, by the way, a late developer and only really began reading intelligently when I was twenty.

I should explain I was born and educated in Cape Town but my mother, born in London, led me to believe from an early age that England was the Promised Land and London Jerusalem, so I was a good deal drawn to books which fed my hunger for Englishness defined by me then, and now, as an ideal of gentleness, culture, countryside and justice.

Enid Blyton, more than any other writer I remember, fulfilled much of that definition, those longings for England, but only in her Famous Five stories. (I could not abide Noddy or any of the others.) The Famous Five, as I remember, lived somewhere in the south of England – Kent, I think – and were amateur detectives who, in their summer holidays, stumbled on crimes and solved them just as it was time to go back to school. Gentle justice triumphed. But it was her ability to share her love of the English landscape which was, to me, her most enduring quality. Enid Blyton described the English rural scene so vividly that I carry to this day what I believe to be her images of tree-tunnels and green hillsides and well-kept careless gardens. I am told now it was a sugary, middle-class idyll she created (a criticism as meaningless to me now as it would have been then), romantic, idealized, nostalgic. The fascinating aspect of her power, however, is that when, many years later, I went to live in a Hampshire village and walked the footpaths and climbed the hangers, my memory was jolted by her descriptions of the England in which the capers of the Famous Five took place and seemed to me accurate. I cannot say she influenced my own writing but as a reader I owe her an enormous debt; and I remember in the 1970s, when censorship was virulent in England, how shocked I was to read of librarians removing Enid Blyton from their shelves for being too middle-class or too twee or too something. They could not have known that to one immigrant, at least, she described a magical world.

I suspect that W. E. Johns with Biggles, and Richmal Crompton (whose first name baffled me because I could not decide his or her gender) with William Brown, were also part of my yearning for England. But there was another excitement and one that has lasted to this day. I must have been ten or eleven when, having finished my first *Biggles,* I discovered in a kind of ecstasy that the author had written a host of other books about the same hero. I devoured them one after the other: by day hiding them behind school textbooks and by night under the bedclothes, reading until the batteries of the torch gave out and the light was no more. I remember much later discovering Graham Greene, Evelyn Waugh, P. G. Wodehouse, and similarly devouring their novels to the exclusion of all else.

With Mark Twain I suppose I took a step up the cultural ladder even though he wasn't English. Huck Finn and Tom Sawyer were more alive to me than any of my real friends or acquaintances for the simple reason that I knew more about them than anyone who crossed my path. I could predict how Huck and Tom would react or what they would say in any given circumstance. They lived and breathed; the Mississippi flowed in Cape Town and Injun Jim stalked my sunlit streets. If Captain Johns was a caricaturist whose colours were stark, Mark Twain made me aware that the life of the characters and one's ability to believe in them were the most important elements in fiction.

The turning-point, however, was Robert Louis Stevenson's *Treasure Island,* which I believe to be a masterpiece. In this book plot and story are perfectly woven to sustain E. M. Forster's two essential requirements of a novel, which are a story and a plot. To the story, Forster explained, you ask the question, 'and then?'; to the plot you ask the question, 'why?'. (He offers this example: the King died and then the Queen died – that's a story. But, the King died and then the

Queen died of grief – that's a plot.) Well, in *Treasure Island*
the story is breathtaking, the invention of incident prolific,
the need to know what happens next unceasing, but the
plot, the why of the novel, is divine. Why all these adventures, why the black spot and Billy Bones and Blind Pew
and Ben Gunn? The answer motivates every event: treasure,
Jim lad, buried treasure. There is also a switch of narrator, a
stunning device, for the tale is told not only by Jim Hawkins
but also by Dr Smollett. Other works by Stevenson I did not
find so rewarding – *Kidnapped* and *Dr Jekyll and Mr Hyde*
were dreadful let-downs – so I read and reread and read yet
again *Treasure Island*. Last year I sailed on the *Hispaniola* for
the umpteenth time and my heart missed a beat, as it always
does, when Israel Hands falls from the rigging.

I am beginning to understand that the books I read as
a child subtly define the adult. I know, too, how influenced I was in my reading by my mother. Her love of
literature, especially poetry, was profound, but she had
prejudices which included an aversion to personifying
animals. (She would shudder with disgust when people
talked to their pets as though they were children.) There
were no copies of Beatrix Potter or Kenneth Grahame
on our shelves and *Jock of the Bushveld,* a South African
classic, she dismissed as ill-written and sentimental. (Some
years ago I was asked to adapt the book for the screen and
found my mother's judgement to be infallible. I wrote the
screenplay. The film, thank God, was never made.) I can
only conclude, therefore, that it was she who bequeathed
to me an ambivalence towards Lewis Carroll. Nevertheless,
he looms large in my formative years. I must have read the

Alice books often because I seem to know them well and rejoice in his imagination and linguistic inventions. But I was wary of him, a little suspicious – as I was of Kipling's *Jungle Book* – and I never surrendered unconditionally to his genius. I warmed to the Carpenter but not the Walrus, to the Mad Hatter but not the Dormouse. The White Rabbit left me cold. And, I now realize, I have never been a great fan of *Animal Farm*.

There was a private lending-library, down the road in Sea Point where I lived, run by Mrs Lipschitz. One night a week, Thursday I think, my mother and I would trot down in the early evening to choose two or three volumes for the coming week. The sections marked 'Sports' and 'Westerns' started to attract me when I was about twelve. Being a cricket fanatic and a promising boxer (until I was knocked out in the second round by a killer named Swart), I read the lives of Don Bradman (as a boy he made himself hit a golf ball with a walking-stick against a jagged wall a hundred times in succession), Jack Dempsey and Gene Tunney (the Long Count – Dempsey was robbed!), Joe Louis (then still the reigning heavyweight champion of the world, the man who had taken his revenge on that arrogant German, Max Schmeling) and Jack Hobbs (a gentleman and a genius). I still place cricket above all other sport and I've no doubt reading about those giants encouraged my undying love for the game. I continue to read books about cricket and cricketers but the fight game is not what it was. As for Westerns, I doubt if any child now reads Zane Grey.

There were three other important strands to my early reading. The first was the Old Testament and the exquisite

liturgy of the synagogue. ('Praised be Thou O Lord Our
God, ruler of the world, by whose law the shadows of
evening fall and the gates of morn are opened.') I was
deeply religious. I bought the Bible stories lock, stock and
tabernacle. The world was created in six days, the Children
of Israel were God's chosen people – although what we
were chosen for was never absolutely clear – and Jehovah
tested poor old Job's faith by causing him to come out in
boils. No work so inflamed my imagination as the Bible,
and the embers still glow. Faith continues to haunt me, like
an ectoplasm, there one moment, gone the next. But, of
course, it is really doubt which haunts me, and is presumably why I now read a good deal of philosophy, although I
am untrained and awkward in my appreciation. The more
I read, the more confused I become, and conclude that
certainty is an early symptom of insanity.

The second strand was encyclopaedias. We had two
sets: one edited by Arthur Mee, the other by Sir John
Hammerton. I spent hours with those volumes and remember especially clearly in Arthur Mee the lives of the famous
composers: reading of Schubert's death from an 'incurable
disease'; of J. S. Bach, as a child, straining his eyes because
he worked too late by candlelight and as a result going
blind in old age (I stopped reading by torchlight under the
bedclothes immediately); and most baffling of all, learning
that Beethoven was deaf – was it possible that a deaf man
could write such sublime music? Exactly how much useful
and useless information I gathered from those tomes I shall
never know, but instinct tells me my inquisitiveness was
quickened and has never died.

The final strand was the discovery of William Shakespeare and the theatre, again my mother's great passions. But it was the cinema which really drove me into his embrace. I was thirteen when I saw Laurence Olivier's film of *Hamlet*. Within a month I had seen it six times and knew the play by heart. *Henry V,* although made first, I saw later and was equally smitten. Thereafter, I read plays compulsively and everything else I could lay hands on about actors and the theatre. A friend, Gerald Masters, and I had a toy theatre – an elaborate structure which we christened the Royal Acropolis – and we would act out an eclectic selection of plays with me taking the leading roles while pushing up and down cardboard cut-outs of the characters. There was little professional theatre in Cape Town but in the Royal Acropolis I discovered Sheridan, Ben Travers, Chekhov, Noel Coward, J. B. Priestley, Elmer Rice, Ibsen, Eugene O'Neill, Wilde and Galsworthy. We had an obsession with Bernard Shaw but that soon wore off and, in my case, has never returned. I did not believe in his characters as real people and so he lost me for ever.

It is impossible, of course, to do justice to all the books which captivated me, but Palgrave's *Golden Treasury* must enter my pantheon. My favourite was Wordsworth – yes, and Keats and Tennyson and, oh, all of them, all of them. And, in the netherworld of adolescence, being given T. S. Eliot's 'The Journey of the Magi' to learn as a punishment and being dropped unwittingly into new, unexplored territory; yes, a cold coming I had of it, and I was no longer at ease in the old dispensation.

My favourite books

The list of my top ten favourite books: I do not really approve of lists but I shall have a go and cheat a little. In no particular order then: Herman Melville's *Moby-Dick*, *War and Peace* by Tolstoy, the complete works of William Shakespeare, *The Interpretation of Dreams* by Sigmund Freud, *Decline and Fall* by Evelyn Waugh, Boswell's *Life of Samuel Johnson LL.D.*, Stevenson's *Treasure Island, The Power and the Glory* by Graham Greene, Dostoyevsky's *Crime and Punishment*, and the Old Testament.

A. S. Byatt

I SPENT much of my childhood in bed, reading. I was handicapped, set apart, greatly blessed by very bad asthma. Much later when I came to read Proust, I recognized certain things in him – a contemplative acute vision, induced by keeping very still in order to be able to breathe, a sense of living most fiercely in the mind, or in books, which were a livelier life. I have tried to remember my first real reading, and failed. There seems to have been nothing between 'Pat can sing. Sing to Mother Pat', and a voracious indiscriminate devouring of all printed words, the *Children's Encyclopaedia*, *Worzel Gummidge*, *Little Grey Rabbit*, *David Copperfield*, *Alice*, *Winnie-the-Pooh*, *The Wind in the Willows*, Sir Walter Scott. I remember not making sense of things – it didn't occur to me that Louisa May Alcott's *Little Women* were *Americans* so I couldn't understand why they had to sail to England. I believed I was threatened with imminent imprisonment in the Marshalsea from reading *Little Dorrit*, and tried *A Midsummer Night's Dream* and got annoyed by being distracted from what I supposed to be the 'real' story, the love of Hermia and Lysander, by fairies. I don't remember finding anything too difficult – I just skipped and struggled to make sense of what I could.

What do I remember? What of all that fiercely explored forest of paper is still alive? I recognized, earlier than Proust, another mirror for myself in Coleridge's remark about his own childhood reading: 'From my early reading of Faery Tales and Genii etc etc – my mind had been habituated *to the Vast* – and I never regarded *my senses* in any way as the criteria of my belief . . .' The roots of my thinking are a tangled maze of myths, folktales, legends, fairy stories. Robin Hood, King Arthur, Alexander of Macedon, Achilles and Odysseus, Apollo and Pan, Loki and Baldur, Sinbad and Haroun al Rashid, Rapunzel and Beauty and the Beast, Tom Bombadil and Cerberus. I have no idea now where I got all this, except for the Norse myths, which came from a turn-of-the-century book, *Asgard and the Gods*, bought by my mother as a crib for her Ancient Norse and Icelandic exams at Cambridge. I read the *Fairy Books* of Andrew Lang and several collections of ballads, and 'How Horatius Kept the Bridge' from Macaulay's *Lays of Ancient Rome*. The tales and myths and legends did, I am now more sure than ever I was, exactly what Coleridge said they did. They made it clear there was another world, beside the world of having to be a child in a house, an inner world and a vast outer world with large implications – good and evil, angels and demons, fate and love and terror and beauty – and the comfort of the inevitable ending, not only the happy ending against odds, but the tragic one too.

At the same time, and just as early, I remember the importance of poetry. Nursery rhymes, ballads, 'The Jackdaw of Rheims' from Richard Barham's *The Ingoldsby Legends* and A. A. Milne's *Now We Are Six*, 'The Rime of the Ancient Mariner' and 'Slowly silently now the moon' by Walter de la Mare. I think one of the most important writers to me ever has been de la Mare, though it is a debt hard to recognize or acknowledge. Partly for the singing strange rhythms of his poetry, partly for the strange worlds and half-worlds he gave one glimpses of, the world of a pike suspended in thick gloom under a bridge, the journeyings of the *Three Mulla-Mulgars*, which I read over and over. The most important poems were three colouring books we had, a page of poetry beside a picture, all three complete stories. *The Pied Piper*, Tennyson's 'The Lady of Shalott', his *Morte d'Arthur*. I knew them all by heart long before I thought to ask who had written them. Their rhythms haunt everything I write, especially the Tennyson. The enclosed weaving lady became my private symbol for my reading and brooding self long before I saw what she meant for him, and for nineteenth-century poetry in general. Truthfulness forces me to admit that we did not have that great anthology of magical and narrative verse, de la Mare's *Come Hither*, but we were brought up on its contents by my mother, who gave us poems and more poems, as though it was unquestionable that this was the best thing she could do for us.

What about fiction, as opposed to fairy tales? What I remember most vividly is learning fear, which I think may be important to all animals – I used to love the song from

Jungle Book – 'It is fear, oh little hunter, it is fear'. And I remember Blind Pew tapping, the terrible staircase and the heather-hunting in *Kidnapped*, I remember Jane Eyre locked in the Red Room, and poor David Copperfield at the mercy of Mr Murdstone, the horrors of Fagin in the condemned cell (I can only have been eight or nine) and worst of all (though I still have nightmares about executions), Pip on the marshes being grabbed by Magwitch in that brilliant and terrible beginning of *Great Expectations*. I must have been very little. I didn't understand any more than Pip that Magwitch's terrible companion was fictive.

I remember my first meeting with evil, too, and it has only just recently struck me how strange that was. I worked my way along my grandmother's shelf of school prizes – was I nine or ten? Or younger? And read *Uncle Tom's Cabin* before anyone had told me that slaves had really existed outside *The Arabian Nights*. Tom's sufferings and the evil of the system and the people who killed him, with cruelty or negligence, made me feel ill and appalled. I never talked to anyone about it. We sang about Christ's suffering in church but that seemed comparatively comfortable and institutional and had after all a happy ending, whereas Tom's story did not. And yet one is grateful for these glimpses of the dark: as long as they do not destroy, they strengthen.

I liked adventures – not Marryat and *The Coral Island* too much, but the wonderfully heartrending stories of Violet Needham, and Dumas and Scott; all the adventures of the Musketeers, *The Talisman* and *Ivanhoe*, *Kenilworth* and *Redgauntlet*, and most of the rest of Scott, though I had trouble with not knowing what Covenanters were in *Old Mortality*, and having to keep several hypotheses open in my mind. I was in love with Athos and with Loki and with the sinful Lancelot and with Ulysses – the clever and complicated and fallible, on the whole.

What I didn't like was children, though I read a lot about them, *faute de mieux*, because I read too fast not to. I didn't like being a child, and I didn't like being with imaginary children, not even the Bastables, not even, really, Arthur Ransome's families, though I read and reread *Swallows and Amazons*, I think mostly for the landscape, and for the very good fear generated by *We Didn't Mean to Go to Sea*. I must make an exception for that anarchic and eternal child, Richmal Crompton's *William*, as much an archetype as Alice. But I hated Enid Blyton's *Famous Five* and all schoolchildren in school stories and the smug kind of children in pony stories who despise children who are interested in clothes or books or anything but tomboy-ishness. I liked *Little Women* better when they were *Good Wives*. They were more interesting. I liked Jane Austen, and believed everything she said about the right way for men and women to behave towards each other – her hero-ines are young things (apart from my favourite, Anne in *Persuasion*) who are about to be able to be women not girls, and be happy, as in fairy stories.

I agree wholly with Tolkien and Auden, in their dispute with Alan Garner about how to write about magical and alien worlds for children. The little groups of wandering Susans and Johns and Erics in their pyjamas and school sandals ruined many good imaginary landscapes and cosmic battles for me. I am too old to have read Tolkien as a child, but the child in me read and reads him as an adult in moments of depression, as I read Dumas and *Asgard and the Gods*, to live in narrative. I can't now read and couldn't then read C. S. Lewis – there is a nasty moral in a sugary pill there, the books have palpable *intentions* on you and the children are horridly childish. It follows from that that I mistrust romantic theories about the wisdom, or truthful vision of children, such as were rife in the 1960s. Children are just people in the process of getting older, vulnerable people learning to be human, and wise children know that being men and women is much more interesting and complicated than the state in which they are temporarily stuck.

I knew a lot about passionate love, from the *Morte d'Arthur* to *Jane Eyre*. I began to learn about sex from E. Arnot Robertson (*Four Frightened People*) and Elizabeth Bowen (*The House in Paris*), a wonderfully double book, bought by my father by mistake for Marjorie Bowen, a tale told through the eyes of a sharp but childish child, which includes adult passion, and has a very odd effect on a reader hardly older than Henrietta herself.

What effect did all this have on my writing? I think there was always a mythic and poetic undertow in my fiction, even at its most realist. *The Game*, for instance, is full of echoes of 'The Lady of Shalott' and the *Morte d'Arthur*, and is essentially a novel about a battle to the death between a realist novelist and an academic with a romantic imagination, in both the medieval and the Coleridgean sense. It turns on a phrase of Dr Johnson's about the hunger of the imagination, which preys incessantly upon life. It asks if books are life-giving or death-dealing, and if so, is it social and emotional truth-telling, or myth and legend which give the power? I have spent much of my career as a writer defending what I call 'self-conscious realism' against the *nouveau roman* or the ideas of Virginia Woolf about life as a series of impressions seen through a luminous halo. I think, although all my books have also been fighting a more or less overt battle with Dr Leavis and the Cambridge-English school of moral seriousness and social responsibility, I have also been deeply influenced by it. But recently – when, for instance, I read Angela Carter saying she wanted to write with the passion with which she read fairy stories as a child, or when I see what Salman Rushdie makes of *The Arabian Nights* as a way of telling truths today – I have felt that the primitive reader in me, too, has been liberated. B. S. Johnson in the 1960s invented various 'experimental' narrative forms based on the premise that 'telling stories is telling lies'. Iris Murdoch said 'All art is adventure stories.' (Or at least the god Apollo said it, in an editorial capacity, in one of her novels.) I agree with Iris Murdoch. And there-fore I find recent movements in the shape of fiction – the new mixtures of fables and myths and quests and hunts, of magic and truth, reality and artifice – very exciting.

My favourite books

One's list of ten, or any other number of books, changes from day to day. I have chosen these really on the principle of whether they stood up to the test of being asked whether I could not do without them, over a period of about three days. I should point out that this is not a list of most admired authors – there are novelists in particular, Balzac, Dickens, George Eliot, Iris Murdoch, Tolstoy, whom I need and love, but *in toto*, and remember well enough to do without particular works. The same goes for many poets – I need Herbert and Donne and Tennyson as much as the included poets, but can do without the *books* with more equanimity. I have included Tolkien, as the narrative to read when ill, rather than Georgette Heyer on the same principle.

The *Collected Poems* of: Wallace Stevens, Emily Dickinson, Robert Browning; *A la recherche du temps perdu*, Marcel Proust; *The Idiot*, Fyodor Dostoyevsky; Nietzsche, *The Birth of Tragedy*; *The Notebooks of S. T. Coleridge*; *Asgard and the Gods* (adapted from the work of Dr W. Wägner by M. W. Macdowell, edited by W. S. W. Anson); *The London Book of English Verse*, ed. Bonamy Dobree (I fear this excellent collection is out of print, but it is still by far my favourite anthology. It was made at the time when my adult taste in poetry was formed by T. S. Eliot, and is full of 'metaphysical' and 'symphonic' poems I love, and a lot of surprises); J. R. R. Tolkien's *The Lord of the Rings* (for reading when very ill or depressed: it is compelling narrative and there is no sex and no real moral problems to agitate the mind).

Simon Gray

I LEARNT to read in Montreal during the war, lisping out the captions and balloon-dialogue of *Captain Marvel* comics, *Batman*, *Superman*, *The Green Hornet*, *Captain Marvel Junior*, *Mary Marvel*, and so forth. I found the very sight of the glossy covers, the feel, the smell, so exciting that to this day I still sometimes swoon at the memory – as potent as the occasional astonished return (one in 50,000 puffs) to the experience of an early cigarette. The first *book* I remember reading was in Hayling Island, when I was about eight, I suppose. The American servicemen based there had gone home, and my brother and I used to haunt the empty barracks, looking for loot. The prize, for me, was a tattered, red-spined but virtually coverless copy of *Sherlock Holmes* stories. So after that more *Sherlock Holmes*, and on to *Father Brown*, and then on to virtually any book I could get hold of – between the age of ten and sixteen I truly believed there was no better place in the world than inside a book.

Among the books I most adored being inside of in my immediate post-pubescence were those by Hank

Janson – the first popular soft-porn merchant – whose covers, as shiny as any *Captain Marvel*, exhibited well-breasted (and partially bra-ed; I'm writing here of the late 1940s and early 1950s) young women, generally bound and gagged, skirts hiked to reveal a stocking-top and a suspender. I used to sell off school textbooks, not only my own, at the second-hand shop in Foyles to find the money (one shilling and sixpence) to keep me in my warm romantic fantasies which were even more important to me than success at cricket. Towards the end of my Hank Janson phase – not that it's ever completely ended; I still stir at the spectacle of a maiden in distress – I was also tucking into the kind of books that chaps with intellectual pretensions at Westminster tucked into. Dostoyevsky, Camus, Sartre – anyone who received a formal education in that era will be poignantly familiar with the bibliography, which extended itself when I found myself back in Canada (Halifax, Nova Scotia, for reasons too boring to explain) to Plato, Aristotle, Kant (I have actually read the whole of *The Critique of Pure Reason*: this is a boast, not a confession), Heidegger, Kummelfliger, Perry Jubb and lots and lots of Raymond Chandler.

Three years later I was in Clermont-Ferrand, France, teaching English at a *collège-technique*, and it was there, suddenly, under the influence of a bearded Leavisite who was doing what I was doing, although at a more exalted level, that I began to read English novels at last. It was he who started me off on Leavis – he'd brought the key texts with him in his knapsack – and through Leavis I read Lawrence, of course and several times, Conrad,

George Eliot, Henry James – the Downing canon. From Clermont-Ferrand I went as first a postgraduate, intending to write a thesis on Henry James, back through the ranks to undergraduate status. When I wasn't playing poker at Cambridge, or going to the cinema, or hunting down ninth-hand copies of long-out-of-print Hank Jansons, I was reading, in a disagreeably professional manner, for the tripos. After the tripos, taken in a heavily hay-fever-ridden summer, I swore I'd never again read a book I didn't actually *want* to read – a pledge I almost managed to stand by even though I eventually got a job teaching literature at London University. It meant I kept my students on a fairly sparse diet – but what the hell!

Now that I've resigned from lecturing my reading is either dilatory or professional – that is, I either pick up books on a whim, going by their cover, the blurb and vaguely recalled reputation, or because they're sent to me with a view to my turning them into film scripts. I try, whenever I can, to avoid the modern novel. I expect lots of modern novels are simply terrific, and that my own experience with them has only been so unfortunate because it's been so haphazard. The problem is, though, that I find them intensely difficult to get stuck into. One is still waiting, waiting, for the absolute immersion, the complete world-deafness of one's childhood reading. When it comes partially it comes from what I now recognize is an entirely expected source, the thriller. After all, it's only in the thriller that a strong story line is mandatory, though no doubt modern critical theorists, who are as anti-coherence as modern educationalists appear to be anti-education, will try to find ways of forcing unreadable fragmentations of thriller-narrative upon us. In fact I have a suspicion that I came across some French (what else?) examples of this some years back. But the truth is you know exactly where you are with a Dick Francis, especially the early ones, which seem to me infinitely superior as works of literature to the razzmatazz stylistics of the highly publicized and award-winning novels by young X, who jives egocentrically across the page, but fails to make one wish to turn it.

One highly celebrated novel of our days I've tried to read three times, and on each occasion, in a state of exhausted admiration, have let it drop to the floor around page fifty, with 400 pages or so still to go. Not only not a patch in narrative flow on Dick Francis, who never insults his readers by turning a phrase unless it's appropriate (i.e. turns a narrative screw), and also not a patch on Barbara Vine (*née* Ruth Rendell, so to speak), whose first three thrillers achieve a genuinely classy atmosphere of excitement and dread that seems to me far beyond the range of all those chaps who write about babies and the bomb – already a decidedly anachronistic subject, though it's true that babies and parental feelings go on and on, and back and back – although you'd think they'd only just been invented, from the surprise with which they're being greeted by a current crop of literary daddies.

Although the above is clearly mere prejudice, feebly masquerading as taste and judgement, it is still an undeniable fact of my nature that I'm unable to follow any prose or indeed verse that doesn't in some sense tell a story. Even polemic, or close-knit political and philosophical argument, seems to me to require a narrative – the feeling that the reader is invited to go on a journey with a terminus in mind, even if that turns out to be somewhere cold and damp, where you'd rather not be. The most perfect example of narrative prose, swift, witty, informative and dramatic, that I know of in the English language is the first chapter of *Mansfield Park*, although every first chapter in Jane Austen is marked by the unmistakable confidence of the writer who knows she has a story to tell, and knows she knows exactly how to tell it. The closing chapters of *Mansfield Park* show all the same qualities corrupted by moral intent. The wit becomes nasty, the drama becomes melodrama, and the confidence becomes simultaneously smug and punitive. I'm not sure why I go into this here, unless it's to register the sense of betrayal, intensely personal betrayal, that books can still induce. To that extent they really are like friends and loved ones.

At one time, about a decade ago, when I was going through an unusually depressing phase, I virtually read only cricket books. Not just the obvious ones, like Neville Cardus and Robertson-Glasgow, but the autobiographies and ghosted autobiographies of players themselves. Edrich, Compton, Evans, Graveney, recently Pat Pocock. One of the most telling bits of drama I've come across in a book is Edrich's account of trying to get Hutton out of bed (to which he had withdrawn in a state of shock and terror) to win the Ashes in Australia, in the great Tyson series. Without doubt, the most astute and witty book I've read in recent years is Mike Brearley's on *The Art of Captaincy*. I thumb it about quite a lot, at all hours of the day and night. But on the whole, though still frequently depressed, I've given them up – there's too much cricket to see, these days, to find the time to read about it seriously. Also, in as much as most of the best books belong to a vanished age, they would probably only add to the depression.

What I'm reduced to, really, is reading the same books again and again. I've read *Mansfield Park* twelve times, most of Jane Austen nearly as often. I've reread Dickens, with as much awe and joy the fifth time around as on the first. I read George Eliot now and again, T. S. Eliot again and again, and Larkin, of course, and George and Weedon Grossmith's *The Diary of a Nobody* and *The Papers of A. J. Wentworth*. The list of great writers I intend never to read again before I die (I can't speak for after. There may well be a Hell) is vastly longer, and includes Proust, all of Joyce except *Dubliners*, E. M. Forster, Virginia Woolf, Shaw, W. H. Auden (for personal reasons too embarrassing to go into), Walter Scott, naturally; and sadly – because I'm still grateful for the intoxicated and bogus sense of manhood he gave me when I was twenty-one and in France and still full of passionate sexual confusions – D. H. Lawrence.

Roger McGough

ONE of my biggest regrets in life is that my own books were not around for me to enjoy when I was a child. In fact, because of the war, very few children's books were available at all. There was a local library with a limited stock, but no bookshops. New books, like bananas, were heard of, but not seen.

My father, an occasional reader who enjoyed stories of the sea, felt embarrassed about entering a library. A working man's fear of being shown up or made to look ignorant, I suppose. He left it to the family to choose the books for him. And it was easy:

'I got this for you, Dad, have you read it?'
'Yes, but it doesn't matter, it's good. It's always good.'

My mother, on the other hand, loved books and was a firm believer in the potency of words to charm, to heal and to educate. It was she who would put me on to a merry-go-round of nursery rhymes and simple prayers, then take me off, dizzy with words. Though books were scarce in those early years Mother made sure that I listened to a bedtime story every night. By the light of a burning factory or a crashed Messerschmitt she would read anything that came to hand: sauce bottle labels, the sides of cornflake packets. All tucked up warm and cosy, my favourite story was a tin of Ovaltine. How well I remember her voice even now: 'Sprinkle two or three heaped teaspoonsful of . . .'

At the age of five I started school and became an infant. At Star of the Sea I learned my letters from wall-charts, so old-fashioned that Ronnie with his Red Rattle and Tired Mother, who sighed 'Hah' as she sat on a large 'h', looked more unreal than the fairies and elves who decorated the picture books.

This method of personifying the alphabet, however, worked too well and overtired my imagination to the extent that I still attribute feelings to individual letters rather than seeing them as mere hieroglyphs. (That's what is good about a word like 'hieroglyph', the letters find themselves in different company, it keeps them on their toes. I digress.)

The first story I remember that touched me deeply was *Greyfriars Bobby* by Eleanor Atkinson, and the fact that it was true made my NHS glasses mist over time after time. To know that there would be no sequel entitled *Bobby to the Rescue,* in which it transpires that the old chap had not really died but had fallen off the top of Ben Nevis and lain injured until finally rescued by the plucky terrier, was a tragic realization. That truth could be crueller than fiction was one of the first lessons that reading taught me, and I didn't want to believe it. What I wanted was *Custer Rides Again, Joan of Arc II* and *Further Adventures of the Princes in the Tower*. Fairytale fiction, of course, was often desperately dark and as scary as any nightmare, and although there were no witches or goblins in the part of Liverpool that I grew up in, I realized that what happened to Hansel and Gretel could happen to any child. The names, places and costumes may have changed but the evil was still there.

But so was goodness of course, courage, and generosity. At the age of seven or eight my heroine was Grace Darling, the lighthouse keeper's daughter who helped rescue sailors from a ship wrecked off the Northumbrian coast. The book featured stirring illustrations of a frail beauty rowing through a storm, and I knew then that when I grew up I wanted to be rescued by someone as lovely as she. (As a matter of fact I was, but that's another story.)

It was at the top end of junior school that I graduated to abridged versions of classics such as *Treasure Island* and *A Christmas Carol* which caused my pulse to race and my hackles tremble. Remember the feeling when turning the page was almost too much to bear? As adults grown weary on clichés and redesigned storylines, we too easily forget the initial jolt, the power, almost drug-like, of those first readings, when imagination flared up and seemed capable of consuming us.

After romping through half-remembered classics (abridged too far, perhaps?), such as *Around the World in a Day-and-a-Half,*

A Tale of One City and *The Lion, the Witch and the Tea-chest*, it was the comic that became my essential reading. Not cartoons but adventure weeklies such as the *Wizard*, *Hotspur* and *Rover*. Here I mixed happily with the public schoolboys of Red Circle, and admired the pluck of 'Limp-along Leslie', the diminutive left-winger who, despite a withered leg, developed an unstoppable shot that unerringly curled into the top right-hand corner of the net two minutes before the final whistle.

Another working-class hero with whom I identified was 'Alf Tupper the Tough of the Track', who trained on fish and chips, ran in hobnailed boots, baggy undies and a borrowed vest and showed the world's best milers a clean pair of heels (well, not that clean, actually). And perhaps my all-time favourite – Wilson, the metaphysical mega-athlete and mystic who lived in a cave on Dartmoor, on a diet of nuts and berries. Clad only in black woolly combinations he would emerge when his country needed him and run like the wind with its tail on fire. Scorning fame and success, he was the outsider, an eccentric loner.

The interesting thing about these comic-book characters is that they were all either deformed, deprived or cuckoo, and yet were capable of extraordinary feats of strength and endurance, thanks to intense concentration, the will to win and an abhorrence of sex.

Unlike me. (It is with some embarrassment that I admit to borrowing my sister's copy of *School Friend* each week to marvel at the drawings of girls wearing tutus or hockey shorts.) *National Geographic* magazines, too, have a lot to answer for.

Verse speaking played an important part in fashioning my reading. As a child I used to mumble, and so when I was eleven my mother sent me to elocution lessons where I learned how to mumble louder. Poems which had been grey indecipherable lumps during Eng. Lit. periods suddenly came to life. Carroll's 'Jabberwocky', 'The Burial of Sir John Moore at Corunna' and Masefield's 'Cargoes' were favourites to recite individually or as part of a chorus. Eventually, as I became unselfconscious about hearing my own voice, I learned to listen to the poet's.

I can't remember what I read from fourteen to seventeen. Set books, I suppose. Or rather, half-hearted attempts. (Thomas Hardy may be credited with having written *The Mayor of Casterbridge* but I wrote at least two thirds of it – the weekly punishment for failing the comprehension test was to write out the chapter in question. Week in, week out . . .)

In late adolescence I became interested in ideas rather than stories: J. D. Salinger, Kerouac and Colin Wilson (could the author of *The Outsider* be the same Wilson who lived in a cave on Dartmoor? Surely not). Cyril Connolly's *The Unquiet Grave*, D. H. Lawrence, Sartre, Joyce and, of course, the poetry.

With an Irish Catholic working-class background it was hardly surprising that I felt ill at ease with the traditional English poet, his Protestantism, his class, his reserve. At university the blackboard was taken down, and through the window behind it the sun streamed in. I discovered the passion and colour of Jiménez and Rimbaud, the surrealism of Morgenstern, of Prévert and Apollinaire. Through

Dylan Thomas and e e cummings to the American Beats and then back, years later, and with some relief, to the English tradition through Eliot and Larkin.

Today I read poetry every day as well as everybody's favourite novelists including Burgess, Theroux, Bainbridge, Lodge, Rendell, etc, etc . . . (there are so many good ones around) Kundera, Vonnegut, etc . . . Keneally, Greene, etc, etc . . . etc.

Emma Tennant

READING for me is tied inextricably to place. The Victorian Gothic house – a 'monstrosity' to some, a 'folly' to others, to all a decidedly odd place for a person to spend their formative years – cast its long shadow over the pages of the books I read. For years no book I read came from anywhere but the bowels and lungs – and in some cases the twisted attics – of the Big House that crouched at the end of a valley still then clad with the last shreds of the Ettrick Forest. I read up and down the house, and I knew fairly early on that I would never begin to be able to get through all of it – even with the help of the terrifying *Demonologie*, property of James VI of Scotland, with its turning paper wheels to aid with the casting of spells.

To begin with that ragged line of Ettrick silver birches outside my bedroom window. This was the Fethan Wood, where James Hogg set fairy tales and metamorphoses: it was dangerous to walk there, to go up to the ring of bright grass and look down at the house through the silver-grey trees. People came out transformed into animals – or didn't come out at all, to be discovered years later as three-legged stools. I read the Hogg stories – or they were read to me – and years before I was able to go on to his great masterpiece, *The Confessions of a Justified Sinner,* the account of a man driven insane by Calvinism, by the dictates of the devil who sends him out to kill as one of the Elect – I could feel the power of Hogg's imagination in the hills and woods and streams that enclosed the house.

The house could be said to be like an archaeological dig, with the basement providing material contemporaneous with the discoveries of archaeologists Arthur Evans or Heinrich Schliemann, and just as startling for a child to discover as it must have been for the archaeologists to unearth the foundations of Knossos or Clytemnestra's tomb. Here were Henty and Ballantyne – and, most important of all, Rider Haggard's *She* – all in low rooms hard to find in a labyrinth of tiled passages, cold and with a strong smell of rot. Here the strong and brave of the Empire fought their battles and had their impossible adventures; and here I lingered, in disused dairies and stillrooms, reading in a world which was a dusty monument to that vanished and glorious past.

From the crepuscular vaults of the house there were two ways up. The back stairs led to the schoolrooms, where tubercular daughters had coughed over books of such spectacular dullness that I remember none of them – except for the fact that some more recent incumbents had left a stash of historical romances by Margaret Irwin and Violet Needham. Here, in the abandoned schoolroom, I was drawn into a past (there were a couple of Georgette

Heyers too) of phaetons and darkly scowling aristocrats and games of faro and the like, and for a while I stopped there, until the discovery of Alexandre Dumas's *The Black Tulip* drew me down the stairs again and out into the garden. For the magnetic quality of that extraordinary book led me to search the grassy paths and flower borders for the elusive tulip – and once I thought I saw it between two yew trees, at the entrance to the garden: a rich, gleaming black flower that would guide me somehow down the paths my own imagination was just beginning to try.

If I had left the basement by the front stairs I would have found myself in the library. Here was the *Witches Book* that the last King of Scotland and the first King of England had used to sentence the women burned to death just a mile or so away at Traquair; and here were the French books, some of great beauty and delicacy, from the library of Madame de Pompadour and other noble families, snapped up by my great-grandfather at the time of the building of the house. All these were unreadable but lovely to touch, with their gold coats of arms and leather binding faded to strawberry pink. Huge atlases were at least of some use, in this room that no one ever sat in; and I would drag them out sometimes. But the temptation to go right up to the top of the house usually proved too strong to resist, and gigantic plates of Africa and Asia lay unstudied on the floor as I ran up the stairs again, this time to the foolish, crenellated summit of the place.

The attics had books in trunks that had split open with age – books no one wanted when they went off to war, or went off to get married, or had no room for anyway.

Bees had once swarmed in the attic, and it's to the smell of wax that I remember finding the early Penguins: the Aldous Huxleys, a book called *A Month of Sundays* which I have never since been able to trace – and the odd Agatha Christie, which kept me up there until dark, amongst children's wicker saddles, pictures of aunts that no one could ever want to look at, and a floor covering of dead bees.

When I was older I would take books from the sitting room, lined with dark green bound volumes of the Brontës, Peacock and Stevenson. But by then the Gothic atmosphere of the place may already have permeated me more than I knew. On coming down for the first time to London and going to school I was obsessed with one poem above all others: Edgar Allan Poe's 'The Bells'. I would shout the words, 'The tintinnabulation of the bells, bells, bells . . .' And my younger brother rolled on the floor with laughter at me.

My favourite books

Street of Crocodiles, Bruno Schulz; *The Master and Margarita*, Mikhail Bulgakov; *Chronicle of a Death Foretold*, Gabriel García Márquez; *Ariel*, Sylvia Plath; *The Confessions of a Justified Sinner*, James Hogg; *Dr Jekyll and Mr Hyde*, R. L. Stevenson; *The White Goddess*, Robert Graves; *Two Serious Ladies*, Jane Bowles; *The Sheltering Sky*, Paul Bowles.

Tom Stoppard

I WAS never a precocious reader. In his *Unreliable Memoirs*
Clive James remembers, or thinks he does, how certain
of his schoolmates, on being asked what they had been
reading in the holidays, would come up with James Joyce
while Clive himself would confess to *Biggles in the South
Seas*. This was pretty much my own experience except that
as far as I know none of us had read James Joyce.

There was a library on the troopship which brought
us from India when I was eight. From the way I tried to
divine the contents of the books purely from their physical appearances, with no sense of authors or titles, I would
guess that I had read little or nothing before then. My
mother qualifies this with her own memory of the two
of us planning to have a bookshop together, but in that
regard all I can recall is buying the *Dandy* and *Beano* in the
shop near the Capital Cinema in Darjeeling.

The first real book I read was *Peter Duck* by Arthur
Ransome. By 'real book' I mean a book which *looked* like
a proper grown-up book, 300 or more pages of solid text.

I was quite surprised to discover that such an intimidating object could turn out to be gripping stuff. This was a few weeks after I arrived in England. I didn't 'know about books'. I noticed from the flyleaf of *Peter Duck* that the author had written other books, and my method of searching for these books had a sort of dim pathos about it; I simply went around picking up any book I saw lying about to see if it was called *Swallows and Amazons*. But it never was.

However, *Peter Duck* broke the dam and when I arrived at my English prep school I started reading books in sets – the collected Arthur Ransome, Richmal Crompton, Captain W. E. Johns, and the usual classics – *The Wind in the Willows*, *Treasure Island*, *The Coral Island*, *Stalky And Co.*, *Three Men in a Boat*. I would say that my reading was utterly conventional except in its voracity. I was the apocryphal child who read the sauce bottle and the cornflakes packet if there was nothing else to hand, and for years afterwards I simply wouldn't contemplate getting on a bus without something to read, to the point, once when I was in my late teens, of spending my bus fare on a second-hand book (I still have it: *Walter Winchell* by St Clair McKelway), preferring the devil of hitchhiking to the deep blue sea of enduring half an hour bookless.

The collected works of Dornford Yates bridged me between schools, and my tastes remained thoroughly unintellectual until I left school, at which time my passion was Damon Runyon. I wrote several Damon Runyon stories.

I'm a very unreliable witness to my own experience but I can recall two significant and very similar incidents at school. In each case I noticed a boy reading a book with such obvious relish and absorption that I wanted to know what the book was. It turned out that one was *Vile Bodies* by Evelyn Waugh, and the other was *England Their England* by A. G. Macdonell. I read the wrong one. Most of my 'light pieces' for the newspaper I joined when I was seventeen – and I wrote hundreds – owed something to Macdonell. It is a book I still have great affection for, but it had a bad effect on me. I would strain for Macdonell's tone when it wasn't appropriate, and end up sounding merely facetious. I was well into my twenties before I caught up with Waugh, who became and remained a literary god.

But where were the great authors, the famous dead? Where were Dickens, Tolstoy, Flaubert? Where was Shakespeare? I become quite shifty when I hear about other people's early reading (this very book is going to cause serious shiftiness, I know). Leaving aside set books (*David Copperfield*, *The Merchant of Venice*, etc, which I found hard going), I never read any 'great literature' till I began to weary of the excitements and pleasures of provincial journalism. I mean no irony here. I loved being a reporter, I loved writing news stories, interviews and my endless series of 'light' pieces.

I must have read a lot of books during this time but I can remember very few of them. Those few, however, went very deep. My Runyon stories were followed by one or two modelled on Truman Capote's *Other Voices, Other Rooms*, and, a few weeks later, on *Miss Lonelyhearts*. A fellow reporter who was considered something of a literary chap (he wore a bow tie, and in fact went on to write thrillers)

told me about a book called *The Catcher in the Rye* by
J. D. Salinger, so next I wrote fake-*Catcher* stories. In other
words, as a (potential) writer I had no personality of my
own; and as a reader I seemed to be a displaced American.
During my twenties I was on an American binge: Fitzgerald,
Steinbeck, Saroyan, Miller, Crane, Cummings, Dos Passos,
Thurber, O'Hara, Lardner, Mailer, Salinger, and, notably, the
first two anthologies of *New Yorker Short Stories*. I bought a
long run of *New World Writing* (I think it was called) and I
remember one exceptional story which was introduced as
coming from a novel-in-progress to be called *Catch*-18 (it
was changed to 22 because Leon Uris had bagged Heller's
number for *Mila* 18).

But above all, there was Hemingway. I read everything,
more or less in the order in which it was written, and I
was knocked sideways. I remained at this angle for years,
as is perfectly clear from Faber's *Introduction 2: Stories by
New Writers* (1963), and I'm not quite perpendicular yet.
Ten years ago I owned Edmund Wilson's copy of *In Our
Time* sent to him by the author fresh off the press. You
can read the letter which accompanied it in Hemingway's
Collected Letters. I sold it in order to buy a statue, a decision so weird that I cannot now bear to think of it, not
least because Wilson is another of my heroes. In the late
1950s I took *Classics and Commercials*, *Axel's Castle* and *To
the Finland Station* on holiday to Spain and spent so much
time in different hotel rooms reading Wilson that I might
as well have stayed in Bristol. *To the Finland Station* was
a seminal book for me, the first book which made me
interested in history and politics with the same *emotional*

involvement exerted by *Peter Duck* fourteen years before. Wilson instantly defined my taste in critical writing, and I still ignore all criticism which isn't descriptive, plain-spoken, concrete.

However, there was a backlash from Wilson. I was impressed by his having learned whatever languages he needed to know for the better understanding of what he was reading (he learned Hebrew when he got inter-ested in the Dead Sea scrolls, and was taking Hungarian lessons when he died), so I decided not to read the great Russians until I could read them in the original. Although I finally gave up in the case of Dostoyevsky, Chekhov stories, Turgenev, Pushkin and Pasternak, I am only now acknowledging to myself that I will never pick up the Russian lessons which I began thirty years ago, so I have not yet read *War and Peace*.

This reading, however, had to compete with my fascin-ation with journalism. I was interested in journalism on every level – its history, its practice, its heroes, and this lasted beyond the time when I stopped writing regularly for newspapers and magazines, in 1962. In 1956 I saw no point in being John Osborne if one could be Noel Barber or Sefton Delmer, who were reporting from Budapest at more or less the same moment that the Royal Court Theatre was becoming the big story on the theatre page.

And of course during this period there were books which one read because 'everyone' read them. Durrell's *The Alexandria Quartet* and Nabokov's *Lolita* were notable examples. But generally I felt out of step. In the late 1950s an English version of the *nouveau roman* had a hot flush;

I couldn't pretend not to be bored. And then, of course, there were the American Beats and their English imitators. With those I pretended more successfully, but my true sympathies were with Capote's remark, 'It's just kind of *typing*, isn't it?' I used the 1960s to do some of the reading which people assumed one had already done, and James Joyce finally joined Captain W. E. Johns in the history of my reading pleasures.

Because I write slowly and because I like to shut out everything which isn't relevant to what I am writing, I read fewer books with each succeeding year. And with each succeeding year, it seems, there are more and more books which one ought to read. I buy them all and read very few of them. How do other people do it? While I have been reading the first half of Ackroyd's *Charles Dickens* at least twenty more 'necessary' books have come out (including, of course, Claire Tomalin's biography of Nelly Ternan). On the whole I tend to put aside these books for my children (who don't read) and spend my time with the books I need for the work I am doing. Almost all the philosophy I have read occupied me, very happily, at the time when I was writing *Jumpers*. This year I must have read a million words about India, because I needed a tiny fraction of that reading for a radio play which I have just finished. Meanwhile, Julian Barnes's *The History of the World in 10½ Chapters*, Martin Amis's *London Fields*, Ian McEwan's *The Innocent*, A. S. Byatt's *Possession* and dozens of others wait hopelessly in a queue for which time, in the end, will run out. But I read every Piers Paul Read as it comes out.

P.S. I have now read the Barnes and the Byatt, so for 'hopelessly' read 'hopefully'.

My favourite books

As for 'ten favourite books' I could spend days trying to arrive at a list which told some kind of truth, but the more definitive one tries to be the more 'favourite' cries out to be defined. Perhaps there is equal truth in naming off the top of my head ten books which, once read, were not put aside:

Winnie-the-Pooh, A. A. Milne; *New Yorker Short Stories*; *The First Forty-Nine Stories*, Ernest Hemingway; *At Swim-Two-Birds*, Flann O'Brien; *Collected Poems*, T. S. Eliot; *A Handful of Dust*, Evelyn Waugh; *Ulysses*, James Joyce; *Pale Fire*, Vladimir Nabokov; *Essays*, Thomas Macaulay; *The Gulag Archipelago*, Solzhenitsyn.

Margaret Atwood

I LEARNED to read before I started school. My mother claims I taught myself because she refused to read comics to me. Probably my older brother helped: he was writing comic books himself, and may have needed an audience.

In any case, the first books I can remember were a scribbled-over copy of *Mother Goose* and several Beatrix Potters, from her Dark Period (the ones with knives, cannibalistic foxes, and stolen babies in them). Then came the complete, unexpurgated *Grimm's Fairy Tales*, which my parents ordered by mail, unaware that it would contain so many red-hot shoes, barrels full of nails, and mangled bodies. This was in the 1940s, just after the war. It was becoming the fashion, then, to rewrite fairy tales, removing anything too bloodthirsty and prettying up the endings, and my parents were worried that all the skeletons and gouged-out eyes in *Grimm's* would warp my mind. Perhaps they did, although Bruno Bettelheim has since claimed that this sort of thing was good for me. In any case I devoured these stories, and a number of them have been with me ever since.

Shortly after this I began to read everything I could get my hands on. At that time my family was spending a lot of time in the northern Canadian bush, where there were no movie theatres and where even radio was unreliable: reading was it. The school readers, the notorious milk-and-water *Dick and Jane* series, did not have much to offer me after *Grimm's. See Jane Run*, indeed. Instead I read comic books and the backs of cereal boxes. I tried 'girls' books' – *The Bobbsey Twins* by Laura Lee Hope, *The Curlytops* series by Howard Garis, *Cherry Ames, Junior Nurse* – but they weren't much competition for *Batman* or for red-hot iron shoes. (*Anne of Green Gables* was an exception; that one I loved.) I made my way through the standard children's classics, some of which I'd already heard, read out loud by my mother – *The Wonderful Wizard of Oz* by L. Frank Baum, the *Alice* books, *Treasure Island. Gulliver's Travels* is not really a children's book, but was considered one because of the giants, so I read that too.

I read Canadian animal stories – those by Sir Charles G. D. Roberts and Ernest Thompson Seton, for instance – in which the animals always ended up dead. Such books appeared regularly at Christmas – adults seemed to think that any book about animals was a children's book – and I would snivel my way through the trapped, shot and gnawed corpses of the various rabbits, grouse, foxes and wolves that littered their pages, overdosing on chocolates. I read Orwell's *Animal Farm*, thinking that it too was a story about animals, and was seriously upset by the death of the horse.

By this time I was about ten or eleven, and I'd begun dipping into the adult shelves. I can recall with great clarity the Dell pocket-book mysteries, the ones with the map of the crime scene on the back and the eye in a keyhole on the front, along with the lurid picture of the strangled blonde in the red strapless gown. One mystery in particular stands out: the murder was done by tying the victim to a tree, naked, during mosquito season. (Living where I did, I found this highly plausible.) I read a junky science-fiction magazine left behind by a guest, and vividly remember a story in which the beautiful women of Planet X hunt men down, paralyse them with a bite on the neck, and lay eggs on them like spiders. I used to drag the really dubious books off into corners, like dogs with bones, where no one would see me reading them. I resorted to flashlights under the covers. I knew good trash when I saw it. I don't think these books influenced my writing, but they certainly influenced my reading.

Around this time too I read the collected works of Edgar Allan Poe, which some fool had put in the school library on the assumption that anything without sex in it was suitable for young minds. This experience disturbed me in a way that *Grimm's Fairy Tales* had not, possibly because Poe is obsessive about detail and sets out to horrify. I had nightmares about decaying or being buried alive, but this did not stop me from reading on.

Attracted by the beautiful woodcuts of whales in our edition, I read Melville's *Moby-Dick*, again expecting animals. I skipped the parts about people; I identified with the whale, and was not at all sad when it wrecked the whaler and drowned most of the crew and got away at the end. After all those trapped wolves and poisoned foxes, it was about time for an animal to come out on top.

When I hit high school, I read *Pride and Prejudice* and *Wuthering Heights*, and developed what was, in those days before rock stars, a standard passion for Mr Darcy and Heathcliff. (Luckily I did not at that time know any bad-tempered, impolite and darkly brooding young men; otherwise I might have run off with them.) These reading choices were approved of by adults, who liked anything called a classic. Other reading choices were not. In grade nine, for instance, I joined a paperback book club which was in the business of parting teenagers from their allowances, and received a satisfying helping of verbal trash through the mail every month. *Donovan's Brain* stands out: it was about an overgrown and demented brain which was being kept alive in a glass jar by scientists – a brain which was trying to take over the world. In addition to colouring my view of politicians, this prepared me for the reading of Marlowe's *Doctor Faustus* and Mary Shelley's *Frankenstein*, later on.

I discovered the cellar. (By this time we were living in Toronto, and had one.) My parents had two vices which I have inherited – they bought a lot of books, and they found it difficult to throw any of them out. The cellar was lined with bookshelves, and I used to go down there and browse among the books, while eating snacks filched from the kitchen – crackers thickly spread with peanut butter and honey, dates prised off the block of them used for baking, handfuls of raisins, and – one of my favourites – lime jelly powder. The whole experience felt like a delicious escape, and my eclectic eating habits complemented what I was reading, which ranged from scientific textbooks on ants and spiders – my father was an entomologist – to H. G. Wells's history of almost everything, to the romances of Walter Scott, to old copies of *National Geographic*, to the theatrical murders of Ngaio Marsh. This is where I came across Churchill's history of the Second World War, Orwell's *Nineteen Eighty-Four*, and Arthur Koestler's *Darkness At Noon* – books which did, much later, actually have an influence on something I wrote myself, as *The Handmaid's Tale* emerged from the same fascination with history and the structure of totalitarian regimes.

All of this took place quite apart from school. At school I was practical, and saw myself as someone who would eventually have a serious job of some kind. The drawback to this was that there were only five careers listed for women in the Guidance textbook: home economist, nurse, teacher, airline stewardess, and secretary. Home economists got paid the most, but I was not good at zippers. This was depressing. I read more.

In English, we were studying a Shakespeare play a year, a good deal of Thomas Hardy and some George Eliot, and a lot of poetry, most of it by the romantics and the Victorians. Writing – unlike reading – appeared to be something that had been done some time ago, and very far away. In those days the Canadian high school curriculum had not yet discovered either modern poetry or Canada itself; 'Canadian writer' seemed to be a contradiction in terms; and when I realized at the age of sixteen that writing was what I wanted to do with the rest of my life, nobody was more surprised than I was.

What do I enjoy reading today? It's hard to say; it varies from day to day. From where I'm writing at this desk I can see, deposited around the floor of the room, eighteen separate piles or nests of books. They aren't all there for purposes of enjoyment – some of them are for work – but, starting from left to right, the things on the tops of the piles are: Virago's catalogue of new books; Márquez's *The General in His Labyrinth*; a newsletter about health; a book on the origins of humanity; a Canadian literary magazine called *Paragraph*; Ethel Wilson's *Hetty Dorval*; a dictionary of French synonyms; two paperback murder mysteries, one by P. D. James, one by Robert Barnard; *Writing the Circle*, an anthology of Native (Indian, Inuit or Eskimo) women writers; Kurt Vonnegut's new novel, *Hocus Pocus*; a book on wind energy in Denmark – well, you get the idea. Every once in a while I root through the piles, picking out something in them I haven't yet read, shuffling them around, trying to figure out where to file the books in the various already overcrowded bookcases. Or I add to the piles, or growl over them, protecting them from being tidied up, or haul something off to another location. I read in bed – what a luxury! – or on aeroplanes, where the phone can never ring; or in the bathtub, or in the kitchen. It's still a random process, and I still love it.

My favourite books

I dislike lists of top ten favourite books, because they don't give you enough room. Novels? Poetry? Non-fiction? Do collected works count? Does the Bible? Does *The Joy of Cooking*?

But here are five novels I've read recently and enjoyed a lot. They have not all been written recently; it's just that I did not get around to them at the time: Lawrence Durrell, *The Alexandria Quartet*; Louise Erdrich, *The Beet Queen*; Toni Morrison, *Beloved*; Chinua Achebe, *Things Fall Apart*; Nawar El Sadawi, *The Fall of the Imam*.

And here are five Canadian novels I've read and reread over the years: Anne Hébert, *Kamouraska*; Alice Munro, *The Lives of Girls and Women*; Margaret Laurence, *The Stone Angel*; Robertson Davies, *Fifth Business*; Timothy Findley, *The Wars*.

Germaine Greer

W HEN I was little I read everything that had letters on it, just for the pleasure of decoding them. 'What does it say?' I would ask, peering over the edge of the breakfast table at the Weeties packet. When no one answered I set about finding out. When I had had my fill of reading about riboflavin and niacin, I set about deciphering the bit of my father's newspaper that drooped over the marmalade pot, so that I can still read upside-down almost as fast as right-way-up.

Reading was my first solitary vice (and led to all the others). I read while I ate, I read in the loo, I read in the bath. When I was supposed to be sleeping, I was reading. So the light would not show under the door I read under the sheets but not by the light of a battery torch, which I had no money to buy. I pinched candle ends from the parish church and burned them in bed, a recollection that makes me shudder. My front hair still stands up in a crinkly quiff from being regularly singed.

While I was doing my household tasks my mother would intone from wherever she was in the house: 'You're reading. Stop reading.' She was trying in vain to prevent my burning a hole in the collar of my school blouse with the iron or from crashing into the skirtings with the vacuum cleaner. If she came into the room where I was supposed to be polishing the silver she was bound to find me reading the sheet of newspaper put down to protect the table. I didn't like having my ears boxed, but I couldn't help myself. If there was a patch of print anywhere within my field of vision, I would read it. Even now I find myself being glared at because, having exhausted my own, I am lost in someone else's newspaper, reading it upside-down or over a shoulder on the Tube.

I don't remember learning to read. I do remember mispronouncing the word 'put' in the first grade because I wanted someone to explain why it wasn't pronounced 'putt' but of course nobody could. After that I stopped pretending I had difficulties and, when my turn came to read aloud, rattled away as fast and shrill as I could until Sister stopped me and slowed us all back down to a crawl. Having read my primer from cover to cover by the second day of school, I was then obliged to listen for a whole year to the other kids boggling for minutes at a time over the simplest words and ignoring the sense altogether; driven beyond my five-year-old endurance I would yell out the right words and so earned an enduring reputation as a know-all creep.

The texts we studied did not repay repeated scrutiny. The second book of the *Victorian Readers,* which was reissued in facsimile in 1989, is as fatuous a collection of fake-childish junk as ever was assembled. It began with something the editors acknowledged only as 'Old Song':

Do you wonder where the fairies are
That folks declare have vanished?
They're very near, yet very far:
But neither dead nor banished, (etc)

Facing it was a foggy reproduction of Reynolds's *The Age of Innocence*. I do not remember having been impressed or otherwise by stories about fairies making rainbows out of ribbons of sunshine and elves using toadstools as umbrellas, but the story of Little Half-Chick, who became a weathercock, and the little foxes, who were scalded to death because the hen in their father's sack replaced herself with a stone, and the dingo who ate up the Hobyahs, who came run-running on the tips of their toes, filled me with angst. The myths that *Child Education* thought appropriate to the age of innocence were redder in tooth and claw than nature herself. The fullest statement of the dog-eat-dog theme was the tale of the old woman who could not get her pig to walk home from market. The old woman's entreaties to the other creatures were fulfilled only when she found milk for the cat.

Then the cat began to kill the rat; the rat began to gnaw the rope; the rope began to hang the butcher; the butcher began to kill the ox; the ox began to drink the water; the water began to quench the fire;

the fire began to burn the stick; the stick began to
beat the dog; the dog began to bite the pig; and the
pig jumped over the stile; and the old woman got
home that night after all.

At home I was reading grown-up books which, though
quite unsuitable, were far less depraving. Before I was eight
I had attempted the entire contents of my parents' small
bird's-eye maple bookcase which included *The Way of a
Transgressor* by Negley Farson, O'Flaherty's *Famine*, Alan
Moorehead's *The End in Africa*, *Through the Forbidden Land*
by Gustav Krist and *The Countess of Rudolstadt* by George
Sand (which is where my mother got my name from). I
discovered voluptuousness by reading an English translation of Gautier's *Mademoiselle de Maupin*. Once a year I
tried to fathom our red-bound Shakespeare with the semi-
pornographic steel engravings. Long before I realized that
neither of the creatures in the title was a reptile, I knew
'The Phoenix and the Turtle' by heart.

By this time I had grown a deep perpetual furrow of
incomprehension in my brow, which prompted the
grown-ups to try to find suitable books that would not be
exhausted in a day and thrown aside. When I was going
on seven my grandmother gave me *Alice in Wonderland* and
The Water-Babies in the Collins Library of Classics edition.
The last time I was in my mother's house I sniffed them
out, drawn by the luxurious scent of the red morocco in
which they were bound. The feel of the book was the
only thing I liked about *The Water-Babies*; which ends
with a moral:

And now, my dear little man, what should we learn from this parable [no question mark].

   We should learn thirty-seven or thirty-nine things, I am not exactly sure which: but one thing, at least, we may learn, and that is this – when we see efts in the ponds, never to throw stones at them, or catch them with crooked pins, or put them into vivariums with sticklebacks, that the sticklebacks may prick them in their poor little stomachs, and make them jump out of the glass into somebody's workbox and so come to a bad end. For these efts are nothing else but the waterbabies who are stupid and dirty and will not learn their lessons and keep themselves clean . . .

What was somebody to make of this *faux naïf* twaddle who was not only not a dear little man, but a girl tall for her age, who had never seen an eft, a vivarium or a stickleback? When I found a dictionary that had the word 'eft' in it I discovered that the Professor of Modern History from the University of Cambridge was an unprincipled liar. The distrust of fiction engendered by this early experience has endured to this very day.

Alice in Wonderland was a different matter. Carroll's prose is elegant and exact where Kingsley's is misshapen, dreary and false. *Alice* was the first thing I read where I didn't care two hoots what happened next because I was so enchanted by how the thing happened that was happening as I read. I wanted to think and speak the way the writing did. I would adopt a word and use it for a whole day until I had got the feel of it, 'fetch' or 'directly' or 'capital' or 'coaxing' or 'melancholy'. Though Lewis Carroll would have scorned to point his moral, *Alice* was a way of being sensible, courteous and interested. You could not read her (for her sensibility is the book) without becoming a little more sensible, courteous and interested yourself.

Most of what I had to read – *Six O'Clock Saints*, and Joyce Lankester Brisley's *Milly-Molly-Mandy*, the Brothers Grimm and Hans Andersen – was nowhere near as intelligent or as intelligible as *Alice*. I didn't read Enid Blyton, or Beatrix Potter. The books I liked best were books that were fat and fact-filled. From our matching dictionary and encyclopaedia, a special offer by the newspaper my father worked for, I learnt the meanings of hundreds of words I had never heard anybody say. I thought the person who casts spells was a 'magican', that a small book was a 'phamphlet' and orphans had to go to an 'aisylum'. The use of words you have seen but not heard is a characteristic of clever Australian children; my godchild at twenty-seven is still saying 'unwieldly' and 'in*t*egral'.

It would be wrong to think that because I read books, any books, some over and over, I enjoyed them. I did not read for pleasure; I was an addict. I read for greed. I jammed books into my brain like a compulsive eater glutting herself gobbling up one book so that I could gobble up another. My reading was mostly displacement activity; when other children were playing, or getting exercise, training in some sport or hanging out with their mates, I was reading. The only alternative was a boredom so heavy and slow that it squashed my soul flat. Conversation with my father did not happen, while conversation with my mother was a torture of calculated illogicality. My brother and sister were each much younger than I. My book, any book, was my fantasy interlocutor, my friend.

For Christmas 1949 my mother gave me a handsome edition of *David Copperfield* with the original illustrations by 'Phiz'. David Copperfield struck me as a weed but, like him, I fell horribly in love with Steerforth, David's Bad Angel, with 'his nice voice, and his fine face, and his easy manner'. This was largely the fault of the illustration of Steerforth confronting Mr Mell. The mixture of feelings that welled in my nearly eleven-year-old bosom when Steerforth seduced Emily while Byronically hating himself for it, to end drowned on the sand at Yarmouth, 'lying with his head on his arm as [David] had often seen him lie at school', was my introduction to grown-up passion. That innocent Oxford edition, bound in brown cloth and lettered in silver on the spine, set me off on a lifetime search for Mr Wrong, including two years' postgraduate work on Byron and a longer infatuation with Rochester.

It was not the writing of Steerforth but the *idea* of him that seduced me. I had yet to discover the real pleasure of reading, which requires a unique combination of educated susceptibility in the reader and greatness in the book. I read on indiscriminately, gorging on print, reading rubbish with the same appetite that I read the best. Because I read so much and so fast I borrowed books from the school library by weight, which was how I came to lug home a vast, badly foxed copy of *Bleak House*. I opened it with some misgiving and read:

Michaelmas Term lately over, and the Lord Chancellor sitting in Lincoln's Inn Hall. Implacable November weather. As much mud in the streets, as if the waters had but newly retired from the face of the earth, and it would not be wonderful to meet a Megalosaurus, forty feet long or so, waddling like an elephantine lizard up Holborn Hill. Smoke lowering down from chimneypots, making a soft black drizzle, with flakes of soot in it as big as full-grown snowflakes – gone into mourning, one might imagine, for the death of the sun. Dogs, undistinguishable in mire. Horses, scarcely better; splashed to their very blinkers. Foot passengers, jostling one another's umbrellas, in a general infection of ill-temper, and losing their foothold at street corners, where tens of thousands of other foot passengers have been slipping and sliding since day broke . . .

By the time I finished that first paragraph I was reading in a different way, letting the phrases swing me along, bouncing through arcs of history, spinning as a hawk's eye to a point of view at once lofty and minute. The rhythm of the writing imposed itself on the rush of my compulsion. I knew that this was an appetite that would not sicken. I would be reading this book for the rest of my life. Dickens had rescued me from both the aversion therapy of the schoolroom and my own perverse nature. I knew real pleasure at last.

My favourite books

Oxford English Dictionary; *Complete Opera Book*, Gustav Kobbé; *Hobson-Jobson Dictionary of Anglo-Indian Usage*; *Trees and Shrubs Hardy in the British Isles*, Bean; *Golden Legend*, Jacobus de Voragine; *English Poets*, Chalmer; *Letters*, Lord Byron (ed. Prothero); *Diaries*, Pepys (ed. Latham and Matthews); *Larousse Illustré*; *Times Atlas of the World*.

Melvyn Bragg

I T was called the sitting room or the front parlour depending how confident you felt in the claim. You can see it today in the D. H. Lawrence museum or in several of the terraced houses reclaimed so affectionately at Beamish. It is overdressed; the horsehair chaise-longue, samplers on the wall, a table decently draped in green velvet tasselled suggestively around the fringe, tiled fireplace with the irons drawn up at attention to one side, shapely womanly paraffin lamp, a piano, cold as frost in winter, in summer a soporific compound of polishes and trapped air. This was where the bodies were laid out in the coffins. This was where the piano was tormented. This was where I could read in peace.

I left that place when I was eight, but I remember reading there, there and in school; in bed, younger, I had been read to. There must have been other private locations but until a full excavation of the past is undertaken they seem beyond reach. So reading was associated with formality and a special place; but the formal, communal place was subverted by its use for something as selfish as reading.

There are many books I remember reading in that parlour. Sunday afternoon, after Sunday School and before evensong, was the best bet for an uninterrupted stretch. *Robin Hood* was an addiction for one season. Whoever put that particular version on paper – I lost it long ago – had great skill in unlocking the imagination of a child. I can still see the print on the page – when Robin met John Little – 'I shall call thee Little John' – after a fierce battle with quarterstaffs on a narrow bridge, a fight which Robin lost – a fine touch of realism there. Will O'Scarlet dropped the 'O'. Friar Tuck 'rubbed his bald pate'. Into the Greenwood they went and I with them. Even today there is no forest on earth which smells or sounds or moves like Sherwood Forest, even though I fear it may well be two stumpy oaks propped up by steel pins, and a motorway cutting through a built-up area. There was grace and goodness in Robin Hood's Greenwood, high cunning for high purposes and the freedom of the forest, a life which would never be circumscribed by a family, Sunday School, sudden mysterious imperatives, and a cold cluttered parlour.

Another of many keen memories is *Kidnapped* – to which the name R. L. Stevenson did not attach itself until years later. What I recall now is how sick I felt when David was isolated on what he mistook for an island and tried to live on the shellfish. I don't suppose I'd ever put a tooth to a shellfish but the scene was felt to be desolate. Perhaps the cold helped.

As a contrast to the solitary books were the comics which seemed to be a common purchase. The *Dandy* and the *Beano* – almost my exact contemporaries – and later the *Wizard, Hotspur, Rover* and *Adventure*. They were gobbled up anywhere. Once a week a woman's magazine, or 'book' as it was called, came in and its romantic short stories were no doubt gulped down like oysters. The daily paper was the *News Chronicle* – used by me at that time for sport and nothing else – the Sunday was the *News of the World* (or the *Empire News*?). Whatever it was the lurid naughty bits were seductive and disturbing. No explanations were asked for, nor were they offered, but the squelch of the stomach on some tale of 1940s vice was a part of the growing habit of reading.

Until eight, then, there are remembered books, quite a few, and acres of sensation illustrated by large block cartoon drawings and disseminated through eye-squinting print. It was either a solitary escape within the respectable protection of hard covers or a gallop among friends through print that stuck to your thumb. The library was visited at least once a week like a dutiful volume which ought to be read.

But perhaps the most intensive reading done at that time was in the Bible and the *Book of Common Prayer* including the psalms and *Hymns Ancient and Modern*. The lessons and the collects of the day were there to be read along as they were read aloud and from the age of six I sat in the choir, part of whose purpose was to be seen to be following the order of service. The psalms were practised several times on Thursday evenings, the words fitted precisely to the demands of the chanting music, and hymns too were bashed out, more perfunctorily, to be replayed on the

Sabbath. In many ways this was the most focused and, I scarcely doubt, the most influential reading I did.

At eight I moved house and was also found to have very poor eyesight and presented with specs, goggles, four-eyes, which changed my childhood. Reading became first a refuge and then even more of an addiction.

The gulping of cheap fiction went on. From that fiction have lingered characters whose life in my mind has outlasted many hundreds from serious and worthy contemporary and even ancient literature. Not an enormous number compared with the comic-book characters such as Wilson, Alf Tupper, Limp Along Leslie, Baldy Hogan, Cannonball Kid, Sergeant Braddock – each one clearly defined by a few notes and able to play variations on simple themes for ever and a day, it appeared. But as the teens crashed in, the diet of hardbacks swelled to a glut and the habit which had plugged gaps of time and taped over boredom, which had been a substitute for play and an excuse for isolation, became a compulsion. In the sporting and games-obsessed culture in which I grew up there was a need to be secretive and so the specs were always whipped off for any scratch ball game going, but I began to look forward to early nights with a book and, if possible, snacks to nibble away the tension.

If we take this up to thirteen or fourteen and call that the end of early reading, then that first clutch takes me from Biggles to D. H. Lawrence, from the Fifth Form at St Dominic's through Psmith to 'grown-up' Wodehouse (if that distinction is permitted), from Blyton's *Famous Five* to John Steinbeck, from Priestley's *The Good Companions* to

Dickens, to Sinclair Lewis, with Tolstoy around or about
to arrive and change everything. At school we read the
set books and were expected to answer detailed questions
on them and read around them. The library was where I
lassoed books for the weekend reading rampage.

As for the influences of this earlier reading, I would
like to spend some long time working that through.
Certainly I can see, or rather hear, the influence of the
steady pressure of religious texts – and see their concerns
in my work still. I wish sometimes I could capture the fast
action of the comics with their *Keystone Cops* version of
Dickens's cliff-hangers. Of the earliest subject matter –
adventure, thrillers, epic events – I see little trace. My
slightly later (when I was about ten) obsession with school
yarns – inevitably public school yarns – could have something to do with a continuing return to a small, enclosed,
almost hermetic community. Once I breasted the teens,
this relationship with my subject matter – the small town
(Steinbeck) tension of intense cohabitation (Lawrence) –
became more noticeable. But in the game of influences
we all like to claim someone like Tolstoy as a father. What
if *Woman's Own* were a truer begetter? Dare one say it?
Who knows what percolates through to fertilize the few
images and words that matter? All of us want to be in a
Great Tradition even if it is an alternative tradition. Indeed
the latter is having a strong innings at present. But what
if the merest, not the greatest, the most banal and not the
most magnificent sets us off? Just as likely – perhaps it
could be argued more likely, in that all but the maddest
egotists would be so intimidated by greatness that they

would flinch from it and would say 'I could do that' of a more humble offering.

Influences, I suspect, are more to do with rhythm than subject, with sound rather than sense, especially at the start, which is when influences most matter. Hearing your tone. Listening to what you hope will be yourself. Excitedly, sometimes desperately spinning through the channels hoping to chance on your own voice. It is there that the singing in the choir, the chanting of the creed, the collective hushed utterance of certain prayers may well have been a more formative influence than anything I've read. Form and subject matter come in any conscious or articulate way later.

There is a stage, much later, when you begin to write and constantly seek not so much influences as models. The boast of the Jesuits, the philosophy of Wordsworth, the discoveries of Freud knead into us the notion that all our deepest experiences occur before we are capable of tabulating them. So to look for influences which would seem to be those which shaped and guided you almost unconsciously is all but a contradiction. Influences look for you. But is even that wholly true? Is the seeking for models which, like many another young writer, caused me to mow down others' first chapters in bookshops and libraries throughout apprentice years, is that wholly different from receiving influences? I hope not. I hope that what one consciously, or especially self-consciously, attaches oneself to might be more than a touchstone, more even than a pole star.

There is a larger issue. Are those most powerful influences on writers the most literary? We are in some way into a phase in our particular literary episode – of a superior knowingness about books, their surfaces, their significations, their interrelatedness. The pleasures of critical recognition are in the ascendant. The begetting of books by bookmen from books can appear the essential matter. But what about the extra-literary influences – the lives led, experiences undergone, emotions enjoyed or endured? Perhaps the nudge or the urge to write could come out of a different source, while the author only turned to books for a way of saying. The influence on a writer of writing cannot be underestimated. It can however be over-estimated.

The next move in this essay on given questions is to list the books one enjoys reading today. The first thing to say is that one of the very greatest pleasures at my age is rereading. To come upon Jane Austen or E. M. Forster, Pushkin, Mann, Svevo, Hawthorne, Joyce and scores of others after some years of neglect proves to be one of the guaranteed pleasures of middle life. I read them more slowly, I read them with more understanding, I hope; I read them with even greater admiration, although perhaps the love one felt so keenly has lost its possessive power.

There are so many dead writers to read again that one welcomes commissions which encourage or, even better, demand that pleasure. And then one is beset by the living – Bellow, Updike, Márquez, Heaney, Hughes, the Amises – the list could fill out the page with easy copy. As could new writers tasted so far only through one book. There is not the time and that is part of the difficulty; there's not the time there was to read. The libraries and

the paperback shelves and the second-hand bookshops are
too full. Nor is there the time to relish as once there was.
Writing itself absorbs much of that time. It will most likely
get worse and soon one will be back to late childhood,
coping with plans and schedules in order to encompass all
the reading one wants to do.

My favourite books

And as for my ten favourite books – that is impossible,
except in the interests of sportsmanship. I assume that
the Bible and Shakespeare are out of this particular lark.
There would have to be something from Tolstoy – *Anna
Karenina* or *The Cossacks*; the short stories of Chekhov
and D. H. Lawrence; Wordsworth's *Prelude* and Twain's
Huckleberry Finn; Joyce's *Portrait of the Artist as a Young Man*
and Dickens's *Bleak House*; a twelve-pack of Wodehouse
and William Faulkner's *The Unvanquished*; Byron's *Don
Juan* and, finally, whatever contemporary work catches my
eye on the pouting rows of paperbacks massed in the new
high street book boutiques.

A completely different list could be just as pleasurable.
Perhaps there are half a dozen such lists. One sure thing
that writing teaches you to do better is to read, and the
pleasure in store in revisiting the list in the above paragraph makes me itch for the silent emptiness of the cold
parlour.

Gita Mehta

'SAHIB. Latest from Plato. *The Republic.* Also, James Hadley Chase and P. G. Wodehouse. You want *Catcher in the Rye*, sahib? *MAD* magazine? But sahib, just now unpacked. At least sample *Little Dorrit* by Charles Dickens.'

To me, that is what it meant to learn to read in India. Having the pleasures of reading shouted at you by pavement booksellers before you even knew how to read. Envying the animation on the face of the grown-up bent over the volumes displayed on a threadbare carpet by the roadside while the bookseller slapped another two books together to loosen the dust kicked up by passing pedestrians, before whispering: '*Anna Karenina*, sahib, *Madame Bovary.* Hot books only this very minute arrived. Believe it or not, sahib. Tomorrow no copies remaining!'

Surely there was no other country in the world where booksellers jumped onto the steps of moving trains, clinging with one hand to the iron bars of the window, with the other pushing forward a basket of books – cajoling, exhorting, begging you to read. Or where the ability to read was thought to be synonymous with the desire to read.

Because illiteracy is so widespread in India, the capacity to read is treated with a respect bordering on awe, and maidservants who could neither read nor write made sure we steered our way past the alphabet into those boring reading primers of English schoolchildren at play. The tedium of the text was only broken by their glee in our achievement, a glee which increased as we were able to repay the stories we had learned at their laps, of gods and kings and ascetics who had cheated their way into immortality, with other tales of sleeping beauties and the extraordinary adventures of Tom Thumb. Because of them the world of the imagination became as tangible to us as the corporeal world, as tangible as the next book read by torchlight when we were sent to bed. And reading became a pleasure so intense it was practically a vice. Indeed, they often treated it as a vice when we could not be drawn from our books to perform our other duties such as eating or sleeping. But however contradictory adults were about our reading habits, they were adamant in demanding respect for the book itself. To deface a book or, worse, to put your feet on a book, were considered acts of such grossness they provoked the contempt of the entire household.

Reading was for us a significant part of the comfort of childhood and a necessary comfort when we were sent off as infants to boarding schools. In darkened dormitories with the monsoon rain beating so heavily on the tin roof it almost drowned our sobs of homesickness we could be tricked out of loneliness by a teacher reading aloud stories of Harry the Horse and his fellow citizens playing games of chance; or the fortunes of Mrs Bennett's daughters; or Mehitabel signing off to her cockroach with the inspiring sentiment: '*Toujours gai*, Archy. *Toujours gai*.'

When we got home from school there were always more books waiting as gifts. Bought for us, like schoolbooks they carried an aura of duty. Fortunately, relatives paying morning calls on our parents would circle our heads with money to remove the evil eye, then press the money into our hands. Now we were in a position to buy our own books and the purchase of two books enabled you to read a hundred, thanks to the lending library.

But these were not the lending libraries of the First World. These were secret shifting Indian lending libraries which fit into garishly painted tin trunks small enough to be strapped on the back of the librarian's bicycle, only learned about by word of mouth. A favourite library took up three rungs on the fire escape behind O. N. Mukherji's Emporium in Calcutta. It contained, my *aficionado* elder brother assured me, the finest collection of westerns in the world. By investing a fraction of a rupee and including your own book in the corpus of the library, you could read as many Louis L'Amour and Zane Grey novels as you could stomach. Or two-in-ones, with a picture of an Apache on one cover and, when you turned the book around and upside down, the picture of a mounted cowboy with drawn six-guns on the other. Sometimes, thanks to the vagaries of the librarian's definition of a western,

you found a Jack London or a Stephen Crane and were
drawn into the worlds of other men of action – Joseph
Conrad, Alexandre Dumas, Leo Tolstoy. Or there would
appear with miraculous suddenness opposite the Chinese
shoemaker's the library which only circulated books by
Denis Wheatley, Edgar Allan Poe and the Brontë sisters.
Then there was the librarian who specialized in Russian
classics – heavily subsidized for the Indian market by the
Soviet Union – and murder mysteries, so that reading
Agatha Christie, Georges Simenon, Rex Stout, was for
us a natural corollary to reading Chekhov, Dostoyevsky,
Gorky.

If this meant our tastes were formed by those books
which the librarians – often clerks moonlighting from
government offices – could buy in second-hand bookstores or trade with other customers, it also meant we were
uninhibited by literary snobbisms, holding an unshakeable
belief that any book we borrowed was a potential source
of delight, that there did not exist the book too difficult
to read.

The only obstacle to our reading appetites was the
tragic absence of a lending library for comics. The steely-
eyed owners of comics shops insisted on full payment,
cash down. Such hard-heartedness enabled them to have
permanent establishments – wooden shacks where they sat
smirking on floors covered with white sheets, surrounded
by unattainable treasure. Leaving our shoes on the roadside we climbed barefoot up the two steps leading into the
shack and disappeared into a brave new world peopled
by Superman, Scrooge McDuck, Archie and Veronica,

Captain Marvel, Nyoka the Jungle Girl. And Classics Illustrated Comics, which enabled us in later years to get degrees in literature from places like Cambridge University because the plots and characters of the great novels were tattooed on our brains.

As we grew older we did of course go to proper bookstores: the cathedral-like Oxford University Press bookshop on Calcutta's Park Street, with its glass-fronted mahogany bookshelves and the hushed voices of the assistants barely audible over the hum of air-conditioning; Ramakrishna and Sons hiding behind stucco Lutyens columns in New Delhi, with its tottering pillars of books piled to the height of the ceiling in a system of cataloguing so mysterious that only the elderly proprietor could locate a book; Faqir Chand's, where the hunchback owner never let you leave without a monogrammed pen or letter opener even if you hadn't bought anything; the Strand Book Stall behind Bombay University, full of advertising executives buying their copies of *Catch-22*.

In these bookstores we struck intellectual attitudes, anxiously awaiting the four new Penguin titles which arrived in India every month while studying on earlier Penguins the portraits of Katherine Anne Porter, Nabokov, Nancy Mitford, Evelyn Waugh. Sometimes we abandoned our orange-covered Penguins, leaving the shop ostentatiously lost between the yellow Faber and Faber covers of Saroyan's *The Daring Young Man on the Flying Trapeze*. Or clutching the blue-covered Methuen editions of Samuel Beckett and Harold Pinter. Or the brightly coloured American paperbacks of Gertrude Stein, Nathanael West,

Kerouac, Capote, J. D. Salinger, which could so effectively be colour co-ordinated with one's clothes.

But our passion for reading was not born in such establishments to visible self-improvement. It was awakened by those pavement bookstalls and lending libraries which so tenaciously offered themselves as a necessary adjunct to every pleasure. If you were taken to a restaurant you had to spend long minutes examining the books spread on the kerb outside. As you did after you had watched a movie. Or been to a cricket match. Or illegally bought a packet of cigarettes. The persistence of such book vendors made us gluttons for books.

The same gluttony characterizes my reading today. And I am as indiscriminate now as I was then. Give me a history or a biography and it will trigger off hours of happy rumination on human behaviour. A contemporary novel, to keep in touch with the Zeitgeist. A golden oldie – *Vanity Fair, War and Peace, Candide,* or any of a hundred others – because each rereading confirms one's original passion for the book. A volume of poetry for that kidney punch: what Emily Dickinson called 'that turning to ice of the limbs' so essential for the enslaved reader. A book on science or philosophy, since who can tell when one might grasp the theory of chaos or Kierkegaard. And give me always a couple of mystery novels in case they cancel my flight.

But then I am an addict, addicted to reading by those magicians sitting cross-legged on the pavements endlessly arranging and rearranging their stock, who lured us away from the little world of the self into whole galaxies of the imagination. How they would have scorned the French observation that 'after every other pleasure proves illusory there remains only the pleasure of the stomach' as they shouted to us like circus barkers, corrupting us with their seductive litany of titles.

Buchi Emecheta

WHEN I was a child, reading was never a major activity in my part of Nigeria. Storytelling was. From the time you are in your mother's belly, you have your own song, your own story. Some Ibo midwives actually sing you praises as you glide from your mother's womb. I belong to this culture.

Going to school and learning to read was not a life planned for me. It happened by accident. My younger brother started school before I did. I used to take him to school and then stand by the school gate watching children from rich homes in their smart uniforms marching to songs played by the band boys. They played songs like 'The Grand Old Duke of York', 'John Brown's Body' and war songs like 'Oh my home'. I used to stand at the gate and march up and down and sing to my heart's content.

Around this time, some Americans (I think they were Baptists) came to our road in Akinwunmi Street and set up a Sunday school. I won the prize for good attendance and was given a beautifully illustrated Gospel according to St Matthew. My father used that to teach me how to read.

I recognized big words like 'generation' and phrases like 'fourteen generations' and 'in this wise'. Curiously enough, almost forty years after, I still write my sentences 'in this wise'.

Our life was strangely very Victorian. Children were expected to be quiet, and girls in particular did a great deal of housework. But because there was no television, and the few radios that existed were intended for adults only, there was still plenty of time to play. I was not good at fighting and hated being beaten up, so I became shy and introspective.

Because I ran away to a Methodist school at the age of eight, my parents consented and promised to keep me in school for two years at least. Some organizations from abroad sent some books of fairy tales to West African schools. Our headmaster said we could borrow them to read. The first story I ever read all by myself was 'Hansel and Gretel'. How I cried and cried for those poor children lying hand in hand in their bed of roses. Snow White and those seven miserable dwarfs made me cry too. But I did not like Goldilocks who had to steal from the bears, and as for that terrible wolf that kept eating up an innocent grandmother, I just did not understand his wickedness. In our families, grandmothers helped a great deal in making life harmonious; they settled cases between young people, they told us stories with songs in the moonlight. So I did not see why the wolf would choose to eat her up. After a while, I knew the words of most of the stories by heart. And I used to start by telling the wolf: 'Now you be a good wolf today and don't eat the grandmother up. She's done nothing to you.'

At the age of ten, I secretly took an entrance exam to a grammar school without telling anybody. I won a scholarship, including my boarding. I refused to stop going to school. My mother said I was bad and selfish, but I loved school and did not 'pay her any mind'. She eventually changed her mind and told me to 'Walk good'. My world changed.

At the Methodist Girls High School, the world of books became open to me. For the first three months we read 'Pinocchio'. I found it silly because I did not understand how a wooden doll's nose could get longer whenever he told a little lie. But by the second term we were in the world of Charles Dickens. With his *David Copperfield*, I cut my first literary tooth. I could identify with David. Those early Methodist missionaries (whom I later discovered to be highly qualified young women from prestigious universities like Oxford and Cambridge) taught us literature in a beautiful, beautiful way. If we were doing Dickens's *Great Expectations*, say, we'd be encouraged to know as much as possible about his world. We were encouraged to use the encyclopaedias and other reference works that threw light on his life. And then we could go on and read as many of his books as we could lay our hands on. Strangely, even when reading for pleasure today, I use the same method. I feel that a single title read from an author is just a glimpse. I like to read more by the author of my choice. Like any other schoolgirl of that period in England, I read all Agatha Christie's books, Conan Doyle, Rider Haggard, Marie Corelli, Joe Clemens and many many others. The difference was that I was in Lagos, Nigeria.

In my fourth year, we studied the Brontë sisters in detail. *Jane Eyre* was the first book written by a woman I studied with my classmates. We could never forget Helen Burns and Mr Rochester.

As for Jane Austen, I came under her spell. This was because I studied for my A level in English literature by myself. I married as soon as I left school at sixteen, and when carrying my first baby I was reading for A levels in English literature, history, geography and Latin. I found *Pride and Prejudice* an all-time masterpiece. I still marvel sometimes how she mastered such delicate irony, humour and yet deep characterization.

The books that influenced my thoughts at the time? All of them did. At school and as a young bride in a boring marriage, I read anything and everything I could lay my hands on. I loved reading so much that I became a library assistant in the American Embassy Library in Lagos.

The third paper for my A level history was on the social history of Britain. I simply chose the period when Jane Austen lived, and for my answers I virtually poured out pages of *Pride and Prejudice, Emma* and *Northanger Abbey.* For the classical background to this paper, I read Oliver Goldsmith's *Vicar of Wakefield* and was always quoting from his *Deserted Village* when describing the great movement from rural areas to the city centres. Another author I liked quoting for a slice of rural England was Thomas Hardy, especially *Far from the Madding Crowd.*

Because we did not have the intrusion of television, the average African child in a good school in the late 1950s and early 1960s could read her heart out. I am afraid it is no longer like that now. Now we have a School of Creative Writing whose main aim is to shorten those long years of apprenticeship we had by sheer reading.

The irony in my literary life was that it was in England that I first came across a book written by a black person. How excited I was that day. I was then a library assistant at the Chalk Farm Library in north London. I did not get the essence of what he was saying in *The Fire Next Time,* but to see Jimmy Baldwin's picture on the cover gave me so much hope.

At the British Museum I saw *Arrow of God* by Chinua Achebe. I read it during my lunch breaks. His book was like listening to a moonlit story of my youth. I could understand every turn of phrase and visualize most of the episodes. Such books gave me another twist of understanding. Books like *Efuru* by Flora Nwapa and *The Man Died* by Wole Soyinka were, to me, landscape in words, the more so because I did not need to stretch my imagination too far. I recognized my youth, my part of Africa in those landscapes and characters created in words. Wole Soyinka's *The Man Died* is an account of the author's time in prison. I had a secret joy when I saw that writing the English language the way it comes from your heart can paint a much more vivid picture. It did not necessarily have to be grammatical, yet the haunting pictures remained.

My favourite books

Choosing my best ten books is difficult, because my taste in reading is quite catholic.

Maybe because I started reading with tragedies, I always read Shakespeare's tragedies over and over again. My all-time favourite is *Hamlet*. I'll try to put my best books list in this order.

Hamlet, William Shakespeare; *Great Expectations*, Charles Dickens; *Their Eyes Were Watching God*, Zora Neale Hurston; *A Short Walk*, Alice Childress; *The Invitation*, Catherine Cookson; *The Coup*, John Updike; *Mila 18*, Leon Uris; *Exodus*, Leon Uris; *Mama Day*, Gloria Naylor; *The Color Purple*, Alice Walker.

Reading is a habit. Once it is formed in childhood, it can be very advantageous later in life. For most writers the habit is invaluable, especially writers like myself who have to use our non-emotional language as the tool of our profession.

My style to date is still very biblical and Dickensian with a great deal of translation from my emotional native language. Equally, most of the protagonists in my works are tragic figures giving my works a kind of sardonic over-tone, and they always start in childhood, not unlike the first books that impressed me as a child, for example *David Copperfield*, *Oliver Twist*, *Great Expectations*, *Little Dorrit* and *Jane Eyre*. And very much like their lives, there is usually an unexpected light at the end of the tunnel.

Until I was asked to do this piece, I did not realize how much I owe to those early classics.

Sally Beauman

I CAN remember the day I learned to read; I can remember the room in which I did so. It was in Bristol, at the top of a tall house overlooking a park; I was with my mother, and the book was Stevenson's *A Child's Garden of Verses* – I have it still. Perhaps this memory, clear as it is, cheats a little, for I loved these poems so much and they had been read to me so often that I almost knew them by heart. Maybe, then, I was only half-reading, half-reciting; nevertheless, some process of decipherment was involved, I am sure. I know that afternoon was momentous.

One of those poems is about a lamplighter, and (this will make me seem very old) there was a lamplighter then in our street, some two years after the end of the war. On winter afternoons we would watch him, my mother and I, as he passed down the hill from gas-lamp to gas-lamp. It seemed a wondrous connection – the sounds that sprang up from the page; the actual man on the hill. I was three years old, and something happened then. In all the years since, I cannot remember a single day that passed without reading.

I liked comedy best, in those days, and for a long time – long after my mother considered I should have outgrown them – I liked A. A. Milne's books, and still do, for that matter. I liked, and still like, the way his fictional characters balance perfectly on that razor edge between clarity and mystery. My favourites were Tigger, because he bounced and boasted, and Eeyore, because he was melancholy. My father, a very tall, very thin man, who could compose his features at will into an expression of heartrending lugu-briousness, was an accomplished Eeyore. But why exactly was Eeyore so sad? Could it be simply that he mourned the flattening of his special thistle bed by a bouncing Tigger? My father and I had long and earnest conversations on the subject. No, we agreed, for Eeyore's melancholy pre-dated that incident. My father's view – a comforting one – was that such vagaries could not always be explained: 'Maybe he just *is*,' he said. He sighed. 'People often just *are*, darling. In my experience, anyway.'

I was not sure then if he was right or wrong – and I still am not. Either way, certain tastes were fixed: I liked books which made you laugh and cry; I liked books in which character propelled the plot; the books I liked best of all were those which moved beyond safe fictional territory, over the horizon and into a hinterland, where anything was possible and for every question the answers stretched to infinity.

That said, I could never claim that my reading was very selective. I read anything and everything. I was an only child; my parents did not acquire a television set (and then only after much ethical anguishing) until I was fourteen years old. There was a wireless set and there was conversation (everyone in my family loved arguing), but much as I enjoyed both of these, I preferred reading. My parents encouraged this; reading by torchlight in bed was sanctioned, though a firm line was taken against reading at mealtimes. They found it a little eccentric (my mother felt girls ought not to be bookworms), but since both were unliterary and liberal they let me read what I liked, neither censoring nor guiding.

The bookshelves at home were a hotchpotch: they were filled with relics to past fashions, past tastes, chance gifts, with the occasional nod towards literary immortality. At boarding school my father had enjoyed Bulldog Drummond and adventures by Buchan, so these were represented, as was a slightly later taste for Somerset Maugham and Dornford Yates. There was a row of leatherbound Dickens (I suspect largely unread), and fat padded volumes of Victorian poetry which had belonged to my grandmother. My father ignored all these; by the time of my childhood his reading was confined to newspapers, and dense analyses of military history he claimed were a sure recipe for sleep.

My mother had more pronounced tastes, and went for a racier read. She liked detective stories, relished murders, but would make do, when pressed, with historical romance. Every week she and I made the lengthy trip to the public library (two buses; a long walk). There she would inform the librarian, with some hauteur, that what she required was something neither too heavy, nor too light. The result of this (treasures like the latest Agatha Christie or Ngaio

Marsh were rare; there was always a long waiting list) were books which were very light indeed. My mother read them with zest. Most, as far as I can remember now, dealt with the wives and daughters of Henry VIII; many were by Jean Plaidy, and most – despite energetic love-interest – ended bloodily: my mother liked this.

So, aged seven or eight, did I. It had not occurred to me then to be critical of any book. I devoured them all: the Buchan, the detective stories, the romances, the *Just William* stories, which had belonged to an uncle, *Peter Pan*, *Alice's Adventures in Wonderland*, *The Wind in the Willows*, *The Arabian Nights*, Nathaniel Hawthorne's *Tanglewood Tales*, *Sherlock Holmes*, the *Katy* books, Kipling, Enid Blyton, Arthur Ransome . . . I loved them all, and reread them all, again and again. I read with a blithe lack of discrimination: *School Friends' Annual* was as delightful to me as Somerset Maugham; Kipling's *Puck of Pook's Hill* and Blyton's *Malory Towers* were equally magical.

I might like to think now that I could differentiate between the imaginative power, the prose style, of Carroll, Blyton or Conan Doyle, or to kid myself that I found the adventures of Alice more resonant than William Brown's run-ins with the housemaid or the perils experienced by those intrepid adventurers Philip, Jack, Dinah and Lucy-Anne (from Blyton's *Adventure* books) – but it would not be the truth. The truth is I was a little heathen and – true god or simulacrum – I loved them all.

Later, this changed. I know exactly when it changed. I can see the room, which smelled of wax polish, and the stern figure who effected the change: Miss Fleur, geography, also in charge of the school library, a whiskery and tweedy woman, possessed of cold blue eyes. I was twelve, new to the school, which was somewhat stern too, and firmly dedicated to the intellectual training of female minds. Miss Fleur informed me, with *froideur*, that Arthur Ransome wrote 'vulgar prose'. She directed me to august, towering, sober shelves: Eliot, Austen, Thackeray, Dickens, Trollope . . .

What? I had never read Austen? Contempt, disbelief, outrage eddied around the room: *Pride and Prejudice* was thrust into my hands – and that was fine, but the next week it was *Barchester Towers,* which was not fine at all. It took me six miserable weeks to finish it, put me off Trollope for the next twenty years (I did not risk him again until I was in my thirties; now I love him) and left me with a residual suspicion of Great World Novels that lasted two years. I could not altogether avoid them, those giants of the past, but I looked at them askance with a mutinous teenage hostility. There was a whiff of cant in the way they were presented; I knew they were supposed to improve my mind – and that set me dead against them. At thirteen and fourteen I preferred my mind unimproved. I knew about 'improving' novels; I'd been given one a few years before by a well-meaning aunt. Louisa M. Alcott's *Little Women:* it was the one book of my childhood that I resolutely despised and detested.

Well, well, I was very obstinate and very stupid. The result was that for two years I read almost no novels. I gave them up; I went cold turkey. But I was fortunate: I met Mrs Culverwell, then aged almost eighty, and with her I rediscovered an old joy – poetry.

It sounds incredibly old-fashioned now (it was the 1950s) but Mrs Culverwell – extra-curricular, on a par with ballet – taught Drama and Poetry Appreciation two afternoons a week, after school, in her drawing room. She was tiny, white-haired, hunch-backed, imperious. Her house, a huge and cavernous place, still lit by gaslight and warmed by coal fires, was a mausoleum to a theatrical youth, when her spine had been straight and her parents had been intimates of Irving. Signed photographs of actors with noble profiles and sorrowful mascara stood ranked upon the piano. Their names meant nothing to me, but their noses were impressive.

Occasionally, looking at these photographs, Mrs Culverwell would go off into a reverie. My recitation of 'The Lady of Shalott', my earnestly rehearsed renditions of 'I know a bank' from *A Midsummer Night's Dream*, or Mercutio's Queen Mab speech from *Romeo and Juliet*, would falter then halt. 'Ah, Ivor,' Mrs Culverwell would sigh towards one of the profiles. Or 'Ah, Sir Frank. Such a very splendid Richard in his day. Then latterly, so sad – you know, his *memory* . . .' Minutes would tick by, then she would rouse herself with a waft of her hand. 'Continue, child,' she would say. 'A little less *fire*. Continue . . .'

Over the next few years we read a great deal of poetry. Mrs Culverwell's taste was firm: verse must be rhythmic, romantic, if possible soulful. We read a great many odes, and came to a halt with Tennyson. We also read our way through Shakespeare, Mrs Culverwell, ex-actress that she was, bagging all the best female parts and leaving me to wrestle with Romeo, Antony, Benedick, Macbeth. I never minded: at night, when I went home to the privacy of my room I played all the parts anyway.

At fifteen, never having seen a Shakespeare play in the theatre, I knew several of them almost by heart, my favourite being *Macbeth*, which I enacted at least once a week, unprompted and alone, giving a no doubt very bad performance not just of the Macbeths themselves but everyone else from the messenger to the porter. Somewhere about this time, meanwhile, when I was fourteen or fifteen, I rediscovered the pleasure of novels. The book which effected the change was *The Catcher in the Rye,* which I read, spellbound, in a single sitting, and which led – for several years afterwards – to a fixation with Salinger. After that, the floodgates opened; the joys came thick and fast – the Brontës, Flaubert, Scott, Tolstoy, Balzac, Camus, Conrad, Stevenson, Austen . . . I cannot remember, now, the order in which I read them, nor the identities of all the other authors with whom they were interspersed. Old habits die hard, and I'm afraid I read as I had always done, voraciously and unsystematically – even the Literature Tripos at Cambridge would not cure me of that.

Later, I did learn to read in a different, less impetuous way: I discovered the pleasures to be found in stripping down the engine of a novel, and – in the process – attempting to decodify the story. That process altered my tastes somewhat: I like Camus and Salinger much less now; I am more suspicious of the constrictions of Austen and the moral piety of George Eliot than I used to be. The novels I love best, and which I reread constantly, have certain qualities in common: their structure is cunning and supple; they can break the heart; there is – always – a whiff of danger. One other common factor, alas: they are all nineteenth-century.

I regret this, for I read modern fiction all the time, some three or four new novels a week; I admire, hugely, the work of such writers as Updike, Bellow, Amis (*fils* – definitely not *père*), Barnes and Chatwin; I look forward to a new detective novel by P. D. James or Ruth Rendell as much as I ever did a Christie – but for the greatest pleasure, the continual capacity to astonish, I would always return to the expansiveness, complexity, and technical audacity of the nineteenth-century novel.

My favourite books

The following list reflects that taste, and also the impossibility of the stern task set. Only *ten* favourite books? I should find it very hard to limit the choice to fifty. However, I abide by the rules of the game. I have included only books reread many times, and I have selected them upon the principles of *Desert Island Discs*: a slight cheat, of course, since that means that, although not listed, I get to hang on to both the Bible and Shakespeare . . .

Emily Brontë, *Wuthering Heights*; Flaubert, *Madame Bovary*; Dickens, *Bleak House* and *Little Dorrit*; Mann, *Buddenbrooks*; Chekhov, *Collected Plays*; John Donne, *Complete Verse & Selected Prose*; Virginia Woolf, *The Complete Diaries*; Anthony Powell, *A Dance to the Music of Time*.

Wendy Cope

THE first book I read to myself was Enid Blyton's *The Buttercup Farm Family*. I can't recall anything about the plot or the characters but I do remember gazing for a long time at the word 'put' before swallowing my pride and asking Nanna to tell me what it said.

Though my parents both left school at fourteen, we were a moderately bookish household, and the grown-ups did all the right things to help me learn to read. Since my grandmother lived with us, there were three of them. It was Nanna who had the most time available to read me stories and to teach me the letter-names and sounds. Once I could read on my own, I wouldn't allow anyone to read to me. This may have been a loss for Nanna. Thinking about it now, I feel very sad.

An inactive and rather depressed child, I began to turn to books for comfort and escape, and much preferred reading to any other pastime. My parents regarded this as a mixed blessing. When they told me off for being unsociable, I thought unsociable sounded like a good thing to be.

Though I was beginning to have some idea of myself as an egghead, I still mostly read Enid Blyton. *The Secret Seven*, *The Famous Five*, the *Malory Towers* stories, and anything else I could get hold of. Except *Noddy*. By the time *Noddy* reached our house, I was too old and sophisticated for such things, and left him to my younger sister. I don't know if Enid Blyton did me any harm. I keep meaning to reread some and find out what's wrong with it.

Then there were horse stories. My mother read me *Black Beauty* before I could read to myself. Not long afterwards I began to have some riding lessons, recommended as a cure for knock knees. Naturally, this gave rise to a desire to have a pony ('*Why* can't we keep a pony in the back garden?') and to read about gymkhanas. But I was discriminating. At the age of nine or ten I abandoned a book after a few chapters because the heroine got keen on a boy and let him kiss her. Boring. Horse stories with romantic interest were unacceptable. Horse stories – or any other kind of stories – with a Christian message were even worse. Since my mother is of the evangelical persuasion, I was sometimes given these. They infuriated me. Religious instruction disguised as a pony book was a cheat and I wasn't having any of it.

Fortunately my mother also directed me towards some children's classics. *Little Women*, *What Katy Did*, Johanna Spyri's *Heidi* and their respective sequels punctuated my addiction to Enid. I remember enjoying *The Jungle Book* more than anything I'd ever read. I loved the characters so much that I dreaded coming to the end and having to leave them behind. This feeling of bereavement on finishing a good novel is something I still experience.

Another vivid memory is the first time I had to put a book down for a few moments because I was afraid that I was going to choke to death with laughter. I was seven and the book was *Winnie-the-Pooh*. This had been read to me when I was too little to see the funny side. Picking it up again was a revelation. I have been rereading the *Pooh* books at intervals ever since and haven't tired of them yet. In fact, they get better as one grows older and understands more about the foibles of human nature. In this respect they resemble the novels of Jane Austen. I particularly admire the way the final chapter of *The House at Pooh Corner* makes the reader laugh (at Eeyore the poet) and then cry within the space of a few pages. I don't think I'd want to be close to anyone who could read this chapter without crying. Or without laughing, for that matter.

Molesworth is another touchstone. Nobody who fails to respond to his wit and wisdom can really be on my wavelength. I first came across *Down with Skool* when I was eleven.

'It looks like a boys' book,' said my mother. 'Are you sure you want it?' I was sure. Though it was Ronald Searle's illustrations that caught my eye in the bookshop, the text, by the late Geoffrey Willans, proved just as wonderful. Nowadays I like the literary theory best: 'Peotry is sissy stuff that rhymes. Weedy people say la and fie and swoon when they see a bunch of daffodils.'

Peotry. As a child, I wasn't much keener than Molesworth. The poems we did at junior school were mostly about nature and fairies. 'Who has seen the wind?' nearly put me off Christina Rossetti for life. Every year, or so it seemed, we had to write a story explaining what was going on in Walter de la Mare's 'The Listeners': '"Is there anybody there?" said the traveller.' I neither kno nor care, as Molesworth might say, if there is anebode there or not.

At home I was subjected to different poetry – recitations by my father of the favourites he knew by heart. We didn't encourage him to give us Tennyson's 'The Charge of the Light Brigade' or excerpts from the *Rubaiyat* over lunch but, if the mood took him, we got it anyway. The poems he made us listen to are now among my favourites too. It's odd how it can go either way. Junior school put me off all sorts of things, including, I am sad to say, *A Midsummer Night's Dream*. Bored to distraction by my early experience of church, I have grown up to love *The Book of Common Prayer* and the hymns we sang.

At school, poetry improved when we began working on the O level English Literature syllabus. I was surprised to find how much I liked certain poems by Yeats, Hardy and James Elroy Flecker. In the sixth form (where I was well taught) I was bowled over by Keats.

But I didn't read poetry in my spare time. At ten or eleven I had discovered detective stories and these were my staple reading during my early teens. Agatha Christie, Dorothy L. Sayers, Margery Allingham, John Dickson Carr, Carter Dickson. And war stories – the name Paul Brickhill comes to mind. From the age of thirteen I also read anything that might have some sex in it. In a girls' boarding school such books were not easy to come by. Some shelves outside the main school library housed the 'fiction library', a collection of historical novels and family

sagas considered suitable for young ladies. Some of them
were known to contain mildly erotic passages and these
were always in demand. The books we brought to school
had to be passed by the authorities but a certain amount
of smuggling went on. After the *Chatterley* trial, someone
brought in a copy of D. H. Lawrence's novel, which was
passed around the sixth form. I went through it looking
for the sex and skipping the rest. Five years ago I read it
properly and thought it very good.

In English lessons we were introduced to Jane Austen
and the Brontës. My pleasure in their novels was modi-
fied by the pernicious business of reading round the class.
To enjoy the book at one's own pace, instead of following
while others stumbled through the text, was bad behaviour.
These lessons didn't achieve their apparent aim – some of
us stubbornly continued to like the books.

University (where I read history) and the years immediately afterwards were a bad time. One of the symptoms was
that I more or less lost the reading habit. It did sometimes
come back. One vacation, severely depressed, no longer
believing in God, and unable to make sense of anything, I
managed to get into *The Brothers Karamazov.* I think it saved
my sanity. Occasionally I would open a book of poems – it
might be T. S. Eliot, or it might be one of J. M. Cohen's
anthologies of *Comic and Curious Verse*, which I acquired in
the early 1960s.

At the age of twenty-seven I went into psychoanalysis
and within six months was reading and writing in every
spare moment. I read psychology books – especially the
work of R. D. Laing and his associates – and poetry.

The New Oxford Book of English Verse, edited by Helen
Gardner, had just been published and it became my guide
to the poetry of past centuries. I began reading contemporary poetry as well – Larkin, Hughes, Sylvia Plath. In
the public library I found the PEN anthologies of new
poetry that Hutchinson used to publish. But there isn't
much poetry in public libraries and there was a limit to
the number of books I could buy on a teacher's salary.
Eventually, and with tremendous gratitude, I discovered
the Arts Council Poetry Library, now housed in the Royal
Festival Hall.

One or two poets of my acquaintance say they never
read novels. Nowadays there are phases when I do, and
phases when I don't. What holds me back is fear of the
child who wants to do nothing but sit and read fiction
all day. If I give in to her, I'll be a penniless hermit. But I
am learning to enjoy novels in moderation. This morning
there's a copy of *Jude the Obscure* on the living-room table,
with page 93/94 turned down. It's going to stay there until
after lunch.

This is the first time I've read *Jude.* Some people would
give a lot to come across a Hardy novel they hadn't read
before, and I'm glad I didn't get round to all the great classics when I was young. Where new fiction is concerned, I
welcome press coverage of the paperback editions. It isn't
just that hardbacks are expensive – they're difficult to carry
around. Authors whose paperbacks I snap up include Anita
Brookner, David Lodge, Julian Barnes, both Amises, P. D.
James, Len Deighton and Alison Lurie. Reading Lurie's
The Nowhere City, I found myself hurrying through the

heroine's love-life to get to the next bit about her sinus trouble. One's preoccupations change with the years.

I haven't opened a history book since I left university but have recently begun to read the occasional biography. *Nancy Mitford* by Selina Hastings got me through an otherwise terrible weekend. Though travel books rarely tempt me, I whiled away some happy hours with Redmond O'Hanlon's two volumes.

When it came to making my list of ten favourites, I asked myself which books come down from the shelves most often. I wouldn't try to argue that Michael Frayn's *Towards the End of the Morning* is better than *War and Peace*, but I haven't read the latter three times. Frayn, whom I first discovered in *The Observer* in about 1960, has frequently made me laugh until I could hardly breathe.

In some cases it seemed a good idea to mention a particular edition of a poet's work. I've chosen the Ricks edition of Housman, despite his peculiar introduction, because it includes the Housman who makes me laugh (in his light verse and letters), as well as the Housman who makes me cry. The *Complete Poems* of Emily Dickinson comprises 1,775 untitled items – it's hard to find the same poem twice, so the ones I know best are all in Ted Hughes's selection. Since my German is elementary, I'm a bit embarrassed about listing the Heine, but it really is a favourite. My copy (a gift, which has great sentimental value) is the Penguin Classics edition, with prose translations at the bottom of each page. As I weep over Heine's lyrics, and memorize some of them, I like to think my knowledge of the language is improving. Next time I'm in a German-speaking country, I'll be well-equipped to express love or grief but still won't know how to ask which tram goes to the shopping centre.

My favourite books

A. E. Housman: *Collected Poems and Selected Prose*, ed. Christopher Ricks; *The Rubaiyat of Omar Khayyam*, trs. Edward Fitzgerald; *A Choice of Emily Dickinson's Verse*, ed. Ted Hughes; *Sonnets*, William Shakespeare; *Heinrich Heine: Selected Verse*, ed. and trans. Peter Branscombe; *Persuasion*, Jane Austen; *Towards the End of the Morning*, Michael Frayn; *The House at Pooh Corner*, A. A. Milne; *The Compleet Molesworth*, Geoffrey Willans and Ronald Searle; *Songs of Praise* (with tunes), ed. Dearmer, Vaughan Williams, Shaw.

Sue Townsend

I WAS eight before I could read. My teacher was a nasty drunken woman who looked like a dyspeptic badger. I'm forty-six now and she is long dead, but my heart almost stops if I see anyone resembling her stomping along the pavement towards me.

I learnt to read during the three weeks I was away from school with a spectacular case of mumps. (Mumps *were* mumps in the 1950s.) My mother went to a rummage sale and came back with a pile of *William* books written by Richmal Crompton, a person I assumed to be a man. I looked at the illustrations and laughed, then I tried to read the captions underneath these delightful scratchy drawings. My mother helped me out and slowly and mysteriously the black squiggles turned into words which turned into sentences, which turned into stories. I could read.

There should have been a hundred-gun salute. The Red Arrows should have flown overhead. The night sky should have blazed with fireworks.

I joined the library thirsting after more *William* books. I read one a day and then two a day, then I ran out and fumbled along the library shelves pulling out books at random. Nothing was ever as good as William, but the die was cast, I was addicted to print.

Christmas came, and with it a stack of books in the Woolworth's classics series. They had serious red covers, and gilt lettering: *Treasure Island* and *Kidnapped*, R. D. Blackmore's *Lorna Doone*, *Heidi*, *Little Women*, Harriet Beecher Stowe's *Uncle Tom's Cabin*. In the front of each book there was a coloured illustration, and when I had read the last page I would turn back to the beginning and study this picture as closely as a Sotheby's expert; trying to extract more meaning and more pleasure. I've always felt a great sadness on finishing a book I've enjoyed. And a strong reluctance to actually close the book and put it on a shelf. I delay the moment of parting as other people might put off finishing a love affair.

During the junior school holidays I would often read three books a day. The local librarian used to interrogate me on the contents, convinced that I was showing off, though there was nobody to impress in my immediate circle. Most adults took my passion for books as a sign of derangement. 'Your brain will burst,' was a common warning, one that I took seriously. When reading I half expected my head to explode and hit the ceiling. It didn't put me off. Reading became the most important thing in my life. My favourite place to read was on my bed, lying on a pink cotton counterpane, and if I had a bag of sweets next to me, I was in heaven.

The first book I lost a night's sleep over was *Jane Eyre*. It was winter and our house wasn't heated – apart from a coal fire in the living room. I read in bed. My fingers and arms froze, my nails went blue. Frost formed on the inside of the window panes, but I could not put *Jane Eyre* down. I loved Jane. Snow fell, a few birds began to sing, my eyes drooped but I had to read on. Who had started the fire? Who was the mad creature in the attic? I ate my porridge reading. I walked to school reading. I read in each lesson until the morning milk break. I finished the last page in the school cloakroom, surrounded by wet gabardine mackintoshes. I felt very lonely. I wanted to talk about *Jane Eyre*. There were so many references I didn't understand, but I made no attempt to talk about that or any other book.

Reading became a secret obsession; I would drop a book guiltily if anyone came into a room. I went nowhere without a book – the lavatory, a bus journey, walking to school.

I began to buy second-hand paperbacks from Leicester market. I soon realized that the orange-covered Penguins were an indication of quality. If I found a writer I liked, I would collect and read everything of theirs I could. The first Orwell I read was *Inside the Whale and Other Essays*. If I am tempted to show off and use an esoteric word, I think of Orwell, who hated esotericism (he would not have approved of the last sentence). I read my tattered copies of P. G. Wodehouse and laughed like a drain in the the middle of the night; more evidence of my derangement, according to my family.

The first erotic book I read was about a Spanish bullfighter. I don't recall the title or the author but I certainly remember the delicious anticipation it aroused in me. I couldn't wait to grow up and have a sexual experience. Though Spanish bullfighters were thin on the ground in Leicester.

I left school one week before my fifteenth birthday and I remember what I was reading on my last day at school. The *Plays* of Oscar Wilde. I took a biography of Ernest Hemingway with me to my first job. It was too large to fit in my narrow office drawer so I hid it inside a brown paper bag and shoved it *under* the desk. I didn't read it during the day, but its presence was a comfort.

I was an emotional reader, I laughed and cried over Dickens and Arnold Bennett, and Nevil Shute made me yearn for a faithful, plodding, Shute-type of man. I imagined us trekking across the Australian outback, finding a rundown hamlet, and then transforming it – together – until death or flood parted us.

When I was sixteen I found a book that did truly change my life – *The Gambler* by Dostoyevsky. Not his best book, but good enough for me at the time. I didn't know that Dostoyevsky was a genius, I knew nothing about Russia, but I found something in *The Gambler* that comforted and satisfied me. I was irritated by the Russian names and baffled by the references to historical events, but I liked the notion of duality; that good and evil coexist inside every human being. I looked on the market stalls for more Dostoyevsky but found nothing. I couldn't borrow more Dostoyevskys from the library because I owed a fortune in library fines (I could never bear to take the books back). I realized that I would have to *buy* a book. Bookshops were intimidating places to me then. They were staffed by wizened old men who knew their stuff and my big problem was that *I didn't know how to pronounce 'Dostoyevsky'.*

One day I was in a café and saw a man with a beard who was wearing a black polo-neck sweater. He was reading a book and smoking a French cigarette. I had *The Gambler* with me and I daringly crossed to this intellectual-looking stranger, showed him the book and asked him how to pronounce the author's name. He pronounced the name 'Dostoyevsky' carefully and we became friends. His name was Bob and he invited me back to his squalid cottage in the country where mice gambolled in the living room. Over the next few years Bob introduced me to Henry Miller, Kafka, Donleavy and Sean O'Casey.

I would trek out to 'Mouse House' as I called it at any hour of the day or night: Bob was always genial and welcoming, but was also, to my great sorrow, homosexual.

I married at eighteen and in that year I discovered Graham Greene, John Steinbeck, George Eliot and the book review pages of the *Manchester Guardian*. I remember the first new hardback book I ever bought: it was Brendan Behan's *Hold Your Hour and Have Another*.

At nineteen I had my first baby (I took Osbert Sitwell's *Laughter in the Next Room* with me in the labour ward). My son was born prematurely and I was forced to leave him in hospital in an incubator while he gained weight. I found Evelyn Waugh's *Scoop* on the hospital trolley – a delightful compensation. Being a very nosy person I have always enjoyed reading diaries, letters and journals, especially Waugh's, Noel Coward's, Pepys's and Virginia Woolf's.

Sylvia Plath's letters to and from her mother prove to me that she was programmed from an early age to take her own life. The standards she set herself were so impossibly high.

My favourite contemporary writers are Kingsley Amis, Paul Theroux, John Updike, Martin Amis, Iris Murdoch . . . but I can't go on, there are so many. I seemed to have spent my whole life reading. God knows how I found the time to rear four children (or conceive them).

What am I reading now? As I write I have a pile of books on my bedside table. The new ones are: *Rabbit at Rest* by John Updike, *Doctor De Marr* by Paul Theroux, *An Immaculate Mistake* by Paul Bailey, *The Body Won't Break* by John McGrath, and six back copies of *Modern Painting*, all but one edited by the late Peter Fuller. I am also rereading, for the fourth time, V. S. Naipaul's *The Enigma of Arrival*.

My favourite books

The books I have most *enjoyed* are: *The House of the Dead*, Fyodor Dostoyevsky; *Lucky Jim*, Kingsley Amis; *Erewhon*, Samuel Butler; *Jane Eyre*, Charlotte Brontë; *Scoop*, Evelyn Waugh; *Resurrection*, Leo Tolstoy; the four *Rabbit* books, John Updike; *Inside the Whale and Other Essays*, George Orwell; *Madame Bovary*, Gustave Flaubert; *Dostoyevsky*, John Jones.

When God rested on the seventh day I'm sure he sat down, kicked off his shoes and opened a book.

Hermione Lee

IKE losing your virginity, if you're that old, or hearing of the assassination of President Kennedy, if you're *that* old, there are some first readings you can always remember. Open the book again, and the place and time of the first impression come back at you, like a sharp smell or a strong flavour. Elizabeth Bowen calls it 'an echotrack of sensation'. The books that retain it are the ones that changed you, however slightly: made you shift your sense of what the world was like, what it was possible to know and to feel.

So Ford Madox Ford's *The Good Soldier*, with its devastatingly low-keyed revelations about treachery and stupidity in love, is forever associated with a late 1960s rainy day in a messy student flat in the Cowley Road, Oxford; Conrad's *Nostromo* with a horrible holiday in the south of France, where the Republic of Costaguana provided a dramatic and absorbing escape from a dismal love affair; Scott Moncrieff's Proust with a cold room in Toxteth where, in my first year of teaching at Liverpool University,

I came home every day, for weeks on end, to Marcel, with the same kind of excitement as if I was going to a secret assignation.

I date the beginning of these kinds of addictive pleasures to when I was nine or ten, in a hotel room in Bordeaux. I had run out of holiday reading, and my mother gave me the book she'd just finished. It was *Far from the Madding Crowd*, in the Macmillan red and cream paperback. Up until then, from the point when she taught me to read at the age of four (I can remember the pleasure of success on making out my first word, which was 'hide-and-seek'), she had been bringing me up on a rich, classical diet of middle-class children's books: *Alice* and *Pooh*, E. Nesbit, the Narnia books and Tolkien, Philippa Pearce's *Tom's Midnight Garden*, Alison Uttley's *A Traveller in Time*, Elizabeth Goudge's *The Little White Horse*, *The Borrowers*, Rosemary Sutcliff, Patricia Lynch, Beverly Nichols, Barbara Leonie Picard, Frances Hodgson Burnett, *The Heroes of Asgard, Tales of King Arthur*, Kipling (I had a peculiar passion for *Stalky & Co.*), Rider Haggard (*She*, not *King Solomon's Mines*), Hugh Walpole (the Jeremy Books – why this weakness for boys' public school stories? – followed by the irresistibly second-rate Herries saga), George MacDonald (*At the Back of the North Wind* rather than the Curdie stories), the Grimm brothers, *Just William* . . . everything a literary child could want except Arthur Ransome. (Like other highbrow literary parents of the 1950s, my mother banned Enid Blyton.) But in Bordeaux I felt I was reading my first adult book. I skipped the descriptions, got bored by the rustics, and fell

passionately in love with Farmer Boldwood. The pattern
was set for adolescence.

Between the ages of ten and seventeen, it seems to me
that I spent most of my time reading. This can't be true, of
course. I went to school (which had more to do with talking, showing off and fighting than reading), I was given a
privileged cosmopolitan musical and theatrical education
(my father played string quartets every weekend, we went
to the opera, I had music lessons, we took well-planned
French holidays and visited art galleries and the Old Vic
and walked in London parks). I had hobbies, but they were
all solemnly, piously literary, like making enormous family
trees of the Greek gods, or indexing my collection of post-
cards of Renaissance nativities (though my half-Jewish,
half-Calvinist background was fiercely sceptical, I was
obsessed, like many young girls, with images of the Virgin
and child).

But what I mostly did was read, and what I mostly read
was novels. I had the run of my mother's bookshelves,
which were extensive, even though she has never ceased
lamenting the loss of half her books in the Blitz. There was
not much parental censorship – they assumed I would give
up the books I didn't understand. Some pleasures to come
simply weren't to my taste at that time – a copy of *David
Copperfield* gathered dust by my bed for about six years,
and I put down *What Maisie Knew* by Henry James in a
hurry, having thought it would be a book for children,
like *What Katy Did*. Some dislikes were settled, at first
sight, for ever: I've always thought life was too short for Sir
Walter Scott.

I liked large complicated books about relationships. A good deal of this diet – Jane Austen and George Eliot and Dostoyevsky and Forster – was intellectually challenging and – I suppose – character-forming, though at the time it all just felt like pleasure. But a great swathe of my adolescent reading, the part I most enjoyed, was – I now recognize – insidiously corrupting. Middle-class literary girls in the 1950s and 1960s were given to read by their mothers the up-market romances which have since brilliantly been given a second life by Virago, safely distanced as historical specimens. We inherited from these wonderful and misleading novels an older generation of women's attitudes to parents and lovers and heroinism. Margaret Kennedy's *The Constant Nymph*, Mary Webb's *Precious Bane*, Antonia White's *Frost in May*, *Olivia* by 'Olivia' (Dorothy Bussy's intense account of her schoolgirl passion for her French teacher), Dodie Smith's delicious *I Capture the Castle*, Rebecca West's *The Fountain Overflows*: these seductive, enchanting, pernicious books sent us into adulthood with highly unrealistic beliefs in the value of intense emotions, powerfully romanticized versions of the male sex, and snobbish commitments to the worlds of art and music and writing where all the really tragic – and therefore true – feelings existed. I suspect that a large number of white British feminists who began their adult life and work in the late 1960s and early 1970s had to do battle – like Virginia Woolf doing battle with the Angel in the House, personified in Coventry Patmore's poem of that name – with the alluring ghosts of these inherited heroines, who all thought the world well lost for love.

Two books, by writers I still dearly love, sum up these powerful influences: Elizabeth Bowen's *To the North* and Rosamond Lehmann's *The Weather in the Streets*. I first read *To the North* when I was about thirteen. It's an edgy, mournful, sexually charged story of two sisters-in-law living together in London, whose controlled lives are disrupted by the predatory Markie, one of Bowen's 1930s cads. It's not her best book (see my list of best books), but I was overwhelmed by its catastrophic ending, with the betrayed, ethereal Emmeline driving Markie at reckless speed on night roads to their death: 'She saw: "TO THE NORTH" written black on white, with a long black immovably flying arrow. Something gave way. An immense idea of departure . . . possessed her spirit, now launched like the long arrow.' I didn't worry at the time at the trap that the Bowen heroine always falls into, of hurling herself unprotected into 'a world of love' and being punished for it – though I see now that was the allure of the book. What I responded to was something extreme, the thrill of reckless speed and letting go, bursting out of the controlled good manners of the writing. Bowen recognized this adolescent desire for extremes. In *The House in Paris* she says: 'Young girls like the excess of any quality . . . they like to have loud chords struck on them.' These books were my loud chords.

The women in Rosamond Lehmann's novels – romantic ingénues, suppressed wives, fragile, long-suffering adulterous heroines – are all victims of a trap, too. They don't want to be déclassée and bohemian, but they don't want to be dull middle-aged, middle-class wives either. So they have catastrophic affairs, and end up lonely and ostracized. Lehmann knows all about the fatal attraction, to these sorts of women, of men with powerful, authoritative public personae and soft centres. As soon as Rollo Spencer comes into the dining car of the train in *The Weather in the Streets*, 'a tall prosperous-looking male figure in a tweed overcoat, carrying a dog under his arm', orders 'sausages, scrambled eggs, coffee, toast and marmalade', and opens *The Times*, you know that Olivia, the victim-heroine, is doomed. What Lehmann does best is the inner voice of women talking to themselves about their hopeless love affairs, seeing their ends already in their beginnings. I remember being overcome with painful romantic bliss, reading her at fifteen, when the heroine of *The Echoing Grove* gives William Blake to her lover: 'And throughout all Eternity/I forgive you, you forgive me.' It was wonderfully high-minded and lacerating, and you could be sure that there was going to be a great deal to forgive. Now I feel that I have to forgive these novels for leading me up the garden path.

When I went to Oxford at seventeen that kind of addictive, enchanted reading began to turn into something different, possibly less pleasant but more complicated and various. There were odd gratifications to be had from the peculiar archaic Oxford English syllabus, still in place in the 1960s, which made you start your first week at university with Milton's *Lycidas* and Anglo-Saxon. I relearnt English as a foreign language. I discovered long poems, the seventeenth and eighteenth century, the romantics. Later, after a year in America, I came to all the magnificent writers who would have been part of my adolescent reading if I had been an American child – Whitman, Dickinson, Twain, Hawthorne – and whom I've been reading and teaching ever since. Discreditably much later, I began to read translations of Eastern European writers, modern American fiction, biography. In the last ten years, I've found other reading pleasures. Making the anthologies of women's short stories for the two volumes of *The Secret Self* led me to some marvellous new discoveries (Alice Munro is at the top of that list). Interviewing a large number of writers for Channel Four's *Book Four,* between 1982 and 1986, gave me the chance to read in areas I'd been ignorant of, such as South African literature (Gordimer, Fugard, Breytenbach, Christopher Hope). And judging the WHSmith prize is a good way of 'keeping up'. But, pleasurable though all these kinds of reading are, they are also jobs of work. It's important to keep time for rogue reading, reading in idleness, casually, accidentally, without a pen in hand. I still miss, and still remember, that phase of passionate early reading: it never quite returns.

I had those privileged years of reading because my mother was a self-educated, dedicated book-lover, my father was a hard-working general practitioner, and both cherished liberal beliefs in the virtues of culture. For many young readers the possibilities of leisured, rich, rewarding reading depend on prolific and uncensored supplies of books in schools and universities, free and well-stocked public libraries, teachers who have time to foster individual or eccentric interests, equal educational opportunities, examination syllabuses which are flexible, imaginative, and not centrally dictated, publishing houses and bookshops willing and able to cater to minority interests, and value ascribed to uneconomical and non-vocational pursuits such as reading and thinking: all things which the Conservative government of the last decade has been busily eradicating.

My favourite books

In memory of my own luxurious years of passionate, leisurely reading, I decided to limit 'my top ten favourite books' to novels. (So Keats's *Letters*, my desert island book, had to go.) To make the game easier for myself, I threw out everything in translation (so no *Anna Karenina*, no Turgenev (*First Love*), no Proust) and everything by contemporaries I have met or know. (Out went a splendid top ten which began with Julian Barnes's *Flaubert's Parrot*, Graham Swift's *Waterland*, *Midnight's Children* by Salman Rushdie, *The Counterlife* by Philip Roth, Anita Brookner's *Look at Me*, and *The Conservationist* by Nadine Gordimer.) Like quarrelling Booker judges, I ruthlessly excluded my second eleven (*The Good Soldier*, Greene's *The End of the Affair*, Stevie Smith's *Novel on Yellow Paper*, Kipling's *Kim* among them.) After that I chose ten books which I have reread at least three times and know that I will read again. They are, in my opinion, ten of the best novels in the language:

Jane Austen, *Persuasion*; Charles Dickens, *Little Dorrit*; George Eliot, *Middlemarch*; Henry James, *The Portrait of a Lady*; Virginia Woolf, *To the Lighthouse*; Elizabeth Bowen, *The Death of the Heart*; Edith Wharton, *Ethan Frome*; F. Scott Fitzgerald, *The Great Gatsby*; Willa Cather, *The Professor's House*; James Joyce, *Ulysses*.

Timberlake Wertenbaker

The Three Musketeers by Alexandre Dumas. Even now I have to say it is my favourite book, the one I don't need to take to a desert island because I know it by heart. I read it at least twenty, thirty times, first in a shortened form at the age of six or so and then again and again until I was sixteen and forced myself to read Dostoyevsky's *Crime and Punishment* instead.

D'Artagnan was from Gascony, which is close enough to the Basque country for me to have thought we came from the same area. The fishing village of my childhood had a mystery and beauty I recognized later, but I was already restless. I wanted to gallop across France and join the musketeers, I wanted adventure and the friendship of such world-weary men as Athos. I also wanted to wear those beautiful hats and outface the intrigues of authority with panache. The book gave me, or rather exacerbated, a thirst for adventure, which I probably transferred later to some of my women characters.

D'Artagnan's rashness. D'Artagnan's loyalty. I wanted to be him. I've often wondered about the gender of identification. At some point, I must have realized that I was a girl reading, instead of some neutral thing that could become d'Artagnan, because I embarked on *Les Petites Filles modèles* by La Comtesse de Ségur. Most of my friends identified with the rebellious Sophie, but I found her rebellion, which consisted mostly of not serving tea with grace, tedious and I identified instead with the most boring and perfect of the little girls. If you can't be a musketeer then you might as well be a perfect female. Moving from the *Musketeers* to *Les Petites Filles* was as painful as the scene in Strindberg's *Dance of Death* when Alice tells her stepdaughter Judith to let down her dress and put up her hair and start taking smaller steps. Alice is not just demanding a physical change, but a confinement of the mind. I had the same sense of restricted space with another of those books one is supposed to like as a girl, *Little Women*. I hated it.

I moved instead to Dostoyevsky, perfect adolescent reading, as far as I was concerned. All those cockroaches. The struggle between good and evil, so strong in adolescence, the Idiot knocking over a precious vase, a common experience, the rage against the father in *The Brothers Karamazov* as well as the longing for forgiveness, for peace, for the kindness of a Father Zossima, based on the wonderful Saint Seraphim of Sarov. There are books that never close, and I think *The Possessed* is such a book. A world crumbling into chaos, the tormented cruelty of Stavrogin, the appearance of little devils proving the existence of God in a world deciding on atheism, scenes from that book still haunt me. I find Dostoyevsky was one of the best novelists of redemption. Redemption is an extraordinary concept, particularly at the end of the twentieth century, when the word could just disappear, along with the word humane.

Although I spent most of my childhood and adolescence reading in French, I had actually learned to read in English, around four, I think, and I remember a jumble of wonderful fantasies. Does anyone remember a book about a cat in a Chinese city? Another about someone who dives into a well and finds a country underneath – I can still touch its landscape. And then, the Hans Christian Andersen stories, in a big red and gold book, with grim illustrations. I grieved for the little mermaid and wanted to stop her from cutting out her tongue for the sake of a boring prince who didn't even notice her. I wonder sometimes if it disturbed me so much it eventually drove me to write *The Love of the Nightingale* about a woman whose tongue is cut out. How can one trace those influences? The power of images is like birthmarks on the memory. The little boy with a splinter of ice in his heart. Who hasn't felt, at times, that splinter of ice? Certainly the fervour of those imagined worlds and complex feelings seemed more real to me and much more interesting than the tedious round of chores and school. In fact, I think the minute I began to read I realized the best way to spend time was to develop one of those convenient childhood diseases and stay in bed and imagine.

At thirteen I discovered the *Odyssey* by mistake in the Lycée Français library. It was new, the pages hadn't yet been cut, and the librarian congratulated me on being serious instead of reading Simone de Beauvoir, gobbled up by my classmates. I had no idea what she meant – the story was wonderful, those travels again, enchanted lands. The Greek was on the opposite page, an indecipherable geography of its own. I wish now I had read the Simone de Beauvoir, as it would have explained or warned me against much of what was to come.

At fifteen, under the influence of my older brother, I switched languages again and started reading and writing in English. He wanted to be the next Hemingway, I decided to be the next Fitzgerald. The new world of American literature: spare writing, subtext (the French are too interested in text to allow much subtext), romantic love often destroyed from within, as opposed to adulterous passion honed by Catholicism. I read voraciously, but too fast, and at second hand. I felt ill at ease in America with its brave, male, woodsman prose and didn't feel at home again until I discovered *Women in Love*, in Italy. I don't know what happened to the children I was supposed to be looking after. I remember lying on my bed, reading, loving the book so much I wanted to eat it. I was never happy with other books by D. H. Lawrence, but that book stayed with me for years. It was the first time I discovered such strong women in a novel; its sexuality enveloped me in that hot summer in which my own body was reeling from discoveries of desire and luxuriance. I remember also being intrigued by the muffled love of the two men for each other. I always have been. Men are often better at loving other men than at loving women because there is no fear, and fear destroys tenderness.

When you really like something I believe you wish to have written it yourself. I felt that way about *Agamemnon* by Aeschylus, which I discovered at university. I was supposed to write an essay on it, I kept trying to rewrite it – no, to write it. Particularly the middle play, *The Libation Bearers*, with its dark and vengeful Electra, the great image of the dispossessed woman, dispossessed even in her tragedy because one never knows what happens to her. The Furies don't pursue her, she is not judged, and therefore never integrated in the state. This still bothers me.

Now that I am writing myself, I read less, which is sad. I've always been a chaotic reader, sniffing my way to books, but that only works if one is reading a lot. I like scientific books I don't understand but with which I can collide imaginatively. I had a good time with Althusser and Gramsci in the 1970s, with Stephen Jay Gould's wonderful essays on animals and evolution and recently with Danah Zohar's *The Quantum Self*, because it makes quantum physics almost comprehensible, and poses important moral questions. And I like writers who cast a clear eye on troubled subjects: Foucault, Germaine Greer, Marina Warner.

I read as much contemporary fiction as I can, which is not much, both grateful to and resentful of the Booker shortlist. The book I read with the greatest pleasure in the last few years must be Graham Swift's *Waterland*. Every time I drive through the fens on my way to Norfolk, I think of his book, which taught me to look at the landscape. I like watery books anyway: Conrad, possibly my favourite novelist, Peter Carey's *Oscar and Lucinda*, Heathcote Williams's *Whale Nation*, Jean Rhys, Margaret Drabble, Angela Carter, Balzac, the poems of Cavafy, of Baudelaire. Too much modern fiction and theatre is dry. I'm for those watery regions of the imagination which you're so close to as a child. The saddest thing about growing up is the threat of desiccation of the imaginative skin, of the mind. It is those memories of those first books that refresh you, like a warm bath after a tedious day of phone calls and shopping. Those knights and mermaids of childhood, sirens calling you back into the sea. The temptation to jump. Of course, you can't, you have to go on, you have to work, but who would want to live without those calls?

Alan Hollinghurst

I WAS an only child, and spent the long afternoons of childhood in rooms full of my father's books. Like many only children I have a certain immunity to loneliness and am content with my own company almost to the point of smugness. Perhaps that is why I squandered the opportunity my singleness gave me to lose myself in reading. The titles of those books – *K2*, *Nanga Parbat*, *Bhowani Junction*, *A Dragon Apparent* – spoke for the adventurousness of a sedentary man's imagination, just as others reflected his need for literature itself: Defoe's *Colonel Jack*, Scott's *Guy Mannering*, *The Crime of Sylvestre Bonnard* by Anatole France. I looked at those that had pictures, but I never read them. I never, in Dickens's phrase, read for life. I learnt soon after, when I had heard the overture to Wagner's *Tannhäuser*, to listen for life, and what followed were holidays planned around the schedules of Radio Three. It was the abstraction of music, and the visionary drama it projected into an inner vacancy of my own, that exercised such a hold on me, and maintained it, too: though I still listen to music every day, I have always been a reluctant reader. I'm not stupid, but I tend to miss the point of certain kinds of book: I read for the feel of an invented world, its colour and shadow. I am quite capable of leaving unfinished a novel I greatly admire. I've never read a thriller, or anything closer to a crime novel than Patricia Highsmith, whose strength I take to be the subversion of formal expectations in favour of the exploration of states of mind. I acknowledge the primacy of story at the same time as being somewhat resistant to it. From my early teens on, what I mainly read was poetry. From my earlier browsings, at six or seven, I bring back most clearly the cartoons in *Pick of Punch* volumes of the immediate post-war years. I loved them not for their humour, which was dim and inaccessible to me, but for the gloomy hatching of jokes about power-cuts, the spidery eccentricity of Emett, the oddly haunting stylish emptiness of Fougasse. All this seemed to deepen the mystery that attaches to the time just before one is born, giving it an air of spectral mobility and impenetrable logic.

I enjoyed classic children's books by A. A. Milne and Kenneth Grahame very much, but I have never made a cult of them. The mood I recall most keenly from my earliest exposure to books was one of alienation. I had no understanding of the rituals enacted in them, or of their alarming and complacent heartiness. Brer Rabbit I remember finding especially remote, and the word Brer itself embodied all the rough presumption of an alien vocabulary. Later I became more adept at the play of exclusive and particular lingos, most obviously in poetry, but also in disciplines which have their own necessary refinements.

From childhood journeys, when I shouted out the styles of successive buildings from the back of the car, I came to take pleasure in the beautiful dry dense language of architectural history and description, and I still derive a keener pleasure from a good architectural essay – James Ackerman on Palladio, say, or Andrew Saint on Norman Shaw, or John Summerson on Soane – than from most good novels. I can lose myself in the plan of a monster Victorian country house the way other people lose themselves in Victorian novels. This was the first language barrier I remember passing, and I was conversant with squints and squinches, strapwork and Flemish bond, could draw you a Herne vault or a four-centred arch or expound the principles of entasis long before the day I still remember when I picked up one of my parents' novels and discovered that grown-up books were somehow or other continuous with children's ones, and felt even a slight disappointment at understanding every word, even if not all that lay behind them.

I am only beginning to see now how deep were the effects of what little voluntary and entirely commonplace reading I did as a prep-school boy. The dominant authors were Tolkien and P. G. Wodehouse. The Wooster stories were on the television at the time, and I brought to what seemed to me close to perfection an imitation of Denis Price's Jeeves; my voice had broken early, and encouraged by the success of my act I assumed a manner of punctilious superiority at all times – a performance oddly akin, it strikes me now, to the sarcastic suavity of our headmaster. I consumed all the Wodehouse I could – Blandings and Psmith as well as Jeeves – and so complete was my identification with them that I was requested to read the stories aloud to the other boys after prep (rather as, informally, I would sing through the entire score of *My Fair Lady* and *The Sound of Music* to the rest of my dorm after lights out). As far as Wodehouse was concerned, I merely thought he was very funny, and didn't understand at the time how enabling he was to me, and how Jeeves in particular had given me a shield of pedantic irony which, like any camp assumption, had become before long an unconscious part of me.

Tolkien, of course, was a laboriously unamusing and I now think bad writer; but he was my obsession between the ages of twelve and fourteen. I took a poor view of *The Hobbit* but read *The Lord of the Rings* six times in succession. Pressure was on me to tackle Trollope, and I did attempt *Barchester Towers* between Tolkien cycles; the repugnance he filled me with has remained irrationally keen to this day. Normally in these intervals I would sulk with a manly Hammond Innes until, at the end of a week or so, the addiction of the Old Forest, the Barrow Downs and Lothlorien could no longer be resisted, and I returned to Bilbo Baggins's eleventh-first birthday party with a happy shudder of familiarity. I went off the book with the abruptness that is an addict's only chance of freedom, but I remain aware of deep feelings it nurtured in me – feelings about place in particular. All its most potent and plausible geography is English, and it conspired with the places where I had grown up – the Berkshire Downs, the Cotswolds, the seclusion and wildness of Dorset, night exercises among tors and standing stones of Dartmoor – to charge all those landscapes with a heroic, elegiac air.

Doubtless I could have got this from other writers too; but as it happened I got it from the derivative fustian of Tolkien, and I feel it keenly still.

It may be partly because I am a very slow reader that I have the recurrent sensation of being if not exactly trapped in a book then at least retained there, subject to a worrying delay. It was a further strength of poetry that, besides its ability to make one weep and shiver, it could, up to a point, be mastered and memorized and didn't go on for too long. Something of a Fotherington-Thomas in my early teens, I would roam the school grounds with *Fifteen Poets*, an anthology that ran, as I recall, from Chaucer to Arnold, and I soon had Keats's Odes, Wordsworth's 'Westminster Bridge', 'Morte d'Arthur' and Matthew Arnold's 'Dover Beach' by heart, for anyone (as a rule only boys very much at a loose end) who wanted to hear them. I didn't read serious novels until I went to Oxford, and even there was practical enough to realize that exam success depended, once one had got beyond absolute ignorance, on containing and even reducing what one knew rather than, as some people madly did, cramming as many books into their heads as they possibly could. Some people were always reading.

It's too soon for me to have worked out the place of reading in my life, or the nature of its pleasure, but writing out these earlier memories for the first time makes me see how ambivalent my relations with books have remained. By day I am on the staff of one of the world's most respected literary papers, and I remember how when I joined I imagined that I would be continuing more or less in the practices I had become accustomed to as a teacher of literature, worrying, without any very lively hope of success, at scholarly questions in Milton or Browning or Pound. Yet as a server or facilitator of such discussions I find myself handling their concerns at a curious remove. The work of a literary editor has a discipline of its own, uncontaminated, unenriched by the materials in which it deals. Only on occasion, as I read extracts in an essay from some dear and great poem like Wordsworth's *Prelude* or Yeats's 'Coole Park, 1929' or Wallace Stevens's 'Sunday Morning', do I feel the vertiginous gap between my business and the primary world of literature itself. And this has to do with writing too, since such moments of recognition make one ache to do as well oneself – or at least to rejoin the abandoned pursuit.

The most innocent and pointless way in which I retain access to the world of donnish reading that I briefly inhabited is through the literary quiz *Nemo's Almanac*, which I used to compete in and have edited for the past four years. This is an annual quotations competition requiring serendipity and an ear for style in both the setter and the solver. Like being a literary editor, it requires a kind of conning pretence of savoir, and gives one equally the illusion of having read the voluminous literature one has merely processed or deployed. Its pleasures are, strictly speaking, bookish rather than literary, yet it too at times brings one – not one, me – to a halt before the greatness of great writing, the hiding-places of my power seem open; I approach, and then they close.

Carol Ann Duffy

I CANNOT recall either of my parents reading for pleasure. The house I grew up in – rented from my father's employers – was virtually bookless. A *Pears' Cyclopaedia*, a mother-of-pearl prayer book, a *Brief History of Glasgow*, are all that I can squeeze from my memory; until I began to read myself. And once I started to read, I stayed reading. Before me now I have my first 'real' book, Lewis Carroll's *Alice's Adventures in Wonderland*, inscribed to me by my paternal grandfather in August 1962. As one who has regularly lost other presents – rings, watches, and so on – it is significant to me that I still possess it. I loved *Alice*. It is the first book that I remember reading all the way through alone – as heady an experience as one's first cigarette – and it changed me. Here was a world to live in, simply through words. Given my strict and undoubtedly clichéd working-class, Catholic background, here was *escape*. Mad Hatters and pools of tears. Language.

But the ending of *Alice* disappointed me. So it was all a dream. Only a dream. Although I immediately reread it, this prompted me to write something myself for the first time; a little story called 'The Further Adventures of Alice'. (Nobody told me about *Through the Looking-Glass*.) I wrote stories and the odd rhyme from then on. Around this time, the whole family joined the local library. Again, I have no memory of either my mother or father using their blue tickets; but I haunted the place with my pink ones, and my four brothers were less frequent visitors. At home one rainy Sunday, having read the latest Enid Blyton far too quickly, as usual (she must have written them in the bath), I picked up one of my brother Frank's library books. Thus began a lifelong love for *William,* which, to this day, has me combing Oxfam shops for early editions. Henceforward (we had no pets) I was accompanied everywhere by an imaginary dog closely modelled on William's Jumble. (*Black Beauty* had a correspondingly equine effect.) Unlike Enid Blyton, Crompton is an author who does not patronize the young reader, and her sophisticated vocabulary gave me the habit of consulting the dictionary. Hubert Lane and Violet-Elizabeth Bott made me top in English. Frank Richards, too, was a favourite writer; and the elegant, violent world of Greyfriars became more vivid than St Austin's R. C. Primary School. I wrote slavishly in imitation of everything I read and vaguely recollect my father taking one story, 'Jo Must Swim', about the triumph of a legless athlete in the swimming-pool, to the local newspaper. I think this embarrassed me.

My birthday falls two days before Christmas and my early addiction to reading ('Get your head out of that book and outside for some fresh air this minute!') solved the present problem. The obligatory doll lay unloved on the floor as I opened my books, often four or five of them at half-a-crown each. Which do I remember now? *Little Women* and *Good Wives*, *What Katy Did*, *Kidnapped*, and Twain's *Tom Sawyer* and *Huckleberry Finn*. Jo, Meg, Beth and Amy, in Alcott's first book, enthralled me. I was, of course, Jo – she wrote stories too – but her marriage to the kindly, dull Professor Bhaer removed some of her glamour as an early role model.

Later birthdays and Christmases yielded *Oliver Twist* and *A Christmas Carol*, and Dickens is an author whom I have read and reread annually, usually over the Christmas holidays or when ill in bed, although I have never dared to read his unfinished *The Mystery of Edwin Drood*. I would point to Dickens's genius with common speech as an influence on my own writing. But maybe not so's you'd notice. Another hero, worshipped early, is P. G. Wodehouse. Champagne to Dickens's red wine. When I meet my friend the poet Kit Wright, we gleefully swop Wodehouse gems. 'Jeeves was there, swinging a dashed efficient shoe.' 'It makes me feel as if I had been chasing rainbows and one of them had turned and bitten me in the leg.' And I still would not be without *Grimm's Fairy Tales* or *The Arabian Nights*, turned to again and again, along with the stories of Robert Louis Stevenson and Conan Doyle's Sherlock Holmes.

At secondary school, a convent, the brilliant, enthusiastic Miss Scriven introduced us to Shakespeare, naturally, and to poetry, her particular interest. Keats's 'Ode to a Nightingale' and, later, John Donne's 'The Flea' and Yeats's

'The Song of Wandering Aengus' inspired my first, imitative poems. All 'thou' and 'dost', but I was lost for ever to prose, for which service Miss Scriven should be thanked. In true adolescent style, I wrote at least one poem a day, and when I discovered Dylan Thomas, the resultant word-diarrhoea was awesome to behold. 'Fleshweathercock' was a pamphlet I published with Outposts while still at school. The title says it all. Still, part of me thought that poets were really dead men and that I would eventually marry Professor Bhaer.

Other books from childhood? Thackeray's *The Rose and the Ring*. Oscar Wilde's fairy tales. The *Narnia* books. (I didn't read *Winnie-the-Pooh* till I was thirty and my lover insisted.) Pamela Brown's *The Swish of the Curtain* prompted a few of us at school to write a small play – or rather, I wrote it, and they were in it. It was called *Egg Flip* and about a magic drink, but I remember little about it. I have written a few since, for radio and theatre. George Eliot's *Silas Marner* was a set book which I devoured in one evening at home, thus leaving me bored stiff (or writing surreptitious poems) in that lesson for the rest of the term. But really, around the age of fourteen and fifteen, I read mostly poetry. Penguin, at that time, published very cheap editions of modern British and European poets, and I used some of my earnings from my Saturday job in a hairdresser's to buy them. Dylan Thomas was replaced by Rilke, Prévert, Pablo Neruda, Stevie Smith, the Liverpool poets and so on, in a random, haphazard method of reading born of enthusiasm alone. I wish I could recapture now the thrill of going home on the bus with a new poetry paperback. My own poems became gradually less archaic, though totally undistinguished.

Forced to choose a 'favourite poet' now, almost an impossibility, I would select T. S. Eliot for his combinations of risk and control, voices and images. 'I should have been a pair of ragged claws/Scuttling across the floors of silent seas' (from 'The Love Song of J. Alfred Prufrock') were the first modern lines of verse that truly gave me the shock of André Breton's 'cold wind brushing the temples'. Behind Eliot, of course, stands Ezra Pound.

There was some fuss when I 'borrowed' my parents' blue library tickets to withdraw adult books from the library, *The Well of Loneliness* by Radclyffe Hall among them. This was confiscated on discovery by my father. I was very moved by this book at the time, around 1969, but trying to reread it a couple of years ago, I found it hilarious. All forms of censorship were discontinued when my grandmother accused me of reading 'a dirty book'. It was John Betjeman's *First and Last Loves,* and dealt with architecture. (This must have been around my Betjeman period.)

For me, the pleasures of reading as an adult seem subtly less intense than reading as a child. This may be to do with time, which does not exist for the child, or the loss of that simplicity which allows one to enter the moment, the fantasy, the book, wholly. One is also more critical, and even the humblest writer is nudged, or provoked, or led by the hand by everything he or she reads – a poem by Ted Hughes, a passage from *Ulysses.* It was via James Joyce that I first came to read Samuel Beckett, the only writer automatically purchased in hardback in our household.

Robert Nye once wrote that Beckett was near to becoming the patron saint of writers, and this is certainly true for me. Beckett's writing is, as he himself said of Joyce's work, *the thing itself.* He is inimitable, yet leads by the most rigorous example. Fail again. Fail better. I remember my lover and I were in Venice when he died and we sent a mournful postcard to a friend – 'On Brink of Shrieks on Bridge of Sighs'.

Sometimes there is a rare day when one is able to disconnect the telephone, open a bottle of wine, and read for sheer self-indulgence. In my case, the book in question on such a day will either be a biography – high-class goss – or the latest *Flashman* by George MacDonald Fraser. The next-best thing to rereading Wodehouse is reading a new *Flashman*. Not having a television, this for me is pure entertainment, total relaxation and much laughter.

Richard Ellmann's biographies of James Joyce and Oscar Wilde have been unequalled, in my opinion, by any other biographer on any subject; though, as I write, I look forward to reading Holroyd on Shaw and, despite the mixed reviews, Ackroyd on Dickens. Richard Holmes's *Coleridge* was also memorable. For the rest, a look at the pile of books on my bedside table gives a fairly typical example of what I read today. There is *The Government of the Tongue* by Seamus Heaney, Ellmann's *a long the riverrun, The Mating Season* by Wodehouse, Richmal Crompton's *William Again, London Fields* by Martin Amis, *Self-Portrait with a Slide* – poems by Hugo Williams (for review) and *The Quincunx* by Charles Palliser. The latter is keeping me awake until two in the morning.

There are probably many books I have forgotten to mention – certainly there are too many poets – and doubtless many books yet to be read that will become favourites. One of the bonuses of friendship is the way in which friends share books and writers from their own past with each other. As with friends and lovers, so it is with books – I have been influenced by all of them.

My favourite books

Just William, Richmal Crompton; *Alice's Adventures in Wonderland*, Lewis Carroll; *Grimm's Fairy Tales*; *A Christmas Carol*, Charles Dickens; *The Jeeves Omnibus*, P. G. Wodehouse; *Molloy / Malone Dies / The Unnamable* (trilogy), Samuel Beckett; *Oscar Wilde*, Richard Ellmann; *Collected Poems*, T. S. Eliot; *Collected Works*, William Shakespeare; *Flashman and the Redskins*, George MacDonald Fraser.

Paul Sayer

CHILDREN make the best readers. As adults, most of them will lose their willingness to be entertained or informed by books of any kind. Might we see this as a regrettable state of affairs, or should we view it coldly as a reflection of the times, which seem to extol the inhibition of artistic curiosity? Either way, there seems no hiding from the fact that a great many supposedly grown-up people do not seem to see reading as a particularly essential pastime. Or do they? Someone must be buying the 50,000 titles reputedly published each year. Has the age of high-technology entertainment really brought about The Death of the Book? Or is there a new hunger for literature, for art, for that lost childlike appetite for the intimate disclosures of the written word?

My own voluntary reading habits probably started at the age of six when the knockabout antics of Dennis the Menace, the Bash Street Kids, Desperate Dan and the other principals of kids' comics were required fare among Jamboree Lucky Bags, home-made catapults, days at the seaside and all the other requisites of one's out-of-school life. Decades later these characters remain impressively durable, having undergone only the most minor physical transformations, and they are still capable of amusing children of all ages with their insatiable pursuits of 'grub' and mischief. 'Roll up! Roll up! More fun on the back page, pals!' exhorts Dennis on the cover of my own son's latest copy of *The Beano*. 'Gnash! Gnash!' goes the Menace's dog Gnasher, rounding up yet another bunch of softies for a bit of teasing.

For many children growing up in the 1960s more formal reading matter often took the form of the ubiquitous novels of Enid Blyton. Looking back one cannot remember having sensed anything objectionable about the perfect organization of the worlds of the Secret Seven and the Famous Five – here were secret rituals, intriguing mysteries, satisfying denouements – though now one must wonder about the white male authority suffused in the tales, the idyllically secure middle-class lives, the moral certainties as dated now as Bakelite and ration books. Perhaps it did all seem a little too perfect for someone growing up on a West Riding council estate, and maybe secretly one felt a little sympathy for the villains who spoke out of the sides of their mouths, living in mortal terror of the police and in utter deference to the English property-owning classes. Good stories, though.

At the time, our parents were doing rather better, with the age of northern realism reaching its peak through novels such as Stan Barstow's *A Kind of Loving*, John Braine's *Room at the Top*, and from the Midlands Alan Sillitoe's *Saturday*

Night and Sunday Morning. Here were the voices of young, obdurate, working-class men who were not going to take the values of the old generation lying down. They were the angry ones who wanted what was on offer for their more socially advantaged counterparts. And, outrageously, they were going to get it.

Someone else who was not going to accept the life mapped out for him was Billy Casper, the estate-scampering hero of Barry Hines's 1968 novel, *A Kestrel for a Knave* (*Kes*). At odds with a hard and unforgiving social landscape, Billy knew one thing for sure – that he was not going to work 'down t'pit' under any circumstances. To this day, I have yet to discover a more trenchant literary evocation of the time and place of my youth than that offered by Hines's memorable book.

I was to discover all these novels a few years after my parents, both indefatigable readers, had enrolled me at a new library which had been built at Sherburn-in-Elmet, a village just a mile or so from where we lived. There I found all the classics, *Treasure Island, Black Beauty, Robinson Crusoe,* virtually all of Dickens, and I went on to develop a precocious interest in Greek and Norse mythology. James Thurber was another great favourite. And I could get two books a week, four if my sister lent me her ticket.

In later years though, I was to fall foul of the Eng. Lit. school of learning, avoiding O level failure with the lowest possible grade. A seasoned window-watcher, I yawned over the deconstruction of Browning and was alienated, for life it seems, from Shakespeare. However, the fiction put before us did inspire some interest: Harper

Lee's *To Kill a Mockingbird*, Laurie Lee's *Cider with Rosie*, and Golding's powerful allegories *Lord of the Flies* and *The Spire*. My private interest in reading continued to flourish with Somerset Maugham – *The Moon and Sixpence* and *The Summing Up* being remembered as particularly gratifying – and the writings of D. H. Lawrence and H. E. Bates, both of whom seemed to appeal to the sensibilities of adolescence.

The fag-end of the 1960s cultural movement led me to Timothy Leary's *The Politics of Ecstasy* and Richard Neville's *Play Power* and some extraordinary messages were being received in the council house garret: 'What to Do When the Vietcong Drop LSD in Our Water Supply.' 'Drop Out. Turn On. Tune In.' 'Man's right to work is the right to be bored for most of his natural life.' 'Fuck the system.' And one really did try to understand the noisy anarchy that both these writers were advocating, though ultimately all I could hear were the voices of spoilt kids railing with a scarcely believable anger against their parents' material and forgivable moral achievements. In my own warm and good-humoured community all of this had a rather hollow ring. I read the books, discarded their ideas, quit school and found a job.

At the age of eighteen I spent my days selling furniture for Habitat and my nights reading Sartre, Mann, Kafka and contemporaries such as Anthony Burgess (*A Clockwork Orange* – reread seven times), Edna O'Brien (*The Love Object*, *A Scandalous Woman*) and Roger McGough (*Watchwords*, *In the Glassroom*, et al.). The Leary book had also prompted an interest in Hermann Hesse, though I made the mistake that this author always warned against by being too young to appreciate the nature of Harry Haller's alienation in *Steppenwolf*, and I came to discount any relevance Hesse's work might have in my own life. Kafka's glacial prose however, especially that of *The Trial*, looks likely to haunt me for the rest of my days. Timeless and inimitable, the nightmare visions of *Metamorphosis*, *The Castle* and, well, all that he wrote, simply refuse to go away, abiding ever in the margins of one's conscious perceptions, as deep and as troubling as the beast that threatens the sanctuary of *The Burrow*.

By the same token, Samuel Beckett's trilogy *Molloy*, *Malone Dies* and *The Unnamable* contains voices which howl against silence; darkly, paroxysmally, in floods of words, contemplating yet never quite explaining the insult of mortality. In *Waiting for Godot*, the two tramps are suspended for eternity. 'Well? Shall we go?' asks Vladimir at the end. 'Yes, let's go,' says Estragon. *They do not move.*

Those who embark on the madcap adventure of trying to create new literature would probably do well to forget the seminal achievements of Beckett and Kafka – nothing can be more intimidating than turning from, say, the second half of *Molloy*, or *In the Penal Settlement*, to a blank page of one's own. That I tried, unsuccessfully, to capture something of both Kafka and Beckett's power in my own first novel *The Comforts of Madness* is testimony more to my own naivety than to my literary convictions. Others who have worked more saliently under these influences include Patrick Süskind – *The Pigeon* and *The Double Bass* – and, closer to home, James Kelman. This latter author seems to have performed one of the most remarkable feats in modern writing by imbuing a specific landscape, Glasgow, with Beckett's universal perspectives. Through such novels as *A Chancer* and *A Disaffection*, and with some brilliant linguistic cameos in the collections of short stories *Not Not While the Giro* and *Greyhound for Breakfast*, Kelman rages and inspires, glancing thunderbolts against Thatcher's Britain, laying bare the blandness and injustices of the 1980s. All of Kelman's work possesses the hallmark of great writing in that it stands up to being read again and again.

I had thought for a long time that the aforementioned age of northern realism had passed, though Pat Barker, with her novels *Union Street* and *Blow Your House Down*, was to prove me wrong. Stylish and uncompromising, this underrated novelist chronicles the lot of working-class women in the north-east and it is to her credit that she does so without a trace of sentiment or moral judgement.

Both Kelman and Barker are recent discoveries. On my way to them I had read a long list of contemporary novels which includes Salman Rushdie's *Midnight's Children* and *Shame*, J. M. Coetzee's *Waiting for the Barbarians*, Anita Brookner's first five elegant offerings, and from earlier times, Solzhenitsyn's *A Day in the Life of Ivan Denisovich* and *Cancer Ward*, Sylvia Plath's *The Bell Jar*, Norman Mailer's *The Executioner's Song* (a book which reaffirmed for life my abhorrence of capital punishment – proof, if any were needed, of the political power of the written word) and probably a thousand others. Some were bad, but hardly any failed to nourish the imagination in one way or another.

They say that when you look back on your life you only remember the good times. Reviewing one's reading history you recall the moments of revelation, of the sublime first paragraph of Hemingway's short story 'In Another Country', of the 'fatal consequence' of Humbert Humbert's first sight of his nymphet in *Lolita*, of the dreamworld of Anna Kavan in *Sleep Has His House*, and of the waking from a psychotic odyssey described by Barbara O'Brien in her lamentably forgotten book *Operators and Things*. And in modern times one must consider the almost unbearably precise prose of Ian McEwan who, with the novels *The Cement Garden*, *The Comfort of Strangers*, *The Child in Time* and *The Innocent*, in addition to his two collections of short stories, *First Love, Last Rites*, and *In Between the Sheets* (I make no apology for listing them all), has proven himself one of those rare jewels: a storyteller who can rise above mere subject matter to produce chillingly durable works of art.

Alongside these cornerstones of modern literature one will, of course, also find ephemera, and students of the untrustworthy science of horse-racing form will doubtless be aware of the allure of the publications of the Timeform organization. Their weekly *Black Books*, with their plain covers suggesting ruggedly concealed 'inside' information about every horse in training, might have a near-mystical appeal for the impecunious and the foolhardy. Here are fairy tales, mysteries, tragedies – the stuff of dreams and seduction. One alights on these books with boundless optimism, all too willing to be charmed by their suggestions, to abandon what common sense one might possess in the pursuit of adventure and profit. The peruser of this and, for that matter, any kind of book is looking for something amongst the words on the page, ready to be informed and entertained. As readers, they become innocent again. And it has been one of the happiest discoveries of my closeted writing life to find that they, readers of all ages, are out there in their millions.

My favourite books

(In alphabetical order): *Blow Your House Down*, Pat Barker; *The Beckett Trilogy*, Samuel Beckett; *Waiting for the Barbarians*, J. M. Coetzee; *A Kestrel for a Knave*, Barry Hines; *The Trial*, Franz Kafka; *Not Not While the Giro*, James Kelman; *The Executioner's Song*, Norman Mailer; *The Cement Garden*, Ian McEwan; *Operators and Things*, Barbara O'Brien; *Timeform Black Book No 19*, 26 Feb 1978/79.

Candia McWilliam

M<small>Y</small> first reading was of course not *mine*. My father is the first person I remember reading to me. Often he smoked at the same time, Senior Service, and he would sometimes be so taken up with the wickedness of Samuel Whiskers or the venal charm of the cat, Simpkin, in Beatrix Potter's *The Tailor of Gloucester* that he burnt his fingers, or, if I was on his knee, my nightdress. These were always slow-burning; my mother bought them at a junk-shop called Mrs Virtue's, famous in Edinburgh in those days. My mother told stories rather than reading them; she could draw illustrations as she went along, using those blocks of paper which are glued together on all four sides and have to be separated with a knife.

When wishing me not to understand what they said, my parents spoke Italian, partly because of attachment to the country and partly because they sent me to the Institut Français when I was very small, so perhaps they thought I might understand if they used French for *pas devant* chat. My French books included the radiant lithographic *Père*

Castor books about animals behaving as animals do, and a nice one about a seal called Jonathan who shoplifted a seabass. My parents' feeling for Italy also influenced the picture books they gave me. I remember two large flat ones published by OUP and written and drawn, I think, by Bettina Ehrlich, called *Carmello* and *Pantaloni*, whose washy yet spot-on illustrations whetted my appetite for Italy – full of amphorae and baskets of fish and pots of flowers.

The *This Is . . .* books by M. Sasek were my introductions, with their wedgy, witty drawings, to the architecture of Paris, New York, Rome and Venice. These idiosyncratic books are not whimsical or patronizing. To a grown-up, I find on returning to them, they are as helpful as to a child. At this time, perhaps my favourite book was a red cloth-bound book by Ana Berry, published in the war. It was called *Art for Children*. It reproduced some well-known and some more obscure paintings, many in black and white, with captions which encouraged prolonged looking. Such books now are tentative, attempting to predigest for small readers. As *Lamb's Tales from Shakespeare*, which I later read and disliked, show, this is not a good idea. I learnt more about human nature from the *Golliwog* books by Bertha Upton. I couldn't stick *Little Grey Rabbit*. Roll on Big Red Myxomatosis.

I had each parent's childhood books from the age I left my cot for a bed you could get out of without climbing. These ranged from cigarette-card albums of the kings and queens of England, through the usuals like *The Water-Babies*, Edward Lear, *Peter Pan in Kensington Gardens* (in my

Edinburgh childhood I thought London a lot more exotic than Never-Never Land), Andrew Lang's *Fairy Books*, and *Kidnapped*. These books – perhaps sixty of them – smelt of cupboards in other houses. Sometimes they yielded shocking booty, a flower pressed by my mother, a bit of writing by my father before he had handwriting. A favourite was *Holiday House*, by an Edinburgh author, Catherine Sinclair, about the rewards of naughtiness. It had a brother and sister, and I was intrigued by those.

The two most indefatigable readers aloud were my paternal grandmother, who read me *Villette* when I was in bed with mumps, and, throughout my childhood, the professor of fine art and Bellini scholar Giles Robertson, who would read to his five children and me the works of Juliana Horatia Ewing. My favourite, for the satisfyingly frequent deaths, was *A Flat Iron for a Farthing*. He read incredibly fast. His children laughed in the right places, but I had to go and read the books for myself. The other great triple-decker, Frances Hodgson Burnett, I encountered first in a double bill, *Sara Crewe* (or: *What Happened at Miss Minchin's*, or: *A Little Princess*) and *Editha's Burglar*. The illustrations were as wonderful to a little girl as Helleus are to a woman – idealized, elegant, just a bit meretricious.

When I was six, my mother began to read E. V. Rieu's translations of the *Iliad* and the *Odyssey*, in the brown and white Penguin. She was useless to talk to at this time. I thought that Homer, the Odyssey was some sort of creature (Caspar the Friendly Ghost, Puff the Magic Dragon) and picked it up. For years after that I was obsessed. I have always talked in my sleep. For those years I would shout

'Odysseus' from time to time. *The Tanglewood Tales* by Nathaniel Hawthorne kept me topped up with the stories of Philemon and Baucis, The Dragon's Teeth, Pandora, the Argonauts and so on. I was besotted, making charts of gods and heroes and their habits, forcing my friends to play a long invented game called 'Siesta Time on Mount Olympus' which involved wrapping up in bedspreads and behaving in character, with much calling for stuffed owls and Hesperidean apples from any parents unlucky enough to be about.

School helped to jostle some of this only-childishness out of me, although my greatest friend, from a large family, had a similar cult on Asgard and we evolved a RomanoGraecoNordic combination of Asgard and Olympus. Her favourite reading was the books of Alan Garner, George Macdonald and E. Nesbit (her family were prolific academic socialists). Later when she took to Tolkien, I could stand it no more, and sheered off towards all sorts of romance, from *Jane Eyre* and *Rebecca* to *Jackie*, a comic whose draughtsmanship arrested my own for ever after countless evenings mimicking its lemur-faced girls and chiselled romantic leads. Muriel Spark arrived in my stocking one Christmas and never departed. I got an itch, predictably, for Huxley, which I wiped out with Waugh. Angus Wilson's short stories bewitched me, good on glitter and on drabness. I kept trying the Bible from start to finish but I skipped.

Before that adolescent separation in taste, though, my friend Harriet had introduced me to Laura Ingalls Wilder's *Little House on the Prairie* books and to *The Cricket in Times*

Square by George Selden, and I got a sense of America's other language, apart from the one we shared. A timid, untravelled Scots child, I had much imagination and little sense of adventure, for I was not physically competent or brave. A fit of reading Arthur Ransome followed by John Buchan and – suddenly, by mistake – P. G. Wodehouse at once made my reading a little less overwhelmingly feminine and attuned my ear to an accent I was not conscious of having heard before, and which I found funny – the accent of the English upper middle class. I became intrigued by voices and began to see the virtue in differences.

Around the age of nine I took up death and poetry. Once or twice a year I would receive a book-token for a pound. This meant eight paperbacks or a lot more books from the second-hand bookshops where I used to hang about at weekends, if I could trade it with my father for cash. I also went through a patch of entering calligraphy competitions and religious essay contests, whose prize – always a book – one might choose. Having decided, defying my innumeracy, that I was going to be a doctor, I requested such tomes as *The Discovery of Nature*, a history of the life sciences, richly published by Thames and Hudson. But I was compelled at this morbid age by Defoe's *Journal of the Plague Year*, on whose – American paperback – cover a pair of burning eyes stared from a sort of rose and khaki chador. Perhaps to redress the balance, my father gave me the *buffo* masterpiece of Harrison Ainsworth, *Old St Paul's*, which combines overwriting, melodrama, history, villainy and unwitting jokes with things you cannot forget. It prints on the mind the burning of the first St Paul's as its second burning must be fixed in the memories of those who were in the Blitz.

Poetry was a natural consequence of liking words very young. I picked them up and rolled them about. We had two enormous broken morocco books called *Animated Nature*. From the age of three these were my treat. Detailed, scenic, unconsciously humorous engravings showed innumerable beasts in imaginative versions of their habitat. The bewitching Latin names curled beneath these and the more diagrammatic *figs*, of dissections. I remember jumping over my skipping rope hundreds of times chanting the formal names of improbable animals, cities, flowers, bones (the 'olecranon process' was my favourite aged five, because I broke it). After nursery rhymes, it was Stevenson's *Child's Garden of Verses* and Walter de la Mare, but eventually the *Dragon Book* pushed me into reading individual poets. The first I picked on were the usual strong flavours, Kipling, Drinkwater, Hopkins, Blake. I wrote poems out again and again and learned them off by heart. I have forgotten most, but Tennyson, Dorothy Parker and Helen Waddell's translations from the silver Latin stick, hardly helpfully. From the age of ten, I lived in the public library. It was next to a huge laundry, so one could return smelling quite respectably of chlorine, as though one had been to the swimming baths.

My favourite comic strip was *The Broons*, about a family of ten living in a tenement. Their name, for English readers, was Brown. It still appears in *The Sunday Post*. My first illicit reading was the pretty, illustrated *Fanny Hill* by John Cleland, which I cannot remember being kept from me.

The absence of censorship at home could have fall-out. The first day at kindergarten, my mother, who was tall and arresting, brought along a wee book she thought my teacher might enjoy. It was *Lady Loverly's Chatter*, a satire in photographs of Lady Chatterley. This was 1959. For all her headscarf and her cigarettes, she was an innocent.

Buying books for my children now, I see visual plenty and some publishing heroes, but a curious gap for voracious readers who will apparently be thrown straight on to the classics or on to mildly souped-up stories about problems with the other sex. I am disconcerted to find this already happening to my six-year-old daughter, but all my children enjoy the picture books I've mentioned, the very same ones. They are, as I was, both pleased and embarrassed to find in them traces that their mother was once a child.

My favourite books

Antony and Cleopatra, William Shakespeare; *Anna Karenina*, Leo Tolstoy; *Middlemarch*, George Eliot; *The Golden Bowl*, Henry James; *Stendhal on Love;The Lives of the Poets*, Samuel Johnson; *Don Juan,* Lord Byron; *Madame Bovary,* Gustave Flaubert; *The Dunciad*, Alexander Pope; *The Stones of Venice,* John Ruskin; *Bleak House,* Charles Dickens; *Religio Medici,* Sir Thomas Browne; *Epistles,* Horace.

Rana Kabbani

WHEN I think of books, I am plunged back into my Damascus childhood and into a world of people who had never been taught how to read. The mountain girl who brought me up, who rolled out the dough for paper-thin *börek*, who dipped a comb in water the better to plait my hair, had never been anywhere near a classroom. In the hungry village she came from, only a handful of boys were lettered, and these had to trek the daily three miles to reach the nearest school.

I can still see our neighbour from the floor above, clattering down the stone staircase in her high-heeled slippers, clutching an airmail letter from a cousin who had long ago made the desperate journey to Brazil. Written in an old-fashioned hand in rose-syrup style, it was read for her by my grandmother.

Of my two grandmothers, only one could read, and it was with her that we lived. This accomplishment marked her out as a lady of wisdom and people sought her advice on all sorts of matters, believing that her access to books gave her powers denied less fortunate souls. She had had an Ottoman education, and her framed Baccalauréat from Istanbul was given pride of place on the sitting-room wall. She read in Arabic, but enjoyed Turkish as well, until that sad day in 1929 when her favourite newspapers arrived in the new Latin script ordained by Kemal Atatürk – which she could not read. She, who had taken such pride in her knowledge of Turkish, now found that this window had closed. The Ottoman era was no more.

My other, illiterate, grandmother would beam with pride when we spread out our homework on her kitchen table, and formed the curvy lines of the Arabic script that would remain mysterious to her. When phones were installed, she found herself unable to work the talking machine unless one of her children was there to dial the number for her.

The world I was raised in was a female one which retained the harem spirit. Three generations of women lived in the house. Together with their relatives, neighbours and friends, they created an intricate society very much preoccupied with 'at home' days and formal visiting. In an age before ready-made foods and electric machines, a great deal of time was spent on domestic chores. Jam was made in huge quantities, enough to last the year. Meat was pickled, as were vegetables, garlic braided, okra threaded into long necklaces which were then put out to dry. Each house made its daily yoghurt and its cheese. The women were forever unstitching mattresses, washing the fleece, combing it out and letting it dry in the sun. Whites had to be boiled in lye and starched by hand. There was no time to read, even if one could! And maybe the need wasn't there, for the women were constantly telling each other stories, and their lives were so strange as to make fiction pale. Banished from rooms where the family sat, our books were kept in a long, narrow corridor, because books gathered dust and dust was a domestic calamity.

As a child, I was so marked by the powerful women I loved that, when I came to read books, I was attracted by those that spoke in female tones. I don't claim to have made the division then, but I was instinctively aware that there was a cruelty in the male voice that repelled me – authoritative, depressive, focused on degradation and punishment. Balzac, Dostoyevsky, Richardson left me cold. I was drawn, I remember, to the literature of the American south which was written by women, perhaps because I saw in the ante-bellum world a mirror image of my own. Carson McCullers was a favourite writer for years. I felt that she too had been offered pistachio nougat from the Grace Kelly handbags of the men-hungry elderly cousins who flitted in and out of our rooms.

As I began reading, life seemed to separate into the life in books and that of the street where the daily sight was of people's hardship: the man who did invisible mending in his hole in the wall, the carpenter's son who had mangled his fingers in a newfangled factory machine, the seamstress whose husband had left her when her children were small. Books provided a means of escape from such pain. In a society where privacy was unheard of and where people retired to their rooms only if they felt very ill, reading was a perfect pretext for solitude. Books seemed to raise one above the mundane, above the chit-chat of the nightly gatherings, or so one little prig liked to think.

In a house where three languages were spoken – Turkish, Arabic and French – English, which no one around me spoke, became my private tongue. It gained me entry into other scenes of domestic life, but also into places untamed by domesticity of any kind. So taken was I by English that I rebelled against reading for pleasure in either Arabic or French, the languages of the classroom. I fled from Chateaubriand exulting the Crusades, and from Victor Hugo lamenting in alexandrines, to explore the heath and the moors.

What made me love English literature so much was the fact that I read as I pleased, bound by no syllabus, and certainly not one designed to instil in natives unbounded respect for Shakespeare's 'scepter'd isle'. I read good books and all sorts of other ones, including a four years' hoard of the *Reader's Digest* stored in our attic next to the jars of olives in brine. *Jane Eyre* was the first English book I read. I was nine, and the experience affected me so much that I was ill with a fever for days, only recovering when my mother took the book out of the room and hid it, breaking its spell over me.

In the heat of our sitting room during the siesta hour, I read about wintry Yorkshire, which for me was as exotic as Araby had been to any English dreamer. Its every detail intrigued me; I would gladly have exchanged my lunch of chicken pilaff for Lowood's thinnest gruel. When I came to England twelve years later, it was as if I had made the journey before.

Books fired in me other expectations, this time of an emotional nature. In the Damascus of my adolescence, it was unusual, even something of a scandal, for a girl to marry for love. This wasn't because parents imposed their own choices, but because the girls themselves preferred Count Paris to Romeo, found it natural to opt for security and respectability rather than the shifting sands of passion. Every other day in my classroom, a girl would arrive with the photographs of her engagement party which everyone, including the teacher, would admire. On that day the lucky bride-to-be would be allowed to come to school with varnished nails, the better to show off the ring, and her hair in a chignon, rather than the usual plait. 'But do you love him?' I would be the only one to ask, to be met with a horrified look, and the retort: 'He's a mechanical engineer!' My emotional expectations were clearly at odds with those of most of my classmates.

My problem was that, at a very early age, I started reading books which described passionate or tragic relationships between men and women, and these turbulent narratives inevitably created a storm inside me. The men I was attracted to were a heady combination of Heathcliff, Baudelaire and Cyrano de Bergerac, crossed with Malcolm X. In retrospect and somewhat ruefully, I recognize that books shaped the sort of love I craved, and determined the marriages I made. I hold the Brontë sisters wholly responsible! Two other girls of my year were, rather like me, unable to make conventional marriages because their emotions had been perverted by novels.

The male–female tug-of-war that books embroiled me in is still being played out. The crude feminism of my early womanhood has not mellowed much; there are few male writers I enjoy unreservedly: Sainte-Beuve is one of them, Márquez is another. The writers I still cannot stomach are the two Lawrences, D. H. and Tee Hee. They belong in the Sea of Offal in which swim the Bully-Boys, the Misogynists, the Pornographers, the Structuralists, the Frauds and the Uncle Toms. I still am determined to think that some writing *is* perfidious and dangerous, even if it is, at any one time, the writing which is most highly lauded, most fêted, and most popular. Ultimately, it belongs in what a Nicaraguan poet recently called the 'latrines of history'.

When I'm feeling low, tired or ill, I find that the best remedy is to curl up with a well-written cookbook, preferably one which dwells on the history of cooking, or with a book of old photographs recalling my grandmother's era. But, at the end of the day, the books I value most are those that speak with compassion, encouraging one to believe that the human condition is surmountable, despite all the evidence.

My favourite books

Charlotte Brontë, *Jane Eyre*; Emily Brontë, *Wuthering Heights*; Carson McCullers, *The Ballad of the Sad Café*; The *Letters* of Emily Dickinson; Colette, *La Vagabonde*; James Baldwin, *Giovanni's Room*; Kobo Abé, *The Woman in the Dunes*; Nikos Kazantzakis, *The Rock Garden*; Adrienne Rich, *The Dream of a Common Language*; Arthur Miller, *After the Fall*.

Jeanette Winterson

MY mother taught me to read from the Book of Deuteronomy because it is full of animals (mostly unclean). Whenever we read 'Thou shall not eat any beast that does not chew the cud or part the hoof' she drew the creature. Horses, bunnies and little ducks were vague fabulous things but I knew all about pelicans, rock badgers, sloths and bats. This tendency towards the exotic has brought me many problems, just as it did for William Blake. My mother drew winged insects and the birds of the air, but my favourite ones were the seabed ones, the molluscs. I had a fine collection from the beach at Blackpool. She had a blue pen for the waves and brown ink for the scaly-backed crab. Lobsters were red biro. She never drew shrimps though, because she liked to eat them in a muffin. I think it had troubled her for a long time. Finally, after much prayer and some consultation with a great Man of the Lord in Shrewsbury, she agreed with St Paul that what God had cleansed we must not call common. After that we went to Molly's Seafoods every Saturday. Deuteronomy had its drawback; it is full of Abominations and Unmentionables. Whenever we read about a bastard or someone with crushed testicles, my mother turned over the page and said 'Leave that to the Lord'. When she'd gone I'd sneak a look. I was glad I didn't have testicles. They sounded like intestines, only on the outside, and the men in the Bible were always having them cut off and not being able to go to church. Horrid.

Oranges are not the only Fruit

I grew up not knowing that language was for everyday purposes. I grew up with the Word and the Word was God. Now, many years after a most secular reformation, I still see language as something holy.

My parents owned six books between them. Two of these were Bibles, the third was Cruden's *Complete Concordance to the Old and New Testaments*, the fourth, *The House at Pooh Corner*, the fifth, *The Chatterbox Annual* 1923, and the sixth, Malory's *Morte d'Arthur*. I was allowed free run of their library when I had learned my first important lesson: Not To Tear. This was achieved by sitting me in my pram with a mail order thermal underwear catalogue. Every time I ripped up a woolly vest or ladies' one-piece, the catalogue was taken away. I could of course have grown up to be a pervert and not a writer. The sad thing is that my parents have never worked out the difference.

I cannot over-emphasize the importance of an outside toilet when there is no room of one's own. It was on the lavatory that I first read Freud and D. H. Lawrence and perhaps, after all, it was the right place. We kept a rubber torch hung on the cistern and I had to juggle my Saturday job money between buying forbidden books and new batteries. It was fairly easy to smuggle books in and out of the house; what was difficult was finding somewhere to keep them. I opted for under the mattress, and anyone with a single bed, standard size, and paperbacks, standard size, will discover that seventy-seven can be comfortably accommodated. But as my collection grew, I began to worry that my mother might notice that her daughter's bed was rising visibly. One day she did. She burned everything.

Not everything. I had already started to shift my hoard to a friend's house and so I still have some of those books, carefully covered in plastic, none of their spines broken.

I discovered a new ruse. I was given a job at the public library which my mother approved of because a) she reckoned that I couldn't read and work at the same time, and b) it meant that she could have unlimited numbers of large-print mysteries. I think too that she hoped that simply being around books would cure me of my obsession for them, rather in the way that retired astronauts are advised to lie and look at the stars. In practice, I went to the library even when I wasn't working, and sat uninterrupted in the reading room under a stained-glass window bearing the legend 'Industry and Prudence Conquer'. I should say too that weekly sackfuls of Ellery Queen seemed to have a sedative effect on my mother. My father continued with the *Beano*. At the library, dutifully stamping out wave upon wave of sea stories, and the battered blossoms of Mills and Boon, I recognized what I had known dimly: that plot was meaningless to me. This was a difficult admission for one whose body was tattooed with Bible stories, but it was necessary for me to accept that my love affair was with language, not with what it said. Art communicates, that is certain. What it communicates, if it's genuine, is something ineffable. Something about ourselves, about the human condition, that is not summed up by the oil painting, or the piece of music, or the poem, but, rather, moves through it. What you say, what you paint, what you can hear is the means not the end of art; there are so many rooms behind.

Freed, then, from the gross weight of how to get from A to B, I came across Gertrude Stein in the humour section. I still don't know why she had been branded with a purple giggle-strip and heaped unalphabetically alongside the usual pile of boys' bad jokes, but I took her away and found a different kind of coherence. At the level of theory rather than practice, she more than any other writer has taught me to think about how language is constructed. Whatever anyone feels about her style and her fiction, she has, in her essays and investigations, left us with an invaluable toolkit. I dismantled a lot of my assumptions about both reading and writing because of her, and most of them weren't worth putting back together again.

I returned Gertrude Stein, to her rightful place under S in the literature section, and was about to embark on two years of undisturbed poetry, when I was disturbed, by my mother, in the public library reading room. She had found me out and come to have a showdown by the photocopier.

'The trouble with books,' she said, 'is that you don't know what's in them until it's too late.' I confronted her with her own taste in murder mysteries and received the reply that if you know there's a body coming, it isn't a shock. So much for plot. However, this didn't help my position: my mother knew that books would lead me astray, and she was right. A short time later I left home and never went back. I didn't take anything with me; the things I loved had already gone.

For some, perhaps for many, books are spare time. For me, the rest of life is spare time: I wake and sleep language. It has always been so. When I was supporting myself by working evenings and weekends, so that I could stay at school, I fought off loneliness and fear by reciting. I had been brought up to memorize very long Bible passages and so memorizing anything is not difficult for me. This was my two years alone with the poets. In the funeral parlour I whispered Donne to the embalming fluids, and later, when I had stopped making up corpses and was working in a mental hospital, I found that Tennyson's 'The Lady of Shalott' was very comforting to the disturbed. Among the disturbed I numbered myself at that time.

I have never been able to give up what I love in return for a quiet life. I didn't notice any hardship in those early years, and although I was exhausted most of the time, I felt, too, the exuberance of a lover when I came back to my tiny borrowed room and there were my books. It seems to me that the limitless world of the imagination is just as crucial as the walled world of the everyday. Inside books there is perfect space and it is that space which allows the reader to deal with the normal problems of gravity. When I talk about books in this way, I'm not talking about the second-rate or the fake. There are plenty of those and bothering with them at all is like eating your meals at McDonald's. If you are surviving on books you soon learn what is and isn't nourishing. I didn't fight to read in order to be slowly poisoned. There is still no room in my life for whatever does not enhance it. I would rather concentrate on the highest, however difficult or challenging, than waste time with the mediocre. I would rather sit quietly and think than pick up a book that reveals nothing.

In 1978 I packed all of my wordly goods into the back of my Morris Minor post office van and drove to Oxford. For the first few weeks I could not rid myself of the suspicion that I had been dropped into the middle of a practical joke. Not only did everyone want to read books, they were expected to do so. They were paid to do so. Did I really not have to prepare for my tutorial in the toilet? If I put my books out on the shelves would they still be there the next day? Whenever someone knocked on my door, I leapt up and stuffed my novel under the pillow. Ridiculous? Yes, but even now I don't keep books in the bathroom because I adore the luxury of just being able to pee.

These days I read in blocks. I choose a writer and read everything over a period of weeks or months. And then, over a further period of weeks or months, I don't read anything. This space allows me to be properly affected by the work and it ensures that I know what I think. I always memorize passages, partly so that I can use them as a measure of experience, but probably because I shall never be altogether convinced that the books will always be on the shelves for me to read. Who knows where the world will take us? If I could only take one thing away with me, or if I was on that ubiquitous desert island, I would choose T. S. Eliot's *Four Quartets*. I read that poem over and over again during the autumn and there is always more to be gleaned from it. It is riches and beauty; there is nothing that it does not say.

I don't have a great many books because there aren't a great many books worth having. I suppose my own library tends to stabilize at around a thousand volumes. Publishers are always sending me jiffy bags full of dross, but fortunately I live near a charity shop. I'm always on the lookout for new things, but I'm usually disappointed. It doesn't matter; whatever's genuine can be read over and over again and the odd thing is that it's not the same book. Art seems to multiply within itself.

My mother and father still have their Bibles, but I have inherited their other four volumes and a music stand with a clamp welded to the bottom so that my mother could fix it on her ironing board and still read the Word of the Lord.

There was a seventh book but I don't know whose it was. It lived in the tallboy under a pile of towels and was further concealed by occupying the cardboard false bottom of a set of bathsalts. It was a 1950s sex manual called *How to Please Your Husband*. I read it and decided that I'd have a lot more fun in the library.

My favourite books (at the moment)

Four Quartets, T. S. Eliot; *Jacob's Room*, Virginia Woolf; *The Prelude*, William Wordsworth; *Wuthering Heights*, Emily Brontë; *Look at me now/Here I am*, Gertrude Stein; *The Consolation of Philosophy*, Boethius; *Collected Poems*, Robert Graves; *Poems*, Elizabeth Bishop; *Invisible Cities*, Italo Calvino; *Collected Poems*, Adrienne Rich.

I don't like lists. They lie.

Kamila Shamsie

I T started with a bear, and a boy in search of his shadow. Winnie-the-Pooh and Peter Pan were the twin companions of my earliest memories (an animal and a child – this has a certain symmetry; in my un-reading life, the primary companions of those days were an Alsatian called Dusty, and my sister). Of the two, it was Peter who lodged himself most deeply in my heart, making me dream of adventurers who would dart in through the open window at night and fly me away to Neverland. In the world of J. M. Barrie parents are understandably wary of Peter and his home 'second to the right and straight on to morning' but in my world it was my mother who pointed out to me that Neverland was just off the coast of Karachi, located on a series of small islets, known as Oyster Rocks by the unknowing; that two of the islets looked like granite sentinels made her claim seem all the more plausible. So although Peter might fly into rooms in London he ended up just off the coast on which I lived; a comforting thought. The only problem with the world of Peter was that girls – or rather, the one girl – was relegated to darning socks and playing mother, but I was happy for my imagination to extend beyond Barrie's and find possibilities for myself other than those of Wendy (who was clearly 'a girly girl' and therefore deserved nothing better than unravelling socks).

It was a few years later that I ran into the most damned of the girly girls, within the world of C. S. Lewis's Narnia. In *The Lion, the Witch and the Wardrobe* and *Prince Caspian* Susan is companion and foil to her younger sister, her role more essential to the family dynamic than that of the oldest brother Peter, but in the last novel of the series, *The Last Battle*, we learn that she is exiled for ever from the world of Narnia because of her interest in lipstick (I may be paraphrasing slightly, but that's the gist). At the age of thirty or so, I confessed to the novelist Michel Faber that when I was eleven and my sister thirteen I called her 'Susan' for daring to grow into an adolescence that I had yet to reach or understand. Did you ever apologize? Michel asked. No, I said, having given it little thought over the years. But you must, he said; it's a terrible thing to have said. It was more in a spirit of amusement at his insistence than from any belief that my sister needed to hear an apology from me two decades later that I offered up my regrets for having Susanned her. It turned out Michel was right. It's the worst thing you've ever said to me, my sister said, and thanked me for the apology.

At eight or nine, I didn't yet see anything problematic about Susan's lipstick exile, though I did have enough sense of how far I was from C. S. Lewis's view of the world to be discomfited by that other Narnia book, *The Horse and His Boy*, in which the villains are dark-skinned people with beards and turbans. But I was far more put out on discovering that the entire Narnia series was an allegory for Christianity and Aslan wasn't a lion, but Christ. My objection, I should say, was not to Christ himself, who I held in high regard, but to the un-lioning of Aslan. I remember very clearly the moment of this discovery – standing in the school library, having pulled a book out of the shelf because it had C. S. Lewis's name in the title. And then, the horror, the horror. I had two choices at that moment. I could decide that the novels I loved so much that my best friend and I liked nothing better than to play imaginative games set in Narnia were not what I thought they were at all; or I could decide that if other people wanted to see Aslan as Christ they were very welcome to do so, but that was no reason for me to disrupt my relationship with the great lion. It really wasn't any kind of choice at all.

When I've had cause to discuss these early books of my childhood, I too often dwell on the lipstick, the turbaned villain, the allegories of Christ in order to talk about the distance between my life in Karachi and those books. This dwelling is always precursor to discussing the enormous sense of exhilaration with which I entered the world of adult reading in adolescence and encountered *Midnight's Children*, in which the English-language novel and the world around me came together in a great starburst of imagination and humour, and made it possible to imagine a space for myself as writer within the changing world of

Anglophone fiction. Prior to that, I simply hadn't known that Karachi could be a location for a novel in English.

But in the process of paying rightful homage to *Midnight's Children* I betrayed my earliest loves. Peter and Aslan and all the characters around them taught me to dream and to imagine. The lipstick and the darned socks were minor notes of discordance, hardly worth my attention amidst the wardrobes that open into a world of eternal winter or the boy whose shadow runs away from him. In the Karachi of my childhood, where we had one state-run television channel and a sheltered life which rarely extended beyond the school yard and private homes, I walked through that wardrobe, flew to Neverland with the boy and his shadow. And in doing so I learnt that novels reach further than their own writers' imagination. *Who do you write for?* I am often asked, the question framed in terms of nation or ethnicity. My own childhood reading makes me impatient of such questions. C. S. Lewis is unlikely to have 'written for' a girl in Karachi, but that doesn't mean any boy in London grew up with a greater claim on Aslan than I did. There were things I didn't understand, of course – *What was Turkish delight to begin with? Why did all the children drink tea, which was clearly a boring beverage for grown-ups?* – but I was happy to read around what I didn't understand, sometimes accepting other rules of living, other times inventing my own explanations. Finding ways of contending with the mystification was as much a part of the joy of reading as was entering fictional worlds and changing their rules (I refer you back to girls and the darning of socks). It is a great gift to a writer, this early knowledge that there will always be people who don't know the world you're writing about, will miss allegories and allusions, and yet will love your books.

Now my reading life covers much wider ground than it did in childhood when writers such as C. S. Lewis and J. M. Barrie simultaneously opened up the universe and circumscribed it – from Tolstoy and Toni Morrison to Ali Smith and Juan Gabriel Vásquez the world sits on my bookshelf. But although I recognize the richness and breadth of my adult library, I miss the deep pleasures of childhood reading, the intensity which sent me back to books – and not just the most loved ones – over and over again. And yet, of all those childhood books the one that is arguably the most important to my life is one I only read once.

I remember clearly the day I found it: I was in my grandfather's study, looking through his intimidating bookshelves in which anything I might have wanted to read (*The Iliad*, *The Odyssey*) was in Greek. I had never yet found anything of interest in those bookshelves, but that didn't stop me returning to them time and again. Gibbon, Pliny, Marx, boring boring boring (in my defence, I was not quite eleven) . . . and then, there, where I must have looked before, in blue binding a book with a title *All Dogs Go to Heaven*. I pulled it out of the shelf with the same sense of wonder with which Lucy might have walked through a wardrobe that led into a world of snow. My grandfather said he had never seen the book before and I was welcome to it. I should say here that the only tragedies of my life that had occurred so far had concerned dogs – first Dusty, the German Shepherd, my earliest companion; and more recently, Topsy, the Russian Samoyed, whose death I was still grieving when some force of benevolence placed a book about dog heaven between Gibbon and Pliny just when I needed to read it.

If I ever howled with tears through a novel prior to *All Dogs Go to Heaven* I don't recall it. In my memory, it was only hours after I finished reading it that my best friend, Asad, came over. Asad and I shared all our books, and to further bind us together he, too, was also deep in mourning for his pet dog. *You have to read this; it's a book set in dog heaven,* I said. He replied: *Why don't we write a book?* And so we did. We called it *A Dog's Life, and After.* I was eleven years old; I haven't stopped writing fiction since.

But there is nothing I can tell you about *All Dogs Go to Heaven,* except that it had a blue cover and was set in dog heaven. I thought Asad borrowed it from me that day we sat down to write our novel together; months later when I asked him if I could have it back he said I never gave it to him. We never lied to each other about books – if one went missing we would say so – and so the disappearance of that novel is as mysterious as its appearance.

A few years ago, while writing something about *All Dogs Go to Heaven* I realized that I could go online and find a copy of it. How strange that the thought had never occurred to me before. It took some searching to uncover it – the unrelated Disney movie of the same name kept leaping into view instead – but I did finally track down a used copy of the novel, which was mine to buy at the click of a button. Reader, I did not buy it. I did not even attempt to remember the author's name. It had come into my life when I needed it, made me into a writer, and disappeared again – life-changing and fleeting, like Aslan, like Peter Pan. I was and am content to leave it as such.

Ten Favourites, at this precise moment in time: *Invisible Cities*, Italo Calvino; *Jazz,* Toni Morrison; *In the Skin of a Lion* and *The English Patient*, Michael Ondaatje; *Midnight's Children,* Salman Rushdie; *To the Lighthouse*, Virginia Woolf; *War and Peace*, Tolstoy; *Housekeeping*, Marilynne Robinson; *Great Expectations*, Charles Dickens; *Meatless Days*, Sara Suleri.

Rory Stewart

RECENTLY, I came across a book by the British monk Gildas. It caught my eye, on a shelf, when I should have been doing something else. I opened it, and was suddenly in the presence of a man from the sixth century. He was speaking, directly to me, in the exact words that he had chosen more than a millennium ago, about the state of Britain after the collapse of the Roman Empire. Here it is, in translation:

> I shall not follow the writings and records of my own country, which (if there were any of them) have been consumed by the fires of the enemy, or have accompanied my exiled countrymen into distant lands, but be guided by the relations of foreign writers, which being broken and interrupted in many places are therefore by no means clear.

He wrote as someone living at the very edge of the known world, one of the last literate men on a distant frontier, conscious of his limitations, and blindness, in a world that had slipped its moorings. He spoke in bewilderment, in distress. He seemed to be writing his sermon-history, as though putting it into a glass bottle, to be thrown from his sinking ship, unsure if anyone would ever read it. And then – fourteen hundred years later – I could.

Later, I found, on a shelf about my local area, an Anglo-Saxon poem about the collapse of a Roman city ('The ruins fell, perished/shattered into mounds of stone, where formerly many a warrior/joyous and bright with gold, with splendour adorned/proud and flushed with wine, in war trappings shone'). Next, I discovered a Cumbrian lullaby, written in the seventh century, about hunting in the Lake District. Then, I came across *Egil's Saga*, in which the tenth-century Norse hero, aged seven, kills a ten-year-old friend with an axe, because of a disagreement at a ball game. I was hearing voices still entirely fresh despite the gap of centuries – apparently undiluted by time, or by a fastidious editor, trying to mask the brutality of the age. They were originally written in four separate languages. And they revealed a period when each valley in the Lake District – near my home – had once been almost a separate nation: when Britain had contained more ethnic, linguistic and religious divisions than Yugoslavia. And yet, without 'reading' these rare texts (Gildas was the first British text, and the last for two hundred years), all such cultures would be almost irretrievable.

I began to understand why reading mattered, in part, because for twenty-one months I was functionally illiterate. Walking, twenty miles or so a day from Turkey to

Bangladesh, I rarely carried a book, and when I learned Farsi, Urdu or Nepali, I did not learn the scripts, so I could not read. Neon advertisements in towns, calligraphy on ancient tiles, and police documents were equally mute to me. The majority of villagers with whom I stayed were also illiterate. In Afghanistan being *besawad* – illiterate – was an insult, used often by city-dwellers against rural people, and it implied stupidity; but in fact I found these illiterate people to be courteous, shrewd, and eloquent. I sensed why, in the late Roman period, people whose ancestors had been able to read and write ceased to do so. Reading, it seemed, wasn't necessary for virtue, for effectiveness, or even, in Charlemagne's case, for running the Holy Roman Empire. But I realized that I, the Afghan villagers and Charlemagne – being illiterate – could not engage in the same way with the languages and voices of the dead. An oral tradition, even relying on bards with astonishing memories, cannot replicate a shelf of books. Only reading can fully resurrect the minds of others.

Once you have taken possession of a book, you can inspect a writer's mind, in all its shades and dimensions. You can establish a relationship, which would be intolerable to a living individual: you can wake the writer at three in the morning, switch her off in mid-sentence, insist she continues for six hours unbroken, skip, go back, repeat the same paragraph again and again, impertinently second-guessing her vocabulary, and metaphors, scrutinizing her structure and tricks.

But a book is not a genie bottle, and the writer is not a slave-mind under your command. The writer remains

always autonomous, never quite obedient to your expect-
ation or understanding. At first, you might flatter yourself
that you have developed an indecorous intimacy. I have
even fancied I had caught a reference which no one else had
caught – as though George Eliot had shared a private joke,
with me and only me, over a distance of a century. But
when I tried to keep up with her, follow her into her most
inaccessible passages, press my mind into hers, burrow into
the ions and synapses of her sub-cervical cortex, I could
never quite possess her.

The writer has from the start the advantage over the
reader. Their minds are more perfected, and clarified over
five hundred pages, than could ever be possible in a real
encounter. If I were to meet Turgenev, I might be frus-
trated by his conversation – aware that he is not focused
in that moment on the things that seem most interesting,
is perhaps repeating an anecdote, rather than thinking. But
reading, I can spend three days, with the most perfected
version of his mind, where every sentence is an exact,
considered, choice.

Sometimes, I have to change to understand a writer.
(Thus, when I was fourteen, I decided that the most inspiring figure in the world was Prince Myshkin in *The Idiot*,
and that Bazarov was the hero of *Fathers and Sons* – now I
can't even guess why I thought those things.) Sometimes,
the writer is simply difficult. Why, for example, instead of
'Kate Croy waited', does Henry James begin *The Wings of
the Dove*: 'She waited, Kate Croy, for her father to come in,
but he kept her unconscionably, and there were moments
at which she showed herself, in the glass over the mantel,

a face positively pale with the irritation that had brought her to the point of going away without sight of him. It was at this point, however, that she remained . . .'? The prose is rebarbative but it is this very resistance that makes it enthralling.

Sometimes I sense that the writer is capable of things beyond anything I could imagine or attempt. Take Oblonsky waking up at the beginning of *Anna Karenina*. Tolstoy can seem essentially a kooky bearded refusenik, in a smock and home-made boots, earnestly imposing his peasant utopia on everyone that surrounded him. And yet he imagines Oblonsky as a sleek, pomaded and grinning society favourite, waking from a dream in which the decanters in a restaurant in America have become dancing-girls singing 'I mio tesoro'. Oblonsky, we learn, had assumed his wife knew of his affair, and connived in it, and is horrified to discover that she was unaware and is now heart-broken. He is so good-humoured that everyone in the household takes his side, against his much better half. He cries, and is shaved, dispatches with competence and common sense his work at the office, shows compassion and understanding towards an awkward visitor, is guilty, troubled, rueful, and buoyant. How is Tolstoy – who would seem, from everything we know of him, to despise Oblonsky – able to make us love him?

Or to take a less canonical example: Peter Brown's new preface to his biography of St Augustine. You can follow the author, as he moves from a memory of a swimming pool in California, to a swimming pool in Cairo, somehow reminded of late Roman Christianity in both locations. You can observe his systematic criticism of his own work, his confession of how much he simplified or misunderstood as a young writer, and his push for a more testing idea of what he might still achieve. And you realize you are in the presence of a mind which makes tough choices on when not to be erudite, whose imagination is poignant: a mind which is resilient, generous to other scholars, and intelligently liberal. And then, there are the moments of fellow-feeling. Just as I conclude Brown is capable of things beyond anything I could imagine or attempt, he settles on a phrase of Foucault, which is also my favourite phrase, and we can recite it for a moment in unison: 'After all, what would be the value of the passion for knowledge if it resulted only in a certain amount of knowingness and not, in one way or another, and to the extent possible, in the knower's straying afield of himself?'

I am, I think, jealous of people who find pleasure in reading, and find this pleasure easy to describe. I am uncomfortable thinking of reading as a pleasure. (I read many thrillers very quickly, but they feel always a bit like fast food, never ultimately satisfying.) And I read so much, that I sometimes worry I am reading when I should be living.

Reading for me is about a relationship with a writer who might be elusive, even intimidating. Reading can make me become a better version of myself, in contact with a finer mind. It is an unstable relationship in which sometimes I, as the reader, can play the tyrant – even fling the book across the room, or close it for ever – but the writer is always more splendid and more autonomous than I. Reading is the love and resurrection of better minds.

My favourite books

Peter Brown, *St Augustine*; V. S. Naipaul, *An Area of Darkness*; *King Lear*; *Egil's Saga*; Erich Auerbach, *Mimesis*; T. S. Eliot, *Four Quartets*; Laurence Sterne, *Tristram Shandy*; Philip Roth, *American Pastoral*; G. K. Chesterton, *Father Brown*; Leo Tolstoy, *Haji Murat*.

Katie Waldegrave

Beside my bed is a wicker basket full of raggedy children's books which I inherited from my grandmother. It is the first possession I would rescue in a fire. Granny had suffered from childhood polio, she broke her back as a teenager and had the first of her seven children when she was nineteen, so by the time I knew her she was fairly immobile. When she was not careering about in her little blue Mini (wicker basket on the passenger seat), she was mostly settled in the high-backed sofa of her Somerset house. She faced the fire and a long coffee table filled with all the things she would need during the day. Her wooden sticks were used for hooking more than for walking. Next to the fire, under her shelf of photo albums, was the wicker basket.

I have no idea how many hours I spent cocooned in that sofa, leaning against her shoulder, turning pages when she nodded. From time to time today, I lift each book carefully out of the basket and leaf through pages which smell just the same as they always did. *Les Malheurs de*

Sophie with its cracked spine: I remember Granny translating as she read while I looked at line drawings of Sophie and her wax doll and wondered which of my aunts had coloured in the pictures so badly. *Le Bon Toto et le méchant Tom*: I think we both preferred Tom, for all that he was so méchant. Ameliaranne Stiggins, Uncle Remus, Mr Buffin, Babar the Elephant, Edward Ardizzone, Shirley Hughes. Granny and I spent many happy hours with Alfie and Brer Rabbit and the rest and in so many of those early books the illustrations are what I remember now. It cut both ways, as my grandmother knew. We read *Struwwelpeter*, but the most frightening of the pictures she had carefully cut out with nail scissors. And then there are the books still in my parents' house. I remember Mum, perched on the side of my bed, reading me *Ernest and Celestine* and *Little Bear* and *Where the Wild Things Are*. As far as I recall none of those had many words at all, but books became and have remained vital. Being without a book on a tube or bus induces a feeling of panic.

At home, my father used to read to me in the drawing room, the one room we were not normally allowed in. Looking back on it, I cannot imagine how he or Mum found so much time. We read E. Nesbit's Psammead series, *Our Island Story*, *The Sword in the Stone*. He would read long past my bedtime, while I tried hard not to look at the gold clock on the mantelpiece in case it drew his attention to the fact. When he chose *The Hobbit* I tended to skip ahead to the end of the recto page and then daydream. My heart did sink slightly when he produced the *Lord of the Rings*, which was even longer. It would never have occurred to me to tell him I found the story dull – and in any case I so loved being curled up with him, he could have read the phone book and I'd have been content. In retrospect, I suppose Tolkien taught me a valuable lesson about beginning to develop and notice my own literary taste.

So being read to was one kind of pleasure, but soon came the great freedom of being able to read at one's own pace. I remember the endless panics my sister Liza and I had rushing to turn off the light whenever we heard a creaking floorboard. Arthur Ransome's *We Didn't Mean to Go to Sea* was the first book I stayed up all night to finish before going blurry-eyed to school. Like so many children I adored series. My brother's generous godfather, Davo, gave him the entire series of *Tintin* for his birthday and I read and reread them endlessly. Between the ages of about eight and eleven all my pocket money went on buying all the *Just William* books which I still think are the greatest comic writing in the English language. They are the first books I pick up when I am ill or unhappy. Despite Ransome's Peggy and Nancy, it was soon clear that being a girl was going to be a disadvantage in life. I had no desire to be of the same sex as Titty and Susan, or Pollyanna, or any of the Little Women – even Jo. I was endlessly given *What Katy Did* as a present – every birthday from about seven to twelve and, ungrateful child that I was, I quickly decided that I didn't care at all what she did, or what she did next. (Although I didn't mind the first one until she falls off a swing and is paralysed, after which she becomes an interminable saintly bore.)

Making up stories for my younger siblings, or reading 'real' stories, became a source of great pleasure for me, if not them. Like most children we most enjoyed the books in which all the parents had disappeared: *The Children Who Lived in a Barn*, *Ballet Shoes*, *Northern Lights*. Rudyard Kipling was the first to make me think about voice. Granny and Dad had both read me the *Just So Stories*, and I'd assumed they were ad-libbing all the 'best beloved' parts. It was only when I came to read them to my younger siblings and we all fell about giggling at me calling them beloved, that I realized my mistake. For the first time I was aware of the author, another presence in all this. Until then I had vaguely assumed that Granny had in fact secretly written the Noel Streatfeild books. How could anyone else have been involved in our private adventures at *The House in Cornwall*? How else could she have known what I'd like to read? I went through an Agatha Christie phase about this time. There is one, *The Murder of Roger Ackroyd*, in which (spoiler alert) the narrator is the killer. I found this oddly spine-tingling. Not for the story, so much as for the sense that Christie had disobeyed the rules; there is a contract with the reader which she had broken. In the correct hands – Ian McEwan's for example – tricksiness can still exhilarate.

There were many books which made me want to write. My best friend Tanya and I spent hours filling exercise books with our own versions of the Swallows and Amazons tales. Like Carroll's Alice we believed in lots of illustrations and conversations. Also as many chapters as possible, each one starting on a new page and neatly underlined in red.

I don't remember what we wrote, but I do remember the satisfaction of filling the paper. Then there were the books which made me want to be a writer. I never liked *Anne of Green Gables*, but L. M. Montgomery's *Emily of New Moon* with its aspiring writer heroine was the first to make me want to be anyone other than William Brown or Tintin.

I think that is one of the wonders of reading as a child. You inhabit the books. In the course of a week I followed a yeti in Tibet, discovered a secret garden in Yorkshire, lived with my miniature family in the skirting boards, watched Aslan die and wreaked havoc with Pippi Longstocking. Michelle Magorian's *Good Night, Mr Tom* was the first book I read which I finished (in tears) and then turned back to the first page to start again. I had to wait for *Anna Karenina* to have that experience again. Now I find however absorbed in a book I am, it's often on the outside. If forced to select favourite books I choose the exceptions to this rule by George Eliot, Jane Austen or Tolstoy.

The Wind in the Willows was the subject of my first literary disagreement. Mrs Marani, a fiercely brilliant teacher at my primary school, taught me about owning an opinion. She argued with us, aged ten, as though we were adults. When I told her I liked *The Wind in the Willows* she had a rant about anthropomorphism. 'Look it up,' she shouted crossly. I did, and considered. It had never particularly occurred to me to discriminate. I just read, anything and everything. Except Enid Blyton and Roald Dahl whom my parents forbade (so with hideous literary snobbishness, I looked down on those of my friends reading *Mallory Towers* and *The Twits* without having a clue why). I knew that Dad loved *The Wind in the Willows*. He thought (and thinks) the Piper at the Gates of Dawn chapter a work of genius. Who to pick? I suggested to Mrs Marani that it wasn't a fair criticism: you could not like or dislike all books about animals. I explained why I liked *The Wind in the Willows* but not *Watership Down*. She disagreed vehemently and then told me I'd made a good argument. It began to make me into a more discriminating reader, but I suppose it was also the beginning of the end of perfect pleasure.

About the age of eleven or twelve those who are lucky make the transition into reading adult books. I had some wonderful schoolteachers who, in various unorthodox ways, helped me make that jump. An English teacher, Mr Fletcher, spent all the lessons for an entire year reading aloud first *Cider with Rosie* and then Saki short stories. I reread Laurie Lee's memoir recently and was disappointed but at the time I adored it. Another teacher gave us copies of Heaney and Hughes's *The Rattlebag* and one lesson a week was devoted to copying poems out of it, as neatly as we could, and illustrating them. Now as a teacher, I recognize this was not particularly sound, pedagogically speaking, for twelve-year-olds, but it opened up the world of poetry to me. Eliza Coutts, who taught us history, had a technique I stole when I became a history teacher. During the course of a lesson about the First World War she told us to read *Birdsong*. Minutes later she took it back with much panic-stricken hand flapping. 'Goodness no, it's full of sex. You mustn't tell your parents.' Needless to say we all went straight to the library. Sex of course was a great incentive for reading as a teenager. *The Chamomile Lawn*, which probably I read too young, alerted me to the fact that I could be reading about astonishing new topics like incest while adults looked on with benign approval.

Several years ago I founded a charity, First Story, with the author William Fiennes. I was a teacher in what is euphemistically known as a challenging secondary school. My students were talented, smart, funny kids but they did not read much – or at least not for pleasure. I don't think that this was necessarily because they were, economically speaking, from deprived backgrounds. I think a lot of teenagers lose the habit of reading. But these teenagers felt detached from the world of reading and writing in a way that depressed me. From the way they spoke and talked it was clear that they did not feel books belonged to them. I remember we asked Gautam Malkani to come and read from his novel *Londonstani* which starts with a fight written in the vernacular. At the end I remember one of my students, Satwinder, saying: 'But miss, I didn't know you were *allowed* to write like that!' Over time Satwinder, like all the students we've worked with since, began to find his own voice, and in doing so his place in the world.

Having worked with teenagers for the past twelve years I have come to believe that pleasures of reading and writing are closely bound to one another. As a small child I knew that each book I read had been produced for me. Richmal Crompton (who was certainly not a woman) had me in mind when writing about William Brown. One of the interesting things about First Story is how writing each week encourages students to read more. They begin with reading each other's work and (with the help of Give a Book) they move out from there. They get closer to the joyful sense I had so often as a child and that I have still with *Middlemarch* or *Persuasion*: how extraordinary – but this book was written for me!

My favourite books

Favourite books are as much an inheritance track as an act of literary discrimination. From my mother: *Persuasion* by way of *Emil and the Detectives* and Antonia White. From my father: *The Leopard* and *Tristram Shandy* by way of *Puck of Pook's Hill*. From both the assumption that reading is essential, like breathing. Beyond this, my approach to an impossible task was to select books which I've read many times before and which I expect to read many more times. Apart from Just William, and perhaps Wodehouse, they are books which seem to change as I grow older. William I hope will stay the same for ever.

Middlemarch, George Eliot; *Galahad at Blandings*, P. G. Wodehouse; *Can You Forgive Her?*, Anthony Trollope; *Pride and Prejudice*, Jane Austen; *William the Pirate,* Richmal Crompton; *Collected Short Stories*, Anton Chekhov; *Hateship, Friendship, Courtship, Loveship, Marriage,* Alice Munro; *Antony and Cleopatra,* William Shakespeare; *The Prelude,* William Wordsworth; *Anna Karenina*, Leo Tolstoy.

Emily Berry

Some of my childhood books are still in my possession. Many of them have strict injunctions penned in the flyleaves to 'Please Be Cafle With This Book' and 'PLEASE DO NOT TEAR', which gives a sense of the importance I attached to them. Even so a few are, regrettably, a little torn.

My childhood can be dangerous territory. It is not a complete circuit but has a break in it, the place where, aged seven, I suddenly lost my mother. Maybe this is why I was so concerned that things should be handled with care. When I think about the books I read and what they gave me, I think about this loss and the work a book can do, at the right moment, to transport you away from something unbearable or, at a different moment – when you're ready to bear it – take you back to it.

Not that I thought about any of this then. Maybe the point of reading is not to have to think or, rather, to think in a way that is so guided and concentrated it becomes a kind of meditation. I've always done a lot of reading.

Recently the mother of a friend I've known since I was small recalled that when we were nine or ten our class were asked how many books we'd read over the summer holidays, and I said I had read twenty-eight!

First there were the talking animals: Squirrel Nutkin, Mrs Tiggy-Winkle (thank goodness for the internet, for a moment I thought she was called Mrs Tiddlywinks); Winnie-the-Pooh . . . There was a great book about a family of pandas or maybe they were koalas (Google tells me this was *Bread and Jam for Frances* by Russell Hoban, and that 'bread and jam for frances what kind of animal is frances' is a popular search. Badger, in fact). There was no such ambiguity in *Frog and Toad Tales*, in which the gloomy and misanthropic Toad is always having to be cheered up by his more upbeat friend Frog – this was probably a familiar dynamic to me even then. '"Toad, Toad!" shouted Frog. "Wake up, it is spring!" "Blah," said a voice from inside the house.' My much-sellotaped copy seems to have been given to me by a family friend who inscribed it: 'Child, Stand no nonsense!' (I was the kind of child who was often being called 'Child!' because I was an only one surrounded by intellectuals who thought this would be an amusing thing to do. I guess it was.)

Children are often given very grown-up tasks in children's books. They go off on important missions and their parents are frequently absent or dead. If this is so that children from intact families can safely play out frightening scenarios, I don't know what it means for the ones who have already experienced those scenarios in real life. Some books that kept me entertained then would terrify me now; like *The Secret Garden*, which opens with a ten-year-old girl in India waking up to discover that her parents and all their servants have died of cholera. Or Maurice Sendak's *Outside Over There*. 'Ida's father was away at sea . . .' it begins (scary enough); meanwhile Sendak's beautiful but nightmarish illustrations show us Ida's little sister being stolen by goblins and replaced with *a replica baby made of ice*. This is the kind of reading that Kafka was probably thinking of when he said: 'The books we need are the kind that act upon us like a misfortune . . . that make us feel as though we were on the verge of suicide, or lost in a forest remote from all human habitation.' I don't think those are the kinds of books I need.

Somewhere beyond or among the talking animals, the stolen babies and dead parents, I found out that what I really wanted was to be growing up in America; and my long-standing commitment to American literature began. Someone gave me a copy of *Eloise* by Kay Thompson and Hilary Knight, a wry illustrated book about a little girl who lives in the Plaza Hotel in New York with her nanny, her dog Weenie and turtle Skipperdee. Eloise is that thing that characters in children's books often are: 'irrepressible'. 'We have a buzzer on our front door / I always lean on it / That's how Nanny knows it's me / ELOISE.' (For some reason the text is laid out as if it's poetry. Which it is, in a way.)

Around the same time I was reading *Little Women* and *What Katy Did*, books I was a big fan of but whose moral stance I was already finding hard to gulp down; in *Little Women* everyone's favourite tomboy Jo March is eventually tamed into a 'good wife' by the paternally mansplainy Professor Bhaer (Jo's refusal of Laurie's advances remains one of the greatest romantic tragedies of my life), while in *What Katy Did* Katy Carr, queen of 'scrapes', is delivered of her waywardness and unto saintliness once she loses the use of her legs in an accident. Because I was myself a very well-behaved little girl, I wanted to read about girls who were not. Maybe I wanted to be reassured that it was possible to break the rules and be all right.

Then I discovered Anastasia Krupnik. Anastasia is not really a rulebreaker, but she's the bolder, more outspoken self any shy, bookish child might dream of becoming. The journal-writing daughter of a poet–academic and an artist, Anastasia is proud to have a wart on her thumb ('it's the loveliest colour I've ever seen in a wart!' says her mother) and a goldfish called Frank. When she is asked to come up with a name for her imminent little brother, she secretly writes down 'the most terrible name she could think of', which turns out to be 'One-Ball Reilly'. Anastasia's creator, Lois Lowry, has said that the inspiration for Anastasia came from the daughter of President Jimmy Carter, Amy: 'There was this one time when this very solemn interviewer asked 10-year-old Amy, "Do you have one message to give to the children of the world?" and she said, "No!"'

Another favourite from this era of my life is *From the Mixed-up Files of Mrs. Basil E. Frankweiler* (maybe one of the best titles ever conceived) by E. L. Konigsburg. The heroine is eleven-year-old Claudia Kincaid, who decides to run away from home and plans her mission meticulously over several weeks, saving up her pocket money by skipping hot fudge sundaes. It's the kind of running away a nervous, organized little girl could get on board with; for a start, there's a destination – 'a large place, a comfortable place [Claudia doesn't like discomfort], an indoor place, and preferably a beautiful place': the Metropolitan Museum of Art in New York City. Once they get there, Claudia and her little brother Jamie (selected as her companion because of his own ability to save money) develop an elaborate routine to elude detection, spending their days attaching themselves to school groups wandering around the museum and their nights sleeping in the collection's sixteenth-century beds. If you want to know how the amazing Mrs. Basil E. Frankweiler comes into it, you'll have to read the book.

As an adult I still like coming-of-age stories in all their iterations (isn't 'coming of age' a permanent condition, really?): *Who Will Run the Frog Hospital?* by Lorrie Moore; *A Boy's Own Story* by Edmund White; *The Virgin Suicides* and *Middlesex* by Jeffrey Eugenides; Alice Walker's *The Color Purple*; Dorothy Allison's *Bastard out of Carolina*; Edna O'Brien's *The Country Girls*; Hanif Kureishi's *The Buddha of Suburbia*; and the classics of the genre, obviously, *The Catcher in the Rye* and *The Bell Jar*.

Certain books I read during adolescence are lodged in me somewhere deep down and are not always easy to access, so that trying to summon them up initiates a kind of queasiness. I was obsessed with the frankly sleazy books of Virginia Andrews, who wrote popular gothic romances heavy on the incest – in the most famous, *Flowers in the Attic*, the blonde, blue-eyed Dollanganger children are hidden away in an 'airless attic' by their grandmother who is slowly poisoning them with arsenic sprinkled on doughnuts. Here's a summary of one of Andrews's novels, *My Sweet Audrina* (which by the way, Wikipedia says, was 'the only standalone book without incest published during Andrews' lifetime'): 'The story features diverse real-world subjects such as brittle bone disease, rape, post-traumatic stress disorder, diabetes and autism in the haunting setting of a Victorian era mansion near the fictitious River Lyle.' I must have been a lot braver back then; I've attempted a few times, out of curiosity, to reread *Flowers in the Attic* as an adult, but I always end up shutting the cover very decisively after scanning the first few lines and wedging it back on the bookshelf. But the aura of Virginia must have stayed with me because I've found it hovering over some of my poems. I have one called 'Sweet Arlene' about a group of sisters being oppressively 'cared for' by a demonic older woman – which all sounds a bit familiar, I realise now.

As a child I was more interested in stories than in poems, until I realized that poems could also be stories. When I was nine or ten I was given by my godmother an elegant edition of the classic anthology *Other Men's Flowers*. It was a grown-up gift that required grown-up treatment. Unfortunately I wrote something on the flyleaf that I later deemed to be embarrassingly juvenile and tore out. Many of the poems in it were over my head, but I discovered the calming practice of incantation and there were some I read aloud many times. I liked the dark ones best – Poe's 'Annabel Lee' ('That the wind came out of a cloud one night, / Chilling and killing my Annabel Lee'),

Wilde's 'The Ballad of Reading Gaol' and Keats's creepiest poem, 'La Belle Dame Sans Merci'. So that was the kind of child I was, earnestly reciting poems about imprisoned and tormented people in my dusty attic bedroom . . . alone and palely loitering.

Don't worry, I had a sense of humour too.

What I remember reading is what it suits me to remember. Nowadays I read slightly fewer novels, a lot more poetry and the occasional memoir or biography. I like reading biographies of writers because it reassures me to find out how mad everyone is. Then I think, oh, maybe I'll be okay then.

While I don't personally want books to act on me 'like a misfortune', I've retained my interest in the darker side of literature and in gothic, troubled characters. I recently discovered Carson McCullers, who immediately became one of my favourite writers because everything she writes – often about the intense romantic infatuations of lonely outsiders – gets to that place where something painful becomes something beautiful.

Otherwise, I struggle with choosing 'favourites' because I feel like you need to be at least ten years beyond something to know whether it's stuck; but I will mention a few other books/writers that have meant something to me at various points: *Giovanni's Room* by James Baldwin; *Are You My Mother?* by Alison Bechdel; John Berryman's *Dream Songs*; Anne Carson; Lydia Davis; Joan Didion; *Half Blood Blues* by Esi Edugyan; *That They May Face the Rising Sun* by John McGahern; Toni Morrison; Frank O'Hara; *Ariel* by Sylvia Plath; 'Bartleby the Scrivener' by Herman Melville;

David Foster Wallace; the anthologies *Emergency Kit: Poems for Strange Times* and *The Horse Has Six Legs* (Charles Simic's translations of Serbian poetry).

I suppose for me the 'pleasure of reading' is in feeling safe. Safe because the act of reading can be containing (and I always feel safest in a bookshop or a library) but also because when you read something that speaks to you, it's a reminder that everything, even and especially the hardest things, has a precedent. So you're not alone, not 'lost in a forest' after all.

Tom Wells

THE thing about books: you get a bit carried away. One minute you're four years old, you've snuck into your Nan's bed first thing and she's teaching you a poem about yellow bananas while the Teasmaid starts up. Next thing you know, you're fourteen, doing your best to cram a cardboard cut-out of a hippogriff into the back of your mum's Corsa. That feels like a good place to start.

It was the last week of the summer holidays, my mum was dragging me into Hull, to British Home Stores, to get some new grey trousers ready for starting back at school. I wasn't keen. Probably I was huffing quite a lot. On the way up Jameson Street though we passed Waterstones and my heart skipped a beat. They were dismantling their Harry Potter window display. I couldn't believe my luck.

All summer, they'd had an amazing cardboard cut-out of Harry and Hermione flying off into the moonlight on Buckbeak's back. Buckbeak was a hippogriff, a winged horse with the head and body of an eagle. He played a very important part in *Harry Potter and the Prisoner of*

Azkaban, which I'd read at least seven times since June. The cardboard cut-out of him looked immense, properly noble – you could see each individually painted feather and feel magical courage coming off him in big, empowering wafts. But they'd taken him down. I begged my mum to go in and ask if they'd still got him, if they were chucking him out, if we could have him. I fibbed a bit, said it was just a very small, very easy-to-carry, very roll-uppable poster. My poor mum wasn't fussed about hippogriffs, she just wanted to get me some school trousers, quickly, before we got a parking ticket, but in she went, heroically, and struggled back out again a couple of minutes later with Buckbeak. His wings were massive – five foot across, at least – they got caught in the security barrier, then the double door, then he was free, free at last and mine to keep. My fourteen-year-old life was complete. Mum was a bit less thrilled. If I wanted him, she said, I'd have to lug him round Hull all afternoon. I did. On just about every street corner he caught a gust of wind and sent me flying. At one point I got trapped behind him, totally lodged in the changing room of BHS, and had to shout for help. I was only in my pants. Still though, I wasn't fussed. Everything's different when you're in love. And I absolutely loved *Harry Potter.*

That's not true, actually – I didn't love Harry. I loved Hagrid, Professor Sprout, the Weasleys, especially Mrs, and Albus Dumbledore. Harry was always a bit preoccupied with the plot, and I've never really got the hang of plots. A good character though – funny and sad and trying their best – feels like making a proper friend. Paddington, the

BFG, the entire population of the Hundred Acre Wood – I knew as I was reading them we were in it for the long haul. I loved Dickon and Martha in *The Secret Garden*, Laura in *The Wreck of the Zanzibar* and Andy in *The Suitcase Kid*. My absolute favourite though was Mildred Hubble, officially *The Worst Witch*. I was (still am) quite a hopeless farmer's son – the only job I ever managed not to mess up was standing in a gap, stopping the cows escaping, like a sort of lanky bollard. Even that was hit-and-miss. Reading about Mildred Hubble gave me hope. She had messy plaits and trailing shoelaces, she fell off her broomstick and couldn't do potions but her heart was in the right place and somehow, in the end, she'd be all right, cheerfully eating crumpets with an elderly wizard she'd rescued from the school pond. Jill Murphy's writing was full of heart and mischief. I absolutely loved it.

As I got a bit older, I got more into Penguin Classics. Partly because they took a bit of reading, partly because I was quite earnest, and partly because they cost a pound – even less if they turned up at jumble sales, which they did. My heroes were Jo March – awkward and spirited, making massive clangers, wearing a dodgy hat to write in when everyone was asleep – and Lizzie Bennett – people-watching with a twinkle in her eye, and loving a good dance. I especially liked how, just by being themselves, they both got their hunks in the end. That felt quite important at the time. I really wanted a hunk.

I grew up in a tiny village called Kilnsea, in East Yorkshire. It is quite beautiful in a windswept, falling-in-the-sea sort of a way, but very isolated. As a joke, my dad's friends would address his birthday cards to 'The Edge of Hell'. They always arrived. Still though: lovely sunsets. Living so far off the beaten track meant that I didn't really know or see anybody who was gay, apart from me, and it wasn't the easiest thing to talk about. As with most things in my life, Hull Central Library came to the rescue. After school I'd stay in town late – I'd got a bus pass and a library card, anything could happen. Mostly I just borrowed books though. I'd try most things – libraries are very low-risk – which is how I ended up reading (and rereading, hundreds of times) *The Hitchhiker's Guide to the Galaxy*, J. D. Salinger's short stories and *I Capture the Castle* by Dodie Smith. Stunning. One day there was a display for LGBT history month. I hovered nearby, pretending to be looking at *Popular Psychology*, waited till no one was about then grabbed *Two Weeks with the Queen* by Morris Gleitzman. I'm really, really glad I did. It was a genuinely funny, open-hearted and properly moving story about a lad called Colin trying to find a doctor who can help his brother to recover from leukaemia. Colin ends up befriending a gay couple, Ted and Griff, who are struggling too. It's a sad story, but full of hope and jokes, and in Ted and Griff's love for each other and Colin's uncomplicated acceptance of them, my worried, fifteen-year-old self took a lot of heart. I started it on the bus home, stayed up as late as I could manage that night once I'd done my geography coursework – limestone pavements, I know – then finished it on the bus next morning. I could've kissed that book. Ten years later, I wandered down Marchmont Street into *Gay's The Word* bookshop, my absolute favourite

place in London, got a cheery welcome and saw shelf after
shelf of brilliant books – Quentin Crisp, Jackie Kay, David
Sedaris, *A Month in the Country* by J. L. Carr and Alan
Bennett's *The Uncommon Reader*. It felt like coming home.
I'm very grateful to Hull Central Library for setting me
off on the way.

My family all relied on the library. My dad liked reading all sorts – Dick Francis, *Angela's Ashes*, Annie Proulx.
One summer he read *Round Ireland with a Fridge* then
we bundled into his Sierra and headed for the ferry at
Holyhead. We didn't take a fridge. Mum was mostly into
Mills and Boons. She read the end first, to check it was
happy, then read the rest to check it wasn't too rude to
pass on to my Nan. Ruth, my sister, loved Marian Keyes. It
was the mixture of romance and baking. She also lent me
Angus, Thongs and Full-Frontal Snogging by Louise Rennison
on a gloomy teenage day, accidentally giving me the funniest book I have ever read (I kept it – she didn't mind). I got
to read some stunning books at uni too – *To the Lighthouse*,
The Canterbury Tales, John Donne's *Songs and Sonnets*, Keats,
the Ranters' pamphlets and everything by Shakespeare that
involved a fool, a fairy or Falstaff. The degree bit felt like
three years of missing the point, but getting all those voices
off my bookshelf and into my head did me the world of
good. Which, in fairness, was probably the point. I trudged
my way through finals – 'for what the world thinks of that
ejaculation – I would not give a groat,' Laurence Sterne,
Tristram Shandy – and headed back to Kilnsea, to wash up
in my mum's café for a bit. It ended up being four years –
my mum's very patient.

One day there was an ad in the *Yorkshire Post* for the West Yorkshire Playhouse's new writing course. You didn't have to have written a play before, which was ideal – I'd written quite a sad poem about the Humber estuary, a haiku about hummus, and nothing else – and it was free. My mum said I should go for it. She knew how much I wanted to be a writer – I'd spent the past few months sitting in the corner reading books by Dan Rhodes and Barbara Pym (*Gold* and *Excellent Women* were my favourites) and sighing. I applied for the course last-minute, and – thank goodness – got on.

Everyone there was thoughtful and full of stories. It was lush. On the train back from Leeds that night I wrote my first joke, about a Mini Milk, and realized this was the exact thing I wanted to be doing for as long as I possibly could. I borrowed some plays – thank you again, Hull Library – read *Talent* by Victoria Wood, *Wit* by Margaret Edson, *A Taste of Honey* by Shelagh Delaney, *Comedians* by Trevor Griffiths, *Waiting for the Telegram* by Alan Bennett, *Bed* by Jim Cartwright – all soulful and scruffy and brimming with life. I sent a script to a theatre company in London called Paines Plough, where I got to work with brilliant directors, met real-life actual playwrights, saw some properly good theatre – *If There Is I Haven't Found It Yet* by Nick Payne, *You Can See the Hills* by Matthew Dunster, *The Aliens* by Annie Baker – and started to find my feet a bit. I watched *The Muppets*, *Gavin & Stacey* and *The Royle Family*, looked at Quentin Blake's illustrations, Beryl Cook's paintings and Jeremy Deller's tea stall, listened to the lyrics of Pulp and Belle and Sebastian and Dolly Parton and The

Smiths, and started seeking out photography books – The Caravan Gallery's *Is Britain Great?* series, Martin Parr's *The Non-Conformists*, *A Day Off* by Tony Ray-Jones and Sefton Samuels's *Northerners*. I wrote down things people said and things people didn't say, stuff I'd just spotted or remembered. In Mike Bradwell's *The Reluctant Escapologist* I learned about the sort of theatre I wanted to make, and Joan Littlewood's autobiography *Joan's Book* was like a radiator, a suit of armour and a proper adventure, all at once. It is the longest book I've ever read. I loved it all.

My favourite books

A Taste of Honey, Shelagh Delaney; *Joan's Book,* Joan Littlewood; *The Worst Witch,* Jill Murphy; *Excellent Women,* Barbara Pym; *Gold,* Dan Rhodes; *Talent,* Victoria Wood; *Angus, Thongs and Full-Frontal Snogging,* Louise Rennison; *The House at Pooh Corner,* A. A. Milne; *The Santaland Diaries,* David Sedaris; *I Capture the Castle,* Dodie Smith.

Notes on the Authors

Stephen Spender was born in 1909. His best-known works are his *Collected Poems* and an autobiography, *World Within World* (first published in 1951). He was married to concert pianist Natasha Litvin with a son, Matthew, and a daughter, Lizzie. He died in 1995.

Michael Foot was born in 1913. He was a politician, journalist and author. He worked for the *Daily Herald*, and was editor of the *Evening Standard* and *Tribune*. He entered Parliament in 1945 and was Leader of the Labour Party (1980–83). He wrote numerous books including a biography of Aneurin Bevan. He died in 2010.

Patrick Leigh Fermor was born in 1915. He joined the Intelligence Corps in 1939, and served as British Liaison Officer with the Resistance on German-occupied Crete. His work includes two books narrating his journey on foot across Europe to the Iron Gate on the Danube in 1933–34, *A Time of Gifts* (1977) and *Between the Woods and the Water* (1986). He died in 2011.

Doris Lessing was born in 1919 in Iran, where she lived for the first five years of her life, and was then brought up on a farm in Southern Rhodesia, now Zimbabwe. She moved to London in 1949 and the following year published her first novel *The Grass is Singing*. She received the Nobel Prize in Literature in 2007 and died in 2013.

Brian Moore was born in Belfast, Northern Ireland, in 1921, and moved to the United States in 1960. His novels include *The Lonely Passion of Judith Hearne* (1955) and *Lies of Silence* (1990). He won several awards for his writing, including the James Tait Black Memorial Prize. He died in 1999.

Robert Burchfield was born in New Zealand in 1923. He edited the four volumes of *A Supplement to the Oxford English Dictionary* (published between 1972 and 1986). He had a long academic career at the University of Oxford and was an Emeritus Fellow of St Peter's College, Oxford. He died in 2004.

Judith Kerr was born in Berlin in 1923. She was educated at eleven schools in four different countries. *The Tiger Who Came to Tea* and *When Hitler Stole Pink Rabbit* are two of her best-known books. Her first picture book started as a bedtime story for her small daughter. She lives in London.

John Mortimer was born in 1923. He was a playwright, novelist and barrister. He wrote many film scripts, radio and television plays, including the Rumpole plays, which won him the British Academy Writer of the Year Award, an adaptation of Evelyn Waugh's *Brideshead Revisited,* and the autobiographical radio and stage play *A Voyage Round My Father.* He died in 2009.

John Fowles was born in 1926. He published several novels, of which *The French Lieutenant's Woman,* which won the WHSmith Literary Award for 1970, and *The Magus* are probably the best-known. He also wrote several non-fiction books. He died in 2005.

Jan Morris was born in 1926. Her works include the *Pax Britannica* trilogy about the Victorian Empire, portraits of cities and autobiographical books. She also edited *The Oxford Book of Oxford*. She divides her time between her home in north Wales, her dacha in the Black Mountains of south Wales and travel abroad.

Philip Ziegler was born in 1929. He began work in the Diplomatic Service, during which time he wrote his first book. After writing five more books, he resigned to devote himself to the official biography of Earl Mountbatten of Burma. He has been chairman of the London Library and of the Society of Authors. He lives in London.

J. G. Ballard was born in 1930 in Shanghai, China. After the attack on Pearl Harbor, Ballard and his family were placed in a civilian prison camp. They returned to England after World War Two. His semi-autobiographical novel *Empire of the Sun* won the 1984 *Guardian* Fiction Prize and James Tait Black Award, and was filmed by Steven Spielberg. He died in 2009.

Ruth Rendell was born in London in 1930. She has been writing suspense fiction and detective stories since the 1960s, both under her own name and using the pseudonym Barbara Vine. Her books have been adapted for film and television, translated into nineteen languages, and have won her many awards. She lives in London.

Edna O'Brien was born in 1930 in County Clare, Ireland. She is the author of many novels and short story collections, including *The Country Girls* trilogy and *A Fanatic Heart*. She has won the Irish PEN Award and the Frank O'Connor International Short Story Award. She lives in London.

John Carey, born in 1934, is emeritus Merton Professor of English Literature at the University of Oxford. His books include critical studies of John Donne, Milton, Dickens and Thackeray, and he edited the best-selling *Faber Book of Reportage*. He has chaired the Man Booker Prize committee twice. He lives in the Cotswolds, where he keeps bees.

Jane Gardam's novels include *The Hollow Land*, which won the Whitbread Literary Award, and *Last Friends*, which was shortlisted for the inaugural Folio Prize 2014. She has also written award-winning short story collections, among them *The Pangs of Love*, which won the Katherine Mansfield Award in 1984. She lives in east Kent.

Ronald Harwood was born in Cape Town in 1934. His plays include *The Dresser*, his films *The Pianist*, for which he won an Academy Award in 2003. He was nominated for an Oscar both for the adapted screenplay of *The Diving Bell and the Butterfly*, and for the film of *The Dresser*. He lives in London.

A. S. Byatt was born in 1936 and studied at Cambridge. Her books include *Possession*, which won the Booker Prize in 1990, *The Children's Book*, awarded the James Tait Black Memorial Prize, and studies of Iris Murdoch, Wordsworth and Coleridge. She lives in London.

Simon Gray was born on Hayling Island in 1936. He wrote more than thirty stage plays, among them *Butley*, *Quartermaine's Terms* and *Japes*. He also wrote five novels and numerous plays for TV, radio and film. His acclaimed works of non-fiction include *The Smoking Diaries* trilogy and *Coda*. He died in 2008.

Roger McGough was born in Lancashire in 1937. His first poems were published in 1965 and his work includes poetry for children as well as adults, and plays for the stage, radio and television. He won a Cholmondeley Award in 1998 and was made a Fellow of the Royal Society of Literature in 2004. He lives in London.

Emma Tennant was born in London in 1937. She is the author of several novels, including a revisionist sequel to *Pride and Prejudice* titled *Pemberley, Two Women of London* and *The Bad Sister*. She has written a play, *Frankenstein's Baby*, for BBC television. She lives in London.

Tom Stoppard was born in Czechoslovakia in 1937. However, English has been his first language since he started school in India. He has written for the stage, television, film and radio. His best-known work includes *Rosencrantz and Guildenstern Are Dead* and *Arcadia*. He also co-wrote the screenplay of *Shakespeare in Love*.

Margaret Atwood was born in 1939. She is the author of many novels, including the classic *The Handmaid's Tale*, and *The Blind Assassin*, winner of the 2000 Man Booker Prize. She has won many awards and was awarded the title of Companion of Literature by The Royal Society of Literature in 2012. She lives in Toronto, Canada.

Germaine Greer is an Australian academic and major feminist voice of the mid-twentieth century, born in 1939. Her ideas have created controversy ever since *The Female Eunuch* became an international bestseller in 1970. Her other books include *Sex and Destiny* and *Shakespeare's Wife*. She lives in Essex.

Melvyn Bragg was born in Cumbria in 1939. He started working for the BBC in 1961. He has written two musicals, screenplays, many novels – including *The Hired Man*, winner of The Time/Life Silver Pen Award, and *The Soldier's Return*, winner of a WHSmith Literary Award – and non-fiction, including books on Laurence Olivier and Richard Burton. He lives in north-west London.

Gita Mehta was born in Delhi in 1943 and educated in India and at the University of Cambridge. She has worked on several television documentaries; her books have been translated into twenty-one languages and include *A River Sutra* and *Karma Cola*. She divides her time between India, London and New York.

Buchi Emecheta was born in 1944, of Ibusa parentage, in Lagos, Nigeria; she came to London in 1962. Her first book, *In the Ditch*, was published in 1972. Since then she has written children's books, plays for BBC and Granada television and many more novels. She lives in north London.

Sally Beauman was born in 1944, and read English Literature at Girton College, Cambridge. She has worked as a journalist and critic in America and the UK, and is the author of eight novels, including *Destiny* and *Dark Angel*, and most recently *The Visitors* (2014). She lives in north London.

Wendy Cope was born in Erith, Kent, in 1945, went to boarding schools in the same county, and then to St Hilda's College, Oxford. Her first collection of poems, *Making Cocoa for Kingsley Amis*, was published in 1986. Since then she has published three additional collections and won a Cholmondeley Award. She lives in Ely.

Sue Townsend was born in Leicester in 1946. She wrote secretly for twenty years and is best-known for creating the character of Adrian Mole. In addition to her novels she wrote twelve plays and two books of non-fiction, and regularly contributed to *The New Statesman*, *Observer* and *Marxism Today*. She died in 2014.

Hermione Lee, born in 1948, has taught at Liverpool, York and Oxford Universities and is now President of Wolfson College, Oxford and a Fellow of the British Academy and of the Royal Society of Literature. Her publications include biographies of Virginia Woolf, Edith Wharton and Penelope Fitzgerald. She lives in Oxford and Yorkshire.

Timberlake Wertenbaker grew up in the Basque Country. A leading British playwright, she has been the recipient of numerous awards including an Olivier Award and the 1990 New York Drama Critics Award for *Our Country's Good* and a Writers' Guild Award for *Three Birds Alighting on a Field*. She lives in north London.

Alan Hollinghurst was born in 1954. He is the author of five novels, including *The Swimming-Pool Library* (1988) and *The Line of Beauty*, which won the Man Booker Prize in 2004 and was adapted by Andrew Davies for BBC2. His most recent novel, *The Stranger's Child*, was published in 2011.

Carol Ann Duffy was born in Scotland in 1955. She was appointed Britain's poet laureate in 2009. She lives in Manchester, where she is Professor of Contemporary Poetry and Creative Director of the Writing School. Her most recent poetry collection is *The Bees*, which received the Costa Prize.

Paul Sayer was born in 1955, near Leeds. A former psychiatric nurse, he is the author of eight novels, including the Whitbread-winning *The Comforts of Madness* and, most recently, *The True Adventures of Richard Turpin*. He lives in York.

Candia McWilliam was born in Edinburgh in 1955. She is the author of *A Case of Knives,* joint winner of the Betty Trask Award, *A Little Stranger*, which won a Scottish Arts Council Book Award, and *Debatable Land*, which won the Guardian Fiction Prize. She lives in Edinburgh.

Rana Kabbani Rana Kabbani was born in Damascus in 1958, and brought up in New York City and Djakarta. She was educated at Georgetown University and Jesus College, Cambridge, where she earned a Ph.D. in English Literature. She is a writer and broadcaster, who has made many radio and television programmes for the BBC. Her book *Imperial*

Fictions has been translated into seven languages. She lives in London.

Jeanette Winterson was born in 1959. In 1985 she published her first novel, *Oranges Are Not the Only Fruit*. Her work has been translated into twenty languages. Her memoir *Why Be Happy When You Could Be Normal* is an international bestseller.

Kamila Shamsie was born in 1973. She is the author of six novels, including *Burnt Shadows*, which was shortlisted for the Orange Prize, and most recently *A God in Every Stone*. She is a Fellow of the Royal Society of Literature and was named a Granta's Best of Young British Novelist. She grew up in Karachi and now lives in London.

Rory Stewart is the author of *The Places in Between*, an account of his solo walk across Afghanistan, and *Occupational Hazards*, which describes his work in Iraq. Formerly a soldier and diplomat, he was the Ryan Professor of Human Rights at Harvard, and is now Chair of the House of Commons Defence Committee.

Katie Waldegrave was born in 1980. Formerly Head of History at Cranford Community College in West London, she founded the charity First Story with author William Fiennes in 2008. Her first book, *The Poets' Daughters*, a biography of the daughters of Wordsworth and Coleridge, was published in 2013. She lives in London.

Emily Berry was born in 1981. Her debut book of poems, *Dear Boy* (Faber & Faber, 2013), won the Forward Prize for Best First Collection and the Hawthornden Prize. She is a contributor to *The Breakfast Bible* (Bloomsbury, 2013). She lives in London, where she grew up.

Tom Wells was born in 1985. His plays include *Me, As a Penguin, The Kitchen Sink, Jumpers for Goalposts* and *Cosmic*. He has also written the short film *Ben & Lump* for Channel 4, the afternoon play *Jonesy* for BBC Radio 4, and the Lyric Hammersmith's panto. He lives in Newcastle.

GIVE A BOOK

Give a Book is a UK based charity that started in May 2011 with the sole aim of giving books where they will be of particular benefit. Our core belief is that to pass on a good read - to give someone a book - is a transaction of worth.

New books are distributed to partner charities and groups, including:

- Magic Breakfast provide breakfasts for hungry children. Give a Book gives books for breakfast book clubs.
- First Story who put writers into challenging schools.
- Age UK who read to isolated elderly people.

- Prison Reading Groups and Six Book Challengers
- Maggie's Centres who help people affected by cancer.

- Doorstep Library Network
- Various schools and other literacy projects where pupils frequently have never had a book in their life.

BECAUSE READING MATTERS

www.giveabook.org.uk

Contact: info@giveabook.org.uk   Registered charity no: 1149664   Patron: Lady Antonia Fraser DBE